ART AND ERROR

ART AND ERROR:

Modern Textual Editing

ESSAYS COMPILED AND EDITED BY

RONALD GOTTESMAN

AND

SCOTT BENNETT

1970

INDIANA UNIVERSITY PRESS

Bloomington / London

Copyright © 1970 by Indiana University Press

Published in Canada by Fitzhenry & Whiteside Limited,
Don Mills, Ontario

Library of Congress catalog card number: 70-103927

SBN: 253-30165-2

MANUFACTURED IN THE UNITED STATES OF AMERICA

To PHILIP B. DAGHLIAN

Contents

Preface

In RECENT YEARS textual editing has engaged the interest of American and English literary scholars who have too often had to teach themselves skills neglected in their professional training. The essays assembled here should make self-education easier. They should also provide a source or textbook useful to those who teach graduate courses in methods of literary research. Even those with no direct professional concern in this area will find several of the essays engaging and instructive.

The volume proceeds from the recognition that textual editing, though an ancient activity, has in recent years undergone important refinements in both its theoretical framework and the application of its principles. The value of bibliographical study and textual editing has long been acknowledged in the case of some classic English authors, but only recently have literary scholars become aware of the significance of textual corruption in works by relatively modern authors. This compilation therefore draws special attention to textual problems presented by post-Renaissance literature and to the rich variety of solutions developed to overcome those problems.

Many of the essays are in effect reports of work in progress. They deal with a wide range of problems, often only partially solved at the time of writing; sometimes they treat problems so general or complex as to admit multiple solutions. In their tentativeness certain essays interestingly reveal the sorts of decisions an editor must face and the options available to him. Others, particularly those written especially for this volume by Professors Dearing, Geduld, Gibson and Petty, and Welland, delineate textual territory that is just beginning to be explored.

The essays were also selected to provide us with samples of the kinds of editorial problems that have been confronted in poetry, fiction, drama, and letters. Manuscript and printed materials in a great many relationships to author and in varying circumstances of textual transmission are considered. It is apparent from these essays that however clear and logical the editorial theory may be, the specific task is likely to be as unique as a set of fingerprints. Accordingly, our intention has been to illuminate the *process* of editing modern literary texts; the end results, new editions, appear monthly.

A. E. Housman's lecture was chosen to open the volume because it reminds us of what everyone concerned with textual criticism —acolyte or high priest, proponent or sceptic—is likely to forget: it is not a mystery or an exact science but "purely a matter of reason and of common sense" informed by facts and devoted to the meticulous discovery of truth. As Housman concludes, "knowledge is good, method is good, but one thing beyond all others is necessary; and that is to have a head, not a pumpkin, on your shoulders, and brains, not pudding, in your head."

R. G.

S. B.

Bloomington, Indiana
9 March 1969

Acknowledgments

THE EDITORS WISH TO THANK THE FOLLOWING PERSONS,
WHO GENEROUSLY OFFERED ADVICE AND SUGGESTIONS
ABOUT THE CONTENTS OF THIS VOLUME.

ROBERT ALLEN	JOSEPH KATZ
O. M. BRACK, JR.	GEORGE LEVINE
MATTHEW J. BRUCCOLI	WILLIAM RILEY PARKER
WILLIAM R. CAGLE	J. ALBERT ROBBINS
PHILIP B. DAGHLIAN	WILLIAM B. TODD
RALPH W. FRANKLIN	ALFRED TOWELL
BRUCE HARKNESS	PHILIP WIKELUND

THE EDITORS WOULD ALSO like to acknowledge their indebtedness to the Bibliographical Society of the University of Virginia for permission to reprint the essays by Russell K. Alspach, R. C. Bald, Fredson Bowers, W. W. Greg, Robert Halsband, and Thomas H. Johnson; to the Bibliographical Society of America for permission to reprint the essays by James B. Meriwether and David M. Vieth; to the Modern Language Association for permission to reprint James Thorpe's essay; to the Society of Authors (London), literary representatives of the estate of A. E. Housman, for permission to reprint his essay; and to A. Francke, Bern, Switzerland, for permission to reprint John Butt's essay.

ART AND ERROR

A. E. HOUSMAN

The Application of Thought

to Textual Criticism

Read to the Classical Association nearly fifty years ago, Hous-man's lecture on the "science of discovering error in texts and the art of removing it" speaks with persistent relevance.

IN BEGINNING to speak about the application of thought to textual criticism, I do not intend to define the term *thought*, because I hope that the sense which I attach to the word will emerge from what I say. But it is necessary at the outset to define *textual criticism*, because many people, and even some people who profess to teach it to others, do not know what it is. One sees books calling themselves introductions to textual criticism which contain nothing about textual criticism from beginning to end; which are all about palaeography and manuscripts and collation, and have no more to do with textual criticism than if they were all about accidence and syntax. Palaeography is one of the things with which a textual critic needs to acquaint himself, but grammar is another, and equally indispensable; and no amount either of grammar or of palaeography will teach a man one scrap of textual criticism.

Reprinted from *Proceedings of the Classical Association*, XVIII (1921), 67–84, with the permission of the Society of Authors.

< Textual criticism is a science, and, since it comprises recension and emendation, it is also an art. It is the science of discovering error in texts and the art of removing it. >That is its definition, that is what the name *denotes*. But I must also say something about what it does and does not *connote*, what attributes it does and does not imply; because here also there are false impressions abroad.

First, then, it is< not a sacred mystery. It is purely a matter of reason and of common sense. We exercise textual criticism whenever we notice and correct a misprint? A man who possesses common sense and the use of reason must not expect to learn from treatises or lectures on textual criticism anything that he could not, with leisure and industry, find out for himself. What the lectures and treatises can do for him is to save him time and trouble by presenting to him immediately considerations which would in any case occur to him sooner or later. And whatever he reads about textual criticism in books, or hears at lectures, he should test by reason and common sense, and reject everything which conflicts with either as mere hocus-pocus.

< Secondly, textual criticism is not a branch of mathematics, nor indeed an exact science at all. It deals with a matter not rigid and constant, like lines and numbers, but fluid and variable; namely the frailties and aberrations of the human mind, and of its insubordinate servants, the human fingers. It therefore is not susceptible of hard-and-fast rules? It would be much easier if it were; and that is why people try to pretend that it is, or at least behave as if they thought so. Of course you can have hard-and-fast rules if you like, but then you will have false rules, and they will lead you wrong; because their simplicity will render them inapplicable to problems which are not simple, but complicated by the play of personality. A textual critic engaged upon his business is not at all like Newton investigating the motions of the planets: he is much more like a dog hunting for fleas. If a dog hunted for fleas on mathematical principles, basing his researches on statistics of area and population, he would never catch a flea except by accident. They require to be treated as individuals; and every problem which presents itself to the textual critic must be regarded as possibly unique.

Textual criticism therefore is neither mystery nor mathematics:

it cannot be learnt either like the catechism or like the multiplication table. This science and this art require more in the learner than a simply receptive mind; and indeed the truth is that they cannot be taught at all: *criticus nascitur, non fit.* If a dog is to hunt for fleas successfully he must be quick and he must be sensitive. It is no good for a rhinoceros to hunt for fleas: he does not know where they are, and could not catch them if he did. It has sometimes been said that textual criticism is the crown and summit of all scholarship. This is not evidently or necessarily true; but it is true that the qualities which make a critic, whether they are thus transcendent or no, are rare, and that a good critic is a much less common thing than for instance a good grammarian. I have in my mind a paper by a well-known scholar on a certain Latin writer, half of which was concerned with grammar and half with criticism. The grammatical part was excellent; it showed wide reading and accurate observation, and contributed matter which was both new and valuable. In the textual part the author was like nothing so much as an ill-bred child interrupting the conversation of grown men. If it was possible to mistake the question at issue, he mistook it. If an opponent's arguments were contained in some book which was not at hand, he did not try to find the book, but he tried to guess the arguments; and he never succeeded. If the book was at hand, and he had read the arguments, he did not understand them; and represented his opponents as saying the opposite of what they had said. If another scholar had already removed a corruption by slightly altering the text, he proposed to remove it by altering the text violently. So possible is it to be a learned man, and admirable in other departments, and yet to have in you not even the makings of a critic.

But the application of thought to textual criticism is an action which ought to be within the power of anyone who can apply thought to anything. It is not, like the talent for textual criticism, a gift of nature, but it is a habit; and, like other habits, it can be formed. And, when formed, although it cannot fill the place of an absent talent, it can modify and minimise the ill effects of the talent's absence. Because a man is not a born critic, he need not therefore act like a born fool; but when he engages in textual criticism he often does. There are reasons for everything, and there are reasons for this; and I will now set forth the chief of them. The *fact* that thought is not sufficiently applied to the subject I shall show hereafter by examples; but at present I consider the causes which bring that result about.

‹ First, then, not only is a natural aptitude for the study rare, but so also is a genuine interest in it. Most people, and many scholars among them, find it rather dry and rather dull. Now if a subject bores us, we are apt to avoid the trouble of thinking about it; but if we do that, we had better go further and avoid also the trouble of writing about it.› And that is what English scholars often did in the middle of the nineteenth century, when nobody in England wanted to hear about textual criticism. This was not an ideal condition of affairs, but it had its compensation. The less one says about a subject which one does not understand, the less one will say about it which is foolish; and on this subject editors were allowed by public opinion to be silent if they chose. But public opinion is now aware that textual criticism, however repulsive, is nevertheless indispensable, and editors find that some pretence of dealing with the subject is obligatory; and in these circumstances they apply, not thought, but words, to textual criticism. They get rules by rote without grasping the realities of which those rules are merely emblems, and recite them on inappropriate occasions instead of seriously thinking out each problem as it arises.

‹ Secondly, it is only a minority of those who engage in this study who are sincerely bent upon the discovery of truth. ᾯe all know that the discovery of truth is seldom the sole object of political writers; and the world believes, justly or unjustly, that it is not always the sole object of theologians: but the amount of subconscious dishonesty which pervades the textual criticism of the Greek and Latin classics is little suspected except by those who have had occasion to analyse it. ❨People come upon this field bringing with them prepossessions and preferences; they are not willing to look all facts in the face, nor to draw the most probable conclusion unless it is also the most agreeable conclusion. ❩Most men are rather stupid, and most of those who are not stupid are, consequently, rather vain; and it is hardly possible to step aside from the pursuit of truth without falling a victim either to your stupidity or else to your vanity. Stupidity will then attach you to received opinions, and you will stick in the mud; or vanity will set you hunting for novelty, and you will find mare's nests. Added to these snares and hindrances there are the various forms of partisanship: sectarianism, which handcuffs you to your own school and teachers and associates, and patriotism which handcuffs you to your own country. Patriotism has a great name as a virtue, and in civic matters, at the present stage of the world's history, it possibly still does more good than harm; but in the sphere of the intellect it is an unmitigated nuisance. I do not know which cuts the worse figure: a German scholar encouraging his countrymen to believe that "wir Deutsche" have nothing to learn from foreigners, or an Englishman demonstrating the unity of Homer by sneers at "Teutonic professors," who are supposed by his audience to have goggle eyes behind large spectacles, and ragged moustaches saturated in lager beer, and consequently to be incapable of forming literary judgments.

⟨ Thirdly, these internal causes of error and folly are subject to very little counteraction or correction from outside. The average reader knows hardly anything about textual criticism, and therefore cannot exercise a vigilant control over the writer: the addlepate is at liberty to maunder and the imposter is at liberty to lie. ⟩ And, what is worse, the reader often shares the writer's prejudices, and is far too well pleased with his conclusions to examine either his premises or his reasoning. Stand on a barrel in the streets of Bagdad, and say in a loud voice, "Twice two is four, and ginger is hot in the mouth, therefore Mohammed is the prophet of God," and your logic will probably escape criticism; or, if anyone by chance should criticise it, you could easily silence him by calling him a Christian dog.

⟨ Fourthly, the things which the textual critic has to talk about are not things which present themselves clearly and sharply to the mind; and it is easy to say, and to fancy that you think, what you really do not think, and even what, if you seriously tried to think it, you would find to be unthinkable.⟩Mistakes are therefore made which could not be made if the matter under discussion were any corporeal object, having qualities perceptible to the senses. The human senses have had a much longer history than the human intellect, and have been brought much nearer to perfection: they are far more acute, far less easy to deceive. The difference between an icicle and a red-hot poker is really much slighter than the difference between truth and falsehood or sense and nonsense; yet it is much more immediately noticeable and much more universally noticed, because the body is more sensitive than the mind. I find therefore that a good way of exposing the falsehood of a statement or the absurdity of an argument in textual criticism is to transpose it into sensuous terms and see what it looks like then. If the nouns which we use are the names of things which can be handled or tasted, differing from one another in being hot or cold, sweet or sour, then we realise what we are saying and take care what we say. But the terms of textual criticism are deplorably intellectual; and probably in no other field do men tell so many falsehoods in the idle hope that they are telling the truth, or talk so much nonsense in the vague belief that they are talking sense.

This is particularly unfortunate and particularly reprehensible, because there is no science in which it is more necessary to take precautions against error arising from internal causes. Those who follow the physical sciences enjoy the great advantage that they can constantly bring their opinions to the test of fact, and verify or falsify their theories by experiment. When a chemist has mixed sulphur and saltpetre and charcoal in certain proportions and wishes to ascertain if the mixture is explosive, he need only apply a match. When a doctor has compounded a new drug and desires to find out what diseases, if any, it is good for, he has only to give it to his patients all round and notice which die and which recover. Our conclusions regarding the truth or falsehood of a MS. reading can never be confirmed or corrected by an equally decisive test; for the only equally decisive test would be the production of the author's autograph. The discovery merely of better and older MSS. than were previously known to us is *not* equally decisive; and even this inadequate verification is not to be expected often, or on a large scale. It is therefore a matter of common prudence and common decency that we should neglect no safe-

guard lying within our reach; that we should look sharp after ourselves; that we should narrowly scrutinise our own proceedings
and rigorously analyse our springs of action. How far these elementary requirements are satisfied, we will now learn from examples.

At the very beginning, to see what pure irrelevancy, what almost
incredible foolishness, finds its way into print, take this instance. It
had been supposed for several centuries that Plautus' name was
M. Accius Plautus, when Ritschl in 1845 pointed out that in the
Ambrosian palimpsest discovered by Mai in 1815, written in the
fourth or fifth century, and much the oldest of Plautus' MSS., the
name appears in the genitive as *T. Macci Plauti,* so that he was really
called *Titus Maccius* (or *Maccus*) *Plautus.* An Italian scholar,
one Vallauri, objected to this innovation on the ground that in all
printed editions from the sixteenth to the nineteenth century the
name was *M. Accius.* He went to Milan to look at the palimpsest,
and there, to be sure, he found *T. Macci* quite legibly written. But
he observed that many *other* pages of the MS. were quite illegible,
and that the whole book was very much tattered and battered;
whereupon he said that he could not sufficiently wonder at anyone
attaching any weight to a MS. which was in such a condition. Is
there any other science, anything calling itself a science, into which
such intellects intrude and conduct such operations in public? But
you may think that Mr. Vallauri is a unique phenomenon. No: if
you engage in textual criticism you may come upon a second Mr.
Vallauri at any turn. The MSS. of Catullus, none of them older
than the fourteenth century, present at 64. 23 the verse:

heroes saluete, deum genus! o bona mater!

The Veronese scholia on Vergil, a palimpsest of the fifth or sixth
century, at *Aen.* v. 80, "salue sancte parens," have the note: "Catul-
lus: saluete, deum *gens,* o bona *matrum* | progenies, saluete iter-
[um]"—giving *gens* for *genus,* *matrum* for *mater,* and adding a
half-verse absent from Catullus' MSS.; and scholars have naturally
preferred an authority so much more ancient. But one editor is
found to object: "the weight of the Veronese scholia, imperfect
and full of lacunae as they are, is not to be set against our MSS."
There is Mr. Vallauri over again: because the palimpsest has large

holes elsewhere and because much of it has perished, therefore what remains, though written as early as the sixth century, has less authority than MSS. written in the fourteenth. If however anyone gets hold of these fourteenth-century MSS., destroys pages of them and tears holes in the pages he does not destroy, the authority of those parts which he allows to survive will presumably deteriorate, and may even sink as low as that of the palimpsest.

Again. There are two MSS. of a certain author, which we will call A and B. Of these two it is recognised that A is the more correct but the less sincere, and that B is the more corrupt but the less interpolated. It is desired to know which MS., if either, is better than the other, or whether both are equal. One scholar tries to determine this question by the collection and comparison of examples. But another thinks that he knows a shorter way than that; and it consists in saying "the more sincere MS. is and must be for any critic who understands his business the better MS."

This I cite as a specimen of the things which people may say if they do not think about the meaning of what they are saying, and especially as an example of the danger of dealing in generalisations. The best way to treat such pretentious inanities is to transfer them from the sphere of textual criticism, where the difference between truth and falsehood or between sense and nonsense is little regarded and seldom even perceived, into some sphere where men are obliged to use concrete and sensuous terms, which force them, however reluctantly, to think.

I ask this scholar, this critic who knows his business, and who says that the more sincere of two MSS. is and must be the better— I ask him to tell me which weighs most, a tall man or a fat man. He cannot answer; nobody can; everybody sees in a moment that the question is absurd. *Tall* and *fat* are adjectives which transport even a textual critic from the world of humbug into the world of reality, a world inhabited by comparatively thoughtful people, such as butchers and grocers, who depend on their brains for their bread. There he begins to understand that to such general questions any answer must be false; that judgment can only be pronounced on individual specimens; that everything depends on the degree of tallness and the degree of fatness. It may well be that an inch of girth adds more weight than an inch of height, or *vice versa*; but that altitude is incomparably more ponderous than obesity, or obesity than altitude, and that an inch of one depresses the scale more than a yard of the other, has never been maintained. The way to find out whether this tall man weighs more or less than that fat man is to weigh them; and the way to find out whether this corrupt MS. is better or worse than that interpolated MS. is to collect and compare their readings; not to ride easily off on the false and ridiculous generalisation that the more sincere MS. is and must be the better.

When you call a MS. *sincere* you instantly engage on its behalf the moral sympathy of the thoughtless: moral sympathy is a line in which they are very strong. I do not desire to exclude morality from textual criticism; I wish indeed that some moral qualities were commoner in textual criticism than they are; but let us not indulge our moral emotions out of season. It may be that a scribe who interpolates, who makes changes deliberately, is guilty of wickedness, while a scribe who makes changes accidentally, because he is sleepy or illiterate or drunk, is guilty of none; but that is a question which will be determined by a competent authority at the Day of Judgment, and is no concern of ours. Our concern is not with the eternal destiny of the scribe, but with the temporal utility of the MS.; and a MS. is useful or the reverse in proportion to the amount of truth which it discloses or conceals, no matter what may be the causes of the disclosure or concealment. It is a mistake to suppose that deliberate change is always or necessarily more destructive of truth than accidental change; and even if it were, the main question, as I have said already, is one of degree. A MS. in which 1 per cent of the words have been viciously and intentionally altered and 99 per cent are right is not so bad as a MS. in which only 1 per cent are right and 99 per cent have been altered virtuously and unintentionally; and if you go to a critic with any such vague enquiry as the question whether the "more sincere" or the "more correct" of two MSS. is the better, he will reply, "If I am to answer that question, you must show me the two MSS. first; for aught that I know at present, from the terms of your query, either may be better than the other, or both may be equal."

But that is what the incompetent intruders into criticism can never admit. They *must* have a better MS., whether it exists or no; because they could never get along without one. If Providence permitted two MSS. to be equal, the editor would have to choose between their readings by considerations of intrinsic merit, and in order to do that he would need to acquire intelligence and impartiality and willingness to take pains, and all sorts of things which he neither has nor wishes for; and he feels sure that God, who tempers the wind to the shorn lamb, can never have meant to lay upon his shoulders such a burden as this.

This is thoughtlessness in the sphere of recension: come now to the sphere of emendation. There is one foolish sort of conjecture which seems to be commoner in the British Isles than anywhere else, though it is also practised abroad, and of late years especially at Munich. The practice is, if you have persuaded yourself that a text is corrupt, to alter a letter or two and see what happens. If what happens is anything which the warmest good-will can mistake for sense and grammar, you call it an emendation; and you call this silly game the palaeographical method.

The palaeographical method has always been the delight of tiros and the scorn of critics. Haupt, for example, used to warn his pupils against mistaking this sort of thing for emendation. "The prime requisite of a good emendation," said he, "is that it should start from the thought; it is only afterwards that other considerations, such as those of metre, or possibilities, such as the interchange of letters, are taken into account." And again: "If the sense requires it, I am prepared to write *Constantinopolitanus* where the MSS. have the monosyllabic interjection *o*." And again: "From the requirements that one should always begin with the thought, there results, as is self-evident, the negative aspect of the case, that one should not, at the outset, consider what exchange of letters may possibly have brought about the corruption of the passage one is dealing with." And further, in his oration on Lachmann as a critic: "Some people, if they see that anything in an ancient text wants correcting, immediately betake themselves to the art of palaeography, investigate the shapes of letters and the forms of abbreviation, and try one dodge after another, as if it were a game, until they hit upon something which they think they can substitute for the corruption, as if forsooth truth were generally discovered by shots of that sort, or as if emendation could take its rise from anything but a careful consideration of the thought."

But even when palaeography is kept in her proper place, as hand-maid, and not allowed to give herself the airs of mistress, she is apt to be overworked. There is a preference for conjectures which call in the aid of palaeography, and which assume, as the cause of error, the accidental interchange of similar letters or similar words, although other causes of error are known to exist. One is presented, for instance, with the following maxim:

> Interpolation is, speaking generally, comparatively an uncommon source of alteration, and we should therefore be loth to assume it in a given case.

Every case is a given case; so what this maxim really means is that we should always be loth to assume interpolation as a source of alteration. But it is certain, and admitted by this writer when he uses the phrase "comparatively uncommon," that interpolation does occur; so he is telling us that we should be loth to assume interpolation even when that assumption is true. And the reason why we are to behave in this ridiculous manner is that interpolation is, speaking generally, comparatively an uncommon source of alteration.

Now to detect a *non sequitur*, unless it leads to an unwelcome conclusion, is as much beyond the power of the average reader as it is beyond the power of the average writer to attach ideas to his own words when those words are terms of textual criticism. I will therefore substitute other terms, terms to which ideas must be attached; and I invite consideration of this maxim and this ratiocination:

> A bullet-wound is, speaking generally, comparatively an uncommon cause of death, and we should therefore be loth to assume it in a given case.

Should we? Should we be loth to assume a bullet-wound as the cause of death if the given case were death on a battlefield? and should we be loth to do so for the reason alleged, that a bullet-wound is, speaking generally, comparatively an uncommon cause of death? Ought we to assume instead the commonest cause of death, and assign death on a battlefield to tuberculosis? What would be thought of a counsellor who enjoined that method of procedure? Well, it would probably be thought that he was a textual critic strayed from home.

< *Why* is interpolation comparatively uncommon? For the same reason that bullet-wounds are: because the opportunity for it is comparatively uncommon. Interpolation is provoked by real or supposed difficulties, and is not frequently volunteered where all is plain sailing; whereas accidental alteration may happen anywhere. Every letter of every word lies exposed to it, and that is the sole reason why accidental alteration is more common. In a given case where either assumption is possible, the assumption of interpolation is equally probable, nay more probable; because action with a motive is more probable than action without a motive. The truth therefore is that in such a case we should be loth to assume accident and should rather assume interpolation; and the circumstance that such cases are comparatively uncommon is no reason for behaving irrationally when they occur.

There is one special province of textual criticism, a large and important province, which is concerned with the establishment of rules of grammar and of metre. Those rules are in part traditional, and given us by the ancient grammarians; but in part they are formed by our own induction from what we find in the MSS. of Greek and Latin authors; and even the traditional rules must of course be tested by comparison with the witness of the MSS. But every rule, whether traditional or framed from induction, is sometimes broken by the MSS.; it may be by few, it may be by many; it may be seldom, it may be often; and critics may then say that the MSS. are wrong, and may correct them in accordance with the rule. This state of affairs is apparently, nay evidently, paradoxical. The MSS. are the material upon which we base our rule, and then, when we have got our rule, we turn round upon the MSS. and say that the rule, based upon them, convicts them of error. We are thus working in a circle, that is a fact which there is no denying; but, as Lachmann says, the task of the critic is just this, to tread that circle deftly and warily; and that is precisely what elevates the critic's business above mere mechanical labour. The difficulty is one which lies in the nature of the case, and is inevitable; and the only way to surmount it is just to be a critic.

The paradox is more formidable in appearance than in reality, and has plenty of analogies in daily life. In a trial or lawsuit the jury's verdict is mainly based upon the evidence of the witnesses; but that does not prevent the jury from making up its mind, from the evidence in general, that one or more witnesses have been guilty of perjury and that their evidence is to be disregarded. It is quite possible to elicit from the general testimony of MSS. a rule of sufficient certainty to convict of falsehood their exceptional testimony, or of sufficient probability to throw doubt upon it. But that exceptional testimony must in each case be considered. It must be recognised that there are two hypotheses between which we have to decide: the question is whether the exceptions come from the author, and so break down the rule, or whether they come from the scribe, and are to be corrected by it: and in order to decide this we must keep our eyes open for any peculiarity which may happen to characterise them.

One of the forms which lack of thought has assumed in textual criticism is the tendency now prevailing, especially among some Continental scholars, to try to break down accepted rules of grammar or metre by the mere collection and enumeration of exceptions presented by the MSS. Now that can never break down a rule: the mere number of exceptions is nothing; what matters is their weight, and that can only be ascertained by classification and scrutiny. If I had noted down every example which I have met, I should now have a large collection of places in Latin MSS. where the substantive *orbis*, which our grammars and dictionaries declare to be masculine, has a feminine adjective attached to it. But I do not therefore propose to revise that rule of syntax, for examination would show that these examples, though numerous, have no force. Most of them are places where the sense and context show that *orbis*, in whatever case or number it may be, is merely a corruption of the corresponding case and number of *urbs;* and in the remaining places it is natural to suppose that the scribe has been influenced and confused by the great likeness of the one word to the other. Or again, read Madvig, *Adu. Crit.*, vol. I, book i, chap. iv, where he sifts the evidence for the opinion that the aorist infinitive can be used in Greek after verbs of saying and thinking in the sense of the future infinitive or of the aorist infinitive with ἄν. The list of examples in the MSS. is very long indeed; but the moment you begin to sort them and examine them you are less struck by their number than by the restriction of their extent. Almost all of them are such as δέξασθαι used for δέξεσθαι, where the two forms differ by one letter only; a smaller number are such as ποιῆσαι for ποιήσειν, where the difference, though greater, is still slight; others are examples like ἥκιστα ἀναγκασθῆναι for ἥκιστ' ἂν ἀναγκασθῆναι, where again the difference is next to nothing. Now if the MSS. are right in these cases, and the Greek authors did use this construction, how are we to explain this extraordinary limitation of the use? There is no syntactical difference between the first and second aorist: why then did they use the 1st aorist so often for the future and the 2nd aorist so seldom? why did they say δέξασθαι for δέξεσθαι dozens of times and λαβεῖν for λήψεσθαι never? The mere asking of that question is enough to show the true state of the case. The bare fact that the aorists thus used in the MSS. are aorists of similar *form* to the future, while aorists of dissimilar form are not thus used, proves that the phenomenon has its cause in the copyist's eye and not in the author's mind, that it is not a variation in grammatical usage but an error in transcription. The number of examples is nothing; all depends upon their character; and a single example of λαβεῖν in a future sense would have more weight than a hundred of δέξασθαι.

In particular, scribes will alter a less familiar form to a more familiar, if they see nothing to prevent them. If metre allows, or if they do not know that metre forbids, they will alter ἐλεινός to ἐλεεινός, οἰστός to ὀϊστός, *nil* to *nihil*, *deprendo* to *deprehendo*. Since metre convicts them of infidelity in some places, they forfeit the right to be trusted in any place; if we choose to trust them we are credulous, and if we build structures on our trust we are no critics. Even if metre does not convict them, reason sometimes can. Take the statement, repeatedly made in grammars and editions, that the Latins sometimes used the pluperfect for the imperfect and the perfect. They did use it for the imperfect; they used it also for the preterite or past aorist; but for the perfect they did not use it; and that is proved by the very examples of its use as perfect which are found in MSS. All those examples are of the 3rd person plural. Why? We must choose between the two following hypotheses:

(a) That the Latins used the pluperfect for the perfect in the 3rd person plural only.

(b) That they did not use the pluperfect for the perfect, and that these examples are corrupt.

If anyone adopted the former, he would have to explain what syntactical property, inviting the author to use pluperfect for perfect, is possessed by the 3rd person plural and not by the two other plural or the three singular persons: and I should like to see some one set about it.

If we adopt the latter, we must show what *external* feature, inviting the *scribe* to write pluperfect for perfect, is possessed by the 3rd person plural exclusively: and that is quite easy. The 3rd person plural is the only person in which the perfect and the pluperfect differ merely by one letter. Moreover in verse the perfect termination *-ĕrunt*, being comparatively unfamiliar to scribes, is altered by them to the nearest familiar form with the same scansion, sometimes *-erint*, sometimes *-erant*: in Ovid's *Heroides* there are four places where the best MS. gives *præbuérunt, stetĕrunt, excidĕrunt, expulĕrunt*, and the other MSS. give *-erant* or *-erint* or both. Accordingly, when the much inferior MSS. of Propertius present pluperfect for perfect in four places, *fuerant* once, *steterant* once, *exciderant* twice, Scaliger corrects to *fuĕrunt, stetĕrunt, excidĕrunt*. Thereupon an editor of this enlightened age takes up his pen and writes as follows: "It is quite erroneous to remove the pluperfects where it can be done without great expenditure of conjectural sagacity (*steterunt* for *steterant* and the like), and not to trouble oneself about the phenomenon elsewhere." I ask, how is it possible to trouble oneself about the phenomenon elsewhere? It does not exist elsewhere. There is no place where the MSS. give *steteram* in the sense of the perfect *steti*, nor *steteras* in the sense of the perfect *stetisti*. Wherever they give examples of the pluperfect which cannot be removed by the change of one letter—

such as *pararat* in i. 8. 36 or *fueram* in i. 12. 11—those are examples where it has sometimes the sense of the imperfect, sometimes of the preterite, but never of the perfect. And the inference is plain: the Latins did not use the pluperfect for the perfect.

Scaliger knew that in the sixteenth century: Mr. Rothstein, in the nineteenth and twentieth, does not know it; he has found a form of words to prevent him from knowing it, and he thinks himself in advance of Scaliger. It is supposed that there has been progress in the science of textual criticism, and the most frivolous pretender has learnt to talk superciliously about "the old unscientific days." The old unscientific days are everlasting; they are here and now; they are renewed perennially by the ear which takes formulas in, and the tongue which gives them out again, and the mind which meanwhile is empty of reflexion and stuffed with self-complacency. Progress there has been, but where? In superior intellects: the rabble do not share it. Such a man as Scaliger, living in our time, would be a better critic than Scaliger was; but we shall not be better critics than Scaliger by the simple act of living in our own time. Textual criticism, like most other sciences, is an aristocratic affair, not communicable to all men, nor to most men. Not to be a textual critic is no reproach to anyone, unless he pretends to be what he is not. To *be* a textual critic requires aptitude for thinking and willingness to think; and though it also requires other things, those things are supplements and cannot be substitutes. Knowledge is good, method is good, but one thing beyond all others is necessary; and that is to have a head, not a pumpkin, on your shoulders, and brains, not pudding, in your head. >

W. W. GREG

The Rationale of Copy-Text

W. W. GREG's *essay is an unquestioned classic in the field, and
like other classic formulations it is deceptively simple and lucid.
His formulation is twofold: first to argue that the data presented
by any text may be differentiated into two classes—substantives
(words as units of meaning) and accidentals (spelling, capitalization, and punctuation); and second to insist on the editor's obligation to discriminate among alterations in authorially revised texts
and thereby avoid falling under the "tyranny of the copy-text."
These two propositions have become axiomatic since Greg's essay
was published, and it is no criticism to suggest that textual editors have since become aware of the practical difficulties of
making distinctions between substantives and accidentals.*

WHEN, IN HIS EDITION OF NASHE, McKerrow invented the term
"copy-text," he was merely giving a name to a conception
already familiar, and he used it in a general sense to indicate that
early text of a work which an editor selected as the basis of his own.
Later, as we shall see, he gave it a somewhat different and more
restricted meaning. It is this change in conception and its implications that I wish to consider.

Reprinted from *Studies in Bibliography*, III (1950–51), 19–36, with the permission of the Bibliographical Society of the University of Virginia.

The idea of treating some one text, usually of course a manuscript, as possessing over-riding authority originated among classical scholars, though something similar may no doubt be traced in the work of biblical critics. So long as purely eclectic methods prevailed, any preference for one manuscript over another, if it showed itself, was of course arbitrary; but when, towards the middle of last century, Lachmann and others introduced the genealogical classification of manuscripts as a principle of textual criticism, this appeared to provide at least some scientific basis for the conception of the most authoritative text. The genealogical method was the greatest advance ever made in this field, but its introduction was not unaccompanied by error. For lack of logical analysis, it led, at the hands of its less discriminating exponents, to an attempt to reduce textual criticism to a code of mechanical rules. There was just this much excuse, that the method did make it possible to sweep away mechanically a great deal of rubbish. What its more hasty devotees failed to understand, or at any rate sufficiently to bear in mind, was that authority is never absolute, but only relative. Thus a school arose, mainly in Germany, that taught that if a manuscript could be shown to be generally more correct than any other and to have descended from the archetype independently of other lines of transmission, it was "scientific" to follow its readings whenever they were not manifestly impossible. It was this fallacy that Housman exposed with devastating sarcasm. He had only to point out that "Chance and the common course of nature will not bring it to pass that the readings of a MS are right wherever they are possible and impossible wherever they are wrong."[1] That if a scribe makes a mistake he will inevitably produce nonsense is the tacit and wholly unwarranted assumption of the school in question,[2] and it is one that naturally commends itself to those who believe themselves capable of distinguishing between sense and nonsense, but who know themselves incapable of distinguishing between right and wrong. Unfortunately the attractions of a mechanical method misled many who were capable of better things.

There is one important respect in which the editing of classical texts differs from that of English. In the former it is the common practice, for fairly obvious reasons, to normalize the spelling, so that (apart from emendation) the function of an editor is limited to choosing between those manuscript readings that offer significant variants. In English it is now usual to preserve the spelling of the earliest or it may be some other selected text. Thus it will be seen that the conception of "copy-text" does not present itself to the classical and to the English editor in quite the same way; indeed, if I am right in the view I am about to put forward, the classical theory of the "best" or "most authoritative" manuscript, whether it be held in a reasonable or in an obviously fallacious form, has really nothing to do with the English theory of "copy-text" at all.

I do not wish to argue the case of "old spelling" *versus* "modern spelling"; I accept the view now prevalent among English scholars. But I cannot avoid some reference to the ground on which present practice is based, since it is intimately connected with my own views on copy-text. The former practice of modernizing the spelling of English works is no longer popular with editors, since spelling is now recognized as an essential characteristic of an author, or at least of his time and locality. So far as my knowledge goes, the alternative of normalization has not been seriously explored, but its philological difficulties are clearly considerable.[3] Whether, with the advance of linguistic science, it will some day be possible to establish a standard spelling for a particular period or district or author, or whether the historical circumstances in which our language has developed must always forbid any attempt of the sort (at any rate before comparatively recent times) I am not competent to say; but I agree with what appears to be the general opinion that such an attempt would at present only result in confusion and misrepresentation. It is therefore the modern editorial practice to choose whatever extant text may be supposed to represent most nearly what the author wrote and to follow it with the least possible alteration. But here we need to draw a distinction between the significant, or as I shall call them "substantive," readings of the text, those namely that affect the author's meaning or the essence of his expression, and others, such in general as spelling, punctuation, word-division, and the like, affecting mainly its formal presentation, which may be regarded as the accidents, or as I shall call them "accidentals," of the text.[4] The distinction is not arbitrary or theoretical, but has an immediate bearing on textual criticism, for scribes (or compositors) may in general be expected to react, and experience shows that they generally do react, differently to the two categories. As regards substantive readings their aim may be assumed to be to reproduce exactly those of their copy, though they will doubtless sometimes depart from them accidentally and may even, for one reason or another, do so intentionally: as regards accidentals they will normally follow their own habits or inclination, though they may, for various reasons and to varying degrees, be influenced by their copy. Thus a contemporary manuscript will at least preserve the spelling of the period, and may even retain some of the author's own, while it may at the same time depart frequently from the wording of the original: on the other hand a later transcript of the same original may reproduce the wording with essential accuracy while completely modernizing the spelling. Since, then, it is only on grounds of expediency, and in consequence either of philological ignorance or of linguistic circumstances, that we select a particular original as our copy-text, I suggest that it is only in the matter of accidentals that we are bound (within reason) to follow it, and that in respect of substantive readings we have exactly the same liberty (and obligation) of choice as has a classical editor, or as we should have were it a modernized text that we were preparing.[5]

But the distinction has not been generally recognized, and has never, so far as I am aware, been explicitly drawn.[6] This is not surprising. The battle between "old spelling" and "modern spelling" was fought out over works written for the most part between 1550 and 1650, and for which the original authorities are therefore as a rule printed editions. Now printed editions usually form an ancestral series, in which each is derived from its immediate predecessor; whereas the extant manuscripts of any work have usually only a collateral relationship, each being derived from the original independently, or more or less independently, of the others. Thus in the case of printed books, and in the absense of revision in a later edition, it is normally the first edition alone that can claim authority, and this authority naturally extends to substantive readings and accidentals alike. There was, therefore, little to force the distinction upon the notice of editors of works of the sixteenth and seventeenth centuries, and it apparently never occurred to them that some fundamental difference of editorial method might be called for in the rare cases in which a later edition had been revised by the author or in which there existed more than one "substantive" edition of comparable authority.[7] Had they been more familiar with works transmitted in manuscript, they might possibly have reconsidered their methods and been led to draw the distinction I am suggesting. For although the underlying principles of textual criticism are, of course, the same in the case of works transmitted in manuscripts and in print, particular circumstances differ, and certain aspects of the common principles may emerge more clearly in the one case than in the other. However, since the idea of copy-text originated and has generally been applied in connexion with the editing of printed books, it is such that I shall mainly consider, and in what follows reference may be understood as confined to them unless manuscripts are specifically mentioned.

The distinction I am proposing between substantive readings and accidentals, or at any rate its relevance to the question of copy-text, was clearly not present to McKerrow's mind when in 1904 he published the second volume of his edition of the Works of Thomas Nashe, which included *The Unfortunate Traveller*. Collation of the early editions of this romance led him to the conclusion that the second, advertised on the title as "Newly corrected and augmented," had in fact been revised by the author, but at the same time that not all the alterations could with certainty be ascribed to him.[8] He nevertheless proceeded to enunciate the rule that "if an editor has reason to suppose that a certain text embodies later corrections than any other, and at the same time has no ground for disbelieving that these corrections, *or some of them at least,* are the work of the author, he has no choice but to make that text the basis of his reprint."[9] The italics are mine.[10] This is applying with a vengeance the principle that I once approvingly described as "maintaining the integrity of the copy-text." But it must be pointed out that there are in fact two quite distinct principles involved. One, put in more general form, is that if, for whatever reason, a particular authority be on the whole preferred, an editor is bound to accept all its substantive readings (if not manifestly impossible). This is the old fallacy of the "best text," and may be taken to be now generally rejected. The other principle, also put in general form, is that whatever particular authority be preferred, whether as being revised or as generally preserving the substantive readings more faithfully than any other, it must be taken as copy-text, that is to say that it must also be followed in the matter of accidentals. This is the principle that interests us at the moment, and it is one that McKerrow himself came, at least partly, to question.

In 1939 McKerrow published his *Prolegomena for the Oxford Shakespeare,* and he would not have been the critic he was if his views had not undergone some changes in the course of thirty-five years. One was in respect of revision. He had come to the opinion that to take a reprint, even a revised reprint, as copy-text was indefensible. Whatever may be the relation of a particular substantive edition to the author's manuscript (provided that there is any transcriptional link at all) it stands to reason that the relation of a reprint of that edition must be more remote. If then, putting aside all question of revision, a particular substantive edition has an over-riding claim to be taken as copy-text, to displace it in favour of a reprint, whether revised or not, means receding at least one step further from the author's original in so far as the general form of the text is concerned.[11] Some such considerations must have been in McKerrow's mind when he wrote (*Prolegomena,* pp. 17–18): "Even if, however, we were to assure ourselves . . . that certain corrections found in a later edition of a play were of Shakespearian authority, it would not by any means follow that that edition should be used as the copy-text of a reprint.[12] It would undoubtedly be necessary to incorporate these corrections in our text, but . . . it seems evident that . . . this later edition will (except for the corrections) deviate more widely than the earliest print from the author's original manuscript. . . . [Thus] the nearest approach to our ideal . . . will be produced by using the earliest 'good' print as copy-text and inserting into it, from the first edition which contains them, such corrections as appear to us to be derived from the author." This is a clear statement of the position, and in it he draws exactly the distinction between substantive readings (in the form of corrections) and accidentals (or general texture) on which I am insisting. He then, however, relapsed into heresy in the matter of the substantive readings. Having spoken, as above, of the need to introduce "such corrections as appear to us to be derived from the author," he seems to have feared conceding too much to eclecticism, and he proceeded: "We are not to regard the 'goodness' of a reading in and by itself, or to consider whether it appeals to our aesthetic sensibilities or not; we are to consider whether a particular edition taken *as a whole* contains variants from the edition from which it was otherwise printed which could not reasonably be attributed to an ordinary press-corrector, but by reason of their style, point, and what we may call inner harmony with the spirit of the play as a whole, seem likely to be the work of the author: and once having decided this to our satisfaction we must accept *all* the alterations of that edition, saving any which seem obvious blunders or misprints." We can see clearly enough what he had in mind, namely that the evidence of correction (under which head he presumably intended to include revision) must be considered *as a whole*; but he failed to add the equally important proviso that the alterations must also be *of a piece* (and not, as in *The Unfortunate Traveller*, of apparently disparate origin) before we can be called upon to accept them *all*. As he states it his canon is open to exactly the same objections as the "most authoritative manuscript" theory in classical editing.

McKerrow was, therefore, in his later work quite conscious of the distinction between substantive readings and accidentals, in so far as the problem of revision is concerned. But he never applied the conception to cases in which we have more than one substantive text, as in *Hamlet* and perhaps in 2 *Henry IV*, *Troilus and Cressida*, and *Othello*. Presumably he would have argued that since faithfulness to the wording of the author was one of the criteria he laid down for determining the choice of the copy-text, it was an editor's duty to follow its substantive readings with a minimum of interference.

We may assume that neither McKerrow nor other editors of the conservative school imagined that such a procedure would always result in establishing the authentic text of the original; what they believed was that from it less harm would result than from opening the door to individual choice among variants, since it substituted an objective for a subjective method of determination. This is, I think, open to question. It is impossible to exclude individual judgement from editorial procedure: it operates of necessity in the all-important matter of the choice of copy-text and in the minor one of deciding what readings are possible and what not; why, therefore, should the choice between possible readings be withdrawn from its competence? Uniformity of result at the hands of different editors is worth little if it means only uniformity in error; and it may not be too optimistic a belief that the judgment of an editor, fallible as it must necessarily be, is likely to bring us closer to what the author wrote than the enforcement of an arbitrary rule.

The true theory is, I contend, that the copy-text should govern (generally) in the matter of accidentals, but that the choice between substantive readings belongs to the general theory of textual criticism and lies altogether beyond the narrow principle of the copy-text. Thus it may happen that in a critical edition the text rightly chosen as copy may not by any means be the one that supplies most substantive readings in cases of variation. The failure to make this distinction and to apply this principle has naturally led to too close and too general a reliance upon the text chosen as basis for an edition, and there has arisen what may be called the tyranny of the copy-text, a tyranny that has, in my opinion, vitiated much of the best editorial work of the past generation.

I will give a couple of examples of the sort of thing I mean that I have lately come across in the course of my own work. They are all the more suitable as illustrations since they occur in texts edited by scholars of recognized authority, neither of whom is particularly subject to the tyranny in question. One is from the edition of Marlowe's *Doctor Faustus* by Professor F. S. Boas (1932). The editor, rightly I think, took the so-called B-text (1616) as the basis of his own, correcting it where necessary by comparison with the A-text (1604).[13] Now a famous line in Faustus's opening soliloquy runs in 1604,

> Bid *Oncaymæon* farewell, *Galen* come

and in 1616,

> Bid *Oeconomy* farewell; and *Galen* come . . .

Here *Oncaymæon* is now recognized as standing for *on cay mæ on* or ὄν καὶ μὴ ὄν: but this was not understood at the time, and *Oeconomy* was substituted in reprints of the A-text in 1609 and 1611, and thence taken over by the B-text. The change, however, produced a rather awkward line, and in 1616 the *and* was introduced as a metrical accommodation. In the first half of the line Boas rightly restored the reading implied in A; but in the second half he retained, out of deference of his copy-text, the *and* whose only object was to accommodate the reading he had rejected in the first. One could hardly find a better example of the contradictions to which a mechanical following of the copy-text may lead.[14]

My other instance is from *The Gipsies Metamorphosed* as edited by Dr. Percy Simpson among the masques of Ben Jonson in 1941. He took as his copy-text the Huntington manuscript, and I entirely agree with his choice. In this, and in Simpson's edition, a line of the ribald Cock Lorel ballad runs (sir-reverence!),

> All wch he blewe away with a fart

whereas for *blewe* other authorities have *flirted*. Now, the meaning of *flirted* is not immediately apparent, for no appropriate sense of the word is recorded. There is, however, a rare use of the substantive *flirt* for a sudden gust of wind, and it is impossible to doubt that this is what Jonson had in mind, for no scribe or compositor could have invented the reading *flirted*. It follows that in the manuscript *blewe* is nothing but the conjecture of a scribe who did not understand his original: only the mesmeric influence of the copy-text could obscure so obvious a fact.[15]

I give these examples merely to illustrate the kind of error that, in modern editions of English works, often results from undue deference to the copy-text. This reliance on one particular authority results from the desire for an objective theory of text-construction and a distrust, often no doubt justified, of the operation of individual judgement. The attitude may be explained historically as a natural and largely salutary reaction against the methods of earlier editors. Dissatisfied with the results of eclectic freedom and reliance on personal taste, critics sought to establish some sort of mechanical apparatus for dealing with textual problems that should lead to uniform results independent of the operator. Their efforts were not altogether unattended by success. One result was the recognition of the general worthlessness of reprints. And even in the more difficult field of manuscript transmission it is true that formal rules will carry us part of the way: they can at least effect a preliminary clearing on the ground. This I sought to show in my essay on *The Calculus of Variants* (1927); but in the course of investigation it became clear that there is a definite limit to the field over which formal rules are applicable. Between readings of equal extrinsic authority no rules of the sort can decide, since by their very nature it is only to extrinsic relations that they are relevant. The choice is necessarily a matter for editorial judgement, and an editor who declines or is unable to exercise his judgement and falls back on some arbitrary canon, such as the authority of the copy-text, is in fact abdicating his editorial function. Yet this is what has been frequently commended as "scientific"—"streng wissenschaftlich" in the prevalent idiom—and the result is that what many editors have done is to produce, not editions of their authors' works at all, but only editions of particular authorities for those works, a course that may be perfectly legitimate in itself, but was not the one they were professedly pursuing.

This by way, more or less, of digression. At the risk of repetition I should like to recapitulate my view of the position of copy-text in editorial procedure. The thesis I am arguing is that the historical circumstances of the English language make it necessary to adopt in formal matters the guidance of some particular early text. If the several extant texts of a work form an ancestral series, the earliest will naturally be selected, and since this will not only come nearest to the author's original in accidentals, but also (revision apart) most faithfully preserve the correct readings where substantive variants are in question, everything is straightforward, and the conservative treatment of the copy-text is justified. But whenever there is more than one substantive text of comparable authority,[16] then although it will still be necessary to choose one of them as copy-text, and to follow it in accidentals, this copy-text can be allowed no over-riding or even preponderant authority so far as substantive readings are concerned. The choice between these, in cases of variation, will be determined partly by the opinion the editor may form respecting the nature of the copy from which each substantive edition was printed, which is a matter of external authority; partly by the intrinsic authority of the several texts as judged by the relative frequency of manifest errors therein; and partly by the editor's judgement of the intrinsic claims of individual readings to originality—in other words their intrinsic merit, so long as by "merit" we mean the likelihood of their being what the author wrote rather than their appeal to the individual taste of the editor.

Such, as I see it, is the general theory of copy-text. But there remain a number of subsidiary questions that it may be worthwhile to discuss. One is the degree of faithfulness with which the copy-text should be reproduced. Since the adoption of a copy-text is a matter of convenience rather than of principle—being imposed on us either by linguistic circumstances or our own philological ignorance—it follows that there is no reason for treating it as sacrosanct, even apart from the question of substantive variation. Every editor aiming at a critical edition will, of course, correct scribal or typographical errors. He will also correct readings in accordance with any errata included in the edition taken as copy-text. I see no reason why he should not alter misleading or eccentric spellings which he is satisfied emanate from the scribe or compositor and not from the author. If the punctuation is persistently erroneous or defective an editor may prefer to discard it altogether to make way for one of his own. He is, I think, at liberty to do so, provided that he gives due weight to the original in deciding on his own, and that he records the alteration whenever the sense is appreciably affected. Much the same applies to the use of capitals and italics. I should favour expanding contractions (except perhaps when dealing with an author's holograph) so long as ambiguities and abnormalities are recorded. A critical edition does not seem to me a suitable place in which to record the graphic peculiarities of particular texts,[17] and in this respect the copy-text is only one among others. These, however, are all matters within the discretion of an editor: I am only concerned to uphold his liberty of judgement.

Some minor points arise when it becomes necessary to replace a reading of the copy-text by one derived from another source. It need not, I think, be copied in the exact form in which it there appears. Suppose that the copy-text follows the earlier convention in the use of u and v, and the source from which the reading is taken follows the later. Naturally in transferring the reading from the latter to the former it would be made to conform to the earlier convention. I would go further. Suppose that the copy-text reads "hazard," but that we have reason to believe that the correct reading is "venture": suppose further that whenever this word occurs in the copy-text it is in the form "venter": then "venter," I maintain, is the form we should adopt. In like manner editorial emendations should be made to conform to the habitual spelling of the copy-text.

In the case of rival substantive editions the choice between substantive variants is, I have explained, generally independent of the copy-text. Perhaps one concession should be made. Suppose that the claims of two readings, one in the copy-text and one in some other authority, appear to be exactly balanced: what then should an editor do? In such a case, while there can be no logical reason for giving preference to the copy-text, in practice, if there is no reason for altering its reading, the obvious thing seems to be to let it stand.[18]

Much more important, and difficult, are the problems that arise in connexion with revision. McKerrow seems only to mention correction, but I think he must have intended to include revision, so long as this falls short of complete rewriting: in any case the principle is the same. I have already considered the practice he advocated (pp. 21–23)—namely that an editor should take the original edition as his copy-text and introduce into it all the substantive variants of the revised reprint, other than manifest errors —and have explained that I regard it as too sweeping and mechanical. The emendation that I proposed (p. 24) is, I think, theoretically sufficient, but from a practical point of view it lacks precision. In a case of revision or correction the normal procedure would be for the author to send the printer either a list of the alterations to be made or else a corrected copy of an earlier edition. In setting up the new edition we may suppose that the printer would incorporate the alterations thus indicated by the author; but it must be assumed that he would also introduce a normal amount of unauthorized variation of his own.[19] The problem that faces the editor is to distinguish between the two categories. I suggest the following frankly subjective procedure. Granting that the fact of revision (or correction) is established, an editor should in every case of variation ask himself (1) whether the original reading is one that can reasonably be attributed to the author, and (2) whether the later reading is one that the author can reasonably be supposed to have substituted for the former. If the answer to the first question is negative, then the later reading should be accepted as at least possibly an authoritative correction (unless, of course, it is itself incredible). If the answer to (1) is affirmative and the answer to (2) is negative, the original reading should be retained. If the answers to both questions are affirmative, then the later reading should be presumed to be due to revision and admitted into the text, whether the editor himself considers it an improvement or not. It will be observed that one implication of this procedure is that a later variant that is either completely indifferent or manifestly inferior, or for the substitution of which no motive can be suggested, should be treated as fortuitous and refused admission to the text—to the scandal of faithful followers of McKerrow. I do not, of course, pretend that my procedure will lead to consistently correct results, but I think that the results, if less uniform, will be on the whole preferable to those achieved through following any mechanical rule. I am, no doubt, presupposing an editor of reasonable competence; but if an editor is really incompetent, I doubt whether it much matters what procedure he adopts: he may indeed do less harm with some than with others, he will do little good with any. And in any case, I consider that it would be disastrous to curb the liberty of competent editors in the hope of preventing fools from behaving after their kind.

I will give one illustration of the procedure in operation, taken again from Jonson's *Masque of Gipsies*, a work that is known to have been extensively revised for a later performance. At one point the text of the original version runs as follows.

> a wise Gypsie . . . is as politicke a piece of Flesh, as most Iustices in the County where he maunds

whereas the texts of the revised version replace *maunds* by *stalkes*. Now, *maund* is a recognized canting term meaning to beg, and there is not the least doubt that it is what Jonson originally wrote. Further, it might well be argued that it is less likely that he should have displaced it in revision by a comparatively commonplace alternative, than that a scribe should have altered a rather unusual word that he failed to understand—just as we know that, in a line already quoted (p. 25), a scribe altered *flirted* to *blewe*. I should myself incline to this view were it not that at another point Jonson in revision added the lines,

> And then ye may stalke
> The *Gypsies* walke

where *stalk*, in the sense of going stealthily, is used almost as a technical term. In view of this I do not think it unreasonable to suppose that Jonson himself substituted *stalkes* for *maunds* from a desire to avoid the implication that his aristocratic Gipsies were beggars, and I conclude that it must be allowed to pass as (at least possibly) a correction, though no reasonable critic would *prefer* it to the original.

With McKerrow's view that in all normal cases of correction or revision the original edition should still be taken as the copy-text, I am in complete agreement. But not all cases are normal, as McKerrow himself recognized. While advocating, in the passage already quoted (p. 23), that the earliest "good" edition should be taken as copy-text and corrections incorporated in it, he added the proviso, "unless we could show that the [revised] edition in question (or the copy from which it had been printed) had been gone over and corrected *throughout* by" the author (my italics). This proviso is not in fact very explicit, but it clearly assumes that there are (or at least may be) cases in which an editor would be justified in taking a revised reprint as his copy-text, and it may be worth inquiring what these supposed cases are. If a work has been entirely rewritten, and is printed from a new manuscript, the question does not arise, since the revised edition will be a substantive one, and as such will presumably be chosen by the editor as his copy-text. But short of this, an author, wishing to make corrections or alterations in his work, may not merely hand the printer a revised copy of an earlier edition, but himself supervise the printing of the new edition and correct the proofs as the sheets go through the press. In such a case it may be argued that even though the earlier edition, if printed from his own manuscript, will preserve the author's individual peculiarities more faithfully than the revised reprint, he must nevertheless be assumed to have taken responsibility for the latter in respect of accidentals no less than substantive readings, and that it is therefore the revised reprint that should be taken as copy-text.

The classical example is afforded by the plays in the 1616 folio of Ben Jonson's Works. In this it appears that even the largely recast *Every Man in his Humour* was not set up from an independent manuscript but from a much corrected copy of the quarto of 1601. That Jonson revised the proofs of the folio has indeed been disputed, but Simpson is most likely correct in supposing that he did so, and he was almost certainly responsible for the numerous corrections made while the sheets were in process of printing. Simpson's consequent decision to take the folio for his copy-text for the plays it contains will doubtless be approved by most critics. I at least have no wish to dispute his choice.[20] Only I would point out—and here I think Dr. Simpson would agree with me—that even in this case the procedure involves some sacrifice of individuality. For example, I notice that in the text of *Sejanus* as printed by him there are twenty-eight instances of the Jonsonian "Apostrophus" (an apostrophe indicating the elision of a vowel that is nevertheless retained in printing) but of these only half actually appear in the folio, the rest he has introduced from the quarto. This amounts to an admission that in some respects at least the quarto preserves the formal aspect of the author's original more faithfully than the folio.

The fact is that cases of revision differ so greatly in circumstances and character that it seems impossible to lay down any hard and fast rule as to when an editor should take the original edition as his copy-text and when the revised reprint. All that can be said is that if the original be selected, then the author's corrections must be incorporated; and that if the reprint be selected, then the original reading must be restored when that of the reprint is due to unauthorized variation. Thus the editor cannot escape the responsibility of distinguishing to the best of his ability between the two categories. No juggling with copy-text will relieve him of the duty and necessity of exercizing his own judgement.

In conclusion I should like to examine this problem of revision and copy-text a little closer. In the case of a work like *Sejanus*, in which correction or revision has been slight, it would obviously be possible to take the quarto as the copy-text and introduce into it whatever authoritative alterations the folio may supply; and indeed, were one editing the play independently, this would be the natural course to pursue. But a text like that of *Every Man in his Humour* presents an entirely different problem. In the folio revision and reproduction are so blended that it would seem impossible to disentangle intentional from what may be fortuitous variation, and injudicious to make the attempt. An editor of the revised version has no choice but to take the folio as his copy-text. It would appear therefore that a reprint may in practice be forced upon an editor as copy-text by the nature of the revision itself, quite apart from the question whether or not the author exercised any supervision over its printing.

This has a bearing upon another class of texts, in which a reprint was revised, not by the author, but through comparison with some more authoritative manuscript. Instances are Shakespeare's *Richard III* and *King Lear*. Of both much of the best text is supplied by the folio of 1623; but this is not a substantive text, but one set up from a copy of an earlier quarto that had been extensively corrected by collation with a manuscript preserved in the playhouse. So great and so detailed appears to have been the revision that it would be an almost impossible task to distinguish between variation due to the corrector and that due to the compositor,[21] and an editor has no choice but to take the folio as copy-text. Indeed, this would in any case be incumbent upon him for a different reason; for the folio texts are in some parts connected by transcriptional continuity with the author's manuscript, whereas the quartos contain only reported texts, whose accidental characteristics can be of no authority whatever. At the same time, analogy with *Every Man in his Humour* suggests that even had the quartos of *Richard III* and *King Lear* possessed higher authority than in fact they do, the choice of copy-text must yet have been the same.

I began this discussion in the hope of clearing my own mind as well as others' on a rather obscure though not unimportant matter of editorial practice. I have done something to sort out my own ideas: others must judge for themselves. If they disagree, it is up to them to maintain some different point of view. My desire is rather to provoke discussion than to lay down the law.

N O T E S

1. Introduction to Manilius, 1903, p. xxxii.
2. The more naive the scribe, the more often will the assumption prove correct; the more sophisticated, the less often. This, no doubt, is why critics of this school tend to reject "the more correct but the less sincere" manuscript in favour of "the more corrupt but the less interpolated," as Housman elsewhere observes ("The Application of Thought to Textual Criticism," *Proceedings of the Classical Association*, 1921, xviii. 75). Still, any reasonable critic will prefer the work of a naive to that of a sophisticated scribe, though he may not regard it as necessarily "better."

3. I believe that an attempt has been made in the case of certain Old and Middle English texts, but how consistently and with what success I cannot judge. In any case I am here concerned chiefly with works of the sixteenth and seventeenth centuries.

4. It will, no doubt, be objected that punctuation may very seriously "affect" an author's meaning; still it remains properly a matter of presentation, as spelling does in spite of its use in distinguishing homonyms. The distinction I am trying to draw is practical, not philosophic. It is also true that between substantive readings and spellings there is an intermediate class of word-forms about the assignment of which opinions may differ and which may have to be treated differently in dealing with the work of different scribes.

5. For the sake of clearness in making the distinction I have above stressed the independence of scribes and compositors in the matter of accidentals: at the same time, when he selects his copy-text, an editor will naturally hope that it retains at least something of the character of the original. Experience, however, shows that while the distribution of substantive variants generally agrees with the genetic relation of the texts, that of accidental variants is comparatively arbitrary.

6. Some discussion bearing on it will be found in the Prolegomena to my lectures on *The Editorial Problem in Shakespeare* (1942), "Note on Accidental Characteristics of the Text" (pp. l–lv), particularly the paragraph on pp. liii–liv, and note 1. But at the time of writing I was still a long way from any consistent theory regarding copy-text.

7. A "substantive" edition is McKerrow's term for an edition that is not a reprint of any other. I shall use the term in this sense, since I do not think that there should be any danger of confusion between "substantive editions" and "substantive readings."

I have above ignored the practice of some eccentric editors who took as copy-text for a work the latest edition printed in the author's lifetime, on the assumption, presumably, that he revised each edition as it appeared. The textual results were naturally deplorable.

8. He believed, or at least strongly suspected, that some were due to the printer's desire to save space, and that others were "the work of some person who had not thoroughly considered the sense of the passage which he was altering" (ii.195).

9. Nashe, ii.197. The word "reprint" really begs the question. If all an "editor" aims at is an exact reprint, then obviously he will choose one early edition, on whatever grounds he considers relevant, and reproduce it as it stands. But McKerrow does emend his copy-text where necessary. It is symptomatic that he did not distinguish between a critical edition and a reprint.

10. Without the italicized phrase the statement would appear much

more plausible (though I should still regard it as fallacious, and so would McKerrow himself have done later on) but it would not justify the procedure adopted.

11. This may, at any rate, be put forward as a general proposition, leaving possible exceptions to be considered later (pp. 30 ff.).

12. Again he speaks of a "reprint" where he evidently had in mind a critical edition on conservative lines.

13. Boas's text is in fact modernized, so that my theory of copy-text does not strictly apply, but since he definitely accepts the B-text as his authority, the principle is the same.

14. Or consider the following readings: 1604, 1609 "Consissylogismes," 1611 "subtile sylogismes," 1616 "subtle Sillogismes." Here "subtile," an irresponsible guess by the printer of 1611 for a word he did not understand, was taken over in 1616. The correct reading is, of course, "concise syllogisms." Boas's refusal to take account of the copy used in 1616 led him here and elsewhere to perpetuate some of its manifest errors. In this particular instance he appears to have been unaware of the reading of 1611.

15. At another point two lines appear in an unnatural order in the manuscript. The genetic relation of the texts proves the inversion to be an error. But of this relation Simpson seems to have been ignorant. He was again content to rely on the copy-text.

16. The proviso is inserted to meet the case of the so-called "bad quartos" of Shakespearian and other Elizabethan plays and of the whole class of "reported" texts, whose testimony can in general be neglected.

17. That is, certainly not in the text, and probably not in the general apparatus: they may appropriately form the subject of an appendix.

18. This is the course I recommended in the Prolegomena to *The Editorial Problem in Shakespeare* (p. xxix), adding that it "at least saves the trouble of tossing a coin." What I actually wrote in 1942 was that in such circumstances an editor "will naturally retain the reading of the copy-text, this being the text which he has already decided is *prima facie* the more correct." This implies that correctness in respect of substantive readings is one of the criteria in the choice of the copy-text; and indeed I followed McKerrow in laying it down that an editor should select as copy-text the one that "appears likely to have departed least in wording, spelling, and punctuation from the author's manuscript." There is a good deal in my Prolegomena that I should now express differently, and on this particular point I have definitely changed my opinion. I should now say that the choice of the copy-text depends solely on its formal features (accidentals) and that fidelity as regards substantive readings is irrelevant—though fortunately in nine cases out of ten the choice will be the same whichever rule we adopt.

19. I mean substantive variation, such as occurs in all but the most faithful reprints.

20. Simpson's procedure in taking the 1616 folio as copy-text in the case of most of the masques included, although he admits that in their case Jonson cannot be supposed to have supervised the printing, is much more questionable.

21. Some variation is certainly due to error on the part of the folio printer, and this it is of course the business of an editor to detect and correct so far as he is able.

R. C. BALD

Editorial Problems —

A Preliminary Survey

Because it is directed to a general scholarly audience rather than to fellow textual editors, R. C. Bald's essay is of particular interest to the curious but uncommitted. Having established by telling illustration the unreliability of machine-printed books, Bald surveys those "problems or ... materials that demand treatment different from that worked out by classical scholars or even by editors of Shakespeare." He then calls our attention to the continuous and radical revision in eighteenth and nineteenth-century works, suggests the necessity of consulting manuscripts, first drafts and work sheets, printer's copy and proofs, points up the special considerations that apply to letters, diaries, and notebooks never intended or prepared for the press, and demonstrates the consequences of careless or willful mutilation of a text. Finally, using Billy Budd *and Eugene Vinaver's edition of* Malory *as examples, he calls attention to the need to adjust editorial procedures to both the material being edited and the proper expectations of readers. His concluding principle for editors bears repeating: "If he has been brought to his task by enthusiasm for an author or a book, he will wish above all things by his work to pass on that enthusiasm."*

B Y COMMON CONSENT the constitution of an author's text is the highest aim that a scholar can set before himself."[1] This, as

Reprinted from *Studies in Bibliography*, III (1950–51), 3–17, with the permission of the Bibliographical Society of the University of Virginia.

one might guess, is the dictum of a classical scholar, and a classical scholar is far more acutely conscious than a student of the modern literatures that for over two thousand years the preservation and elucidation of the texts of the great writers have been the primary concern of literary study. Yet to many, and not to lay minds alone, textual criticism is an arid activity, almost synonymous with pedantry. Nevertheless, the text must be established before a just critical appraisal is possible, as a simple illustration will make clear.

The 13th of Donne's *Holy Sonnets* is one of the better known of his *Divine Poems*. It begins,

> What if this present were the worlds last night?
> Marke in my heart, O Soule, where thou dost dwell,
> The picture of Christ crucified, and tell
> Whether that countenance can thee affright.

In all the editions before Grierson's the poem concluded:

> so I say to thee
> To wicked spirits are horrid shapes assign'd,
> This beauteous form assumes a pitious mind,

but Grierson, on the authority of the manuscripts, altered "assumes" to "assures." "Assumes" gives the poem the flatness of a geometrical demonstration, even though it might be argued that the word would come naturally enough from one so soaked as Donne in the dialectic of scholastic philosophy. "Assures," on the other hand, alters the whole effect of the poem and brings it to the triumphant climax which Donne surely intended.

The present disrepute of textual criticism, it would seem, arises from an excessive faith in our mechanical means of reproducing books. We take our texts on trust. Modern scholarship, Dr. R. W. Chapman has remarked, seems to proceed on the assumption that the texts of books published after 1700 are sound, or, if not, that "it is useless, if not improper, to correct them." But, he continues, "The first position has only to be stated to reveal its absurdity; every book, every newspaper, reminds us of human fallibility. The second position . . . arises from cowardice."[2] Whether due to indifference or cowardice, textual corruption can go unchecked for a surprisingly long time, and can produce some very disconcerting results. Let me illustrate.

A correspondent in *The Times Literary Supplement* not long ago pointed out that the very titles of certain books, quite frequently reprinted, have been altered, and the original titles almost forgotten. How many readers of Dickens, for instance, know that *The Adventures of Oliver Twist: or, The Parish Boy's Progress* is the title which the author gave his novel? And if title pages are so unreliable, what can be expected of the text? An examination of modern reprints of *Tristam Shandy* revealed widespread divergences from Sterne's final text:

> Errors in punctuation amount on many pages to 15 to 20 to the page . . . . Modern reprints have frequently set in lower case words which Sterne required to be set in small capitals. Alterations in spelling have not been confined to modernizations; . . . errors destroying Sterne's sense and meaning have been perpetuated, like *area* for *aera, clause* for *cause, port* for *post, timber* for *tinder, catching* for *catechising,* and *caravans* for *caverns.*[3]

Many of these errors apparently originated in some popular nineteenth-century reprint, and have been repeated ever since.

Another class of book in which textual laxity is frequent is one in which, theoretically, it should be rarest: the textbook. Textbooks profess to be edited by competent scholars, and should thus be in a class quite apart from the popular reprint, mass-produced as economically as possible. It would be easy to cite examples of indifferent, scissors-and-paste editing, and even of culpable carelessness, but it will be more effective to refer to books otherwise immune from the ordinary criticism of slipshod work. Within the past year or so two new college *Shakespeares* have appeared,[4] whose editors are perhaps the two most active and distinguished Shakespearian scholars in the country. For range and interest of material presented in introductions and notes, the two books are a marked improvement on anything previously available, and they are bound to exert a strong influence on the teaching of Shakespeare for a generation or so. Yet both reproduce the Globe text. It is not as if there had been no advances in the textual study of Shakespeare during the present century, nor are these two editors ignorant of the work of Pollard, McKerrow, Greg, and Dover Wilson; but is there any other branch of study in which a teacher would be satisfied to present students, as these books do, with the results achieved by scholarship up to, but not beyond, the year 1864?

A third example may be given to show how neglect of textual matters may distort or nullify an argument. In a recent investigation into the origins and development of what we call the Victorian attitude of mind the Reverend Thomas Bowdler's *Family Shakespeare* almost inevitably came up for discussion. In *I Henry IV*, it was alleged, Bowdler showed a certain squeamishness about Falstaff's oaths, though, rather surprisingly, he was somewhat erratic in his elimination of them. "Zounds," " 'Sblood," "By the Lord," and "By the mass" are frequently omitted, and in one place "God" is replaced by "heaven."[5] But such omissions and substitutions were not due to Bowdler at all. The more forcible expressions are all found, it is true, in most modern editions, and they also appear in the early quartos, but they do not appear in the First Folio. This half-hearted censorship of Shakespeare's text took place in the theatre, and was the result of the Act of 1606 which forbade the profane "use of the holy name of God or of Jesus Christ or of the Holy Ghost or of the Trinitie" on the stage; Bowdler was merely working from an eighteenth-century text of Shakespeare based on the First Folio and in actual fact did not concern himself in any way with Falstaff's oaths.

If, then, we are aware of the value of textual studies, we must pay them more than lip service, and no scholar is properly trained unless he knows something of the mechanics of preparing a text. In the remarks which follow I shall confine myself to English texts from the period of the Renaissance onwards, that is, to the age of the printed book, since the texts of the manuscript age are to be the subject of another paper in this series. A distinction between the texts of the manuscript age and those of the age of the printed book is fully justified. I am aware, of course, that certain early texts and editions have survived in unique exemplars, and that the twelve surviving copies of the first edition of *King Lear* contain ten different combinations of corrected and uncorrected sheets, so that such texts may present problems closely analagous to those of texts found only in manuscript. In the main, however, it is true to say that the printed book presents the text in a fixed and standardized form, whereas every manuscript is unique, and its value as an authority for the text must be separately investigated.

Although there have been authors, from Ben Jonson in Shakespeare's day to Housman in our own, who have been extremely meticulous about the form in which their work has appeared in print, most of the conventions of English spelling and punctuation are the creation of printers and compositors, especially in the seventeenth century. Most authors, provided their words and sense have been accurately reproduced, have been content to have current printers' usage superimposed upon their writings. In other words, though a manuscript copied out fair to be sent to the publisher may represent the work in its final form as far as the author is concerned, it is not necessarily yet in the form in which it will be offered to the reader, or in which the author expects it to be offered. Thus Wordsworth sent the copy for the second edition of *Lyrical Ballads* to Humphry Davy, requesting him before the manuscript went to press to adjust the punctuation—"a business in which I am ashamed to say I am not adept." Similarly the manuscript of his *Ode on Intimations of Immortality* (first published in the *Poems* of 1807), which is in the handwriting of his sister-in-law Sara Hutchinson with notes and corrections in Wordsworth's hand, has had emphatic changes in capitalization and punctuation added, presumably by a reader at the publisher's.[6] Coleridge's *Friend* may be cited for another example. The manuscript is extant, partly in Coleridge's hand, but mainly in Sara Hutchinson's. It was originally printed by a provincial printer at Penrith, with the result that the first edition reproduces many of the eccentricities of spelling, punctuation, italicization, and capitalization of Coleridge and his amanuensis. A few years later, when a revised edition was brought out in London, most of these eccentricities were normalized. By comparison with the edition of

1818 the original edition looks more like a piece of eighteenth than of nineteenth-century typography, but there is no shred of evidence that Coleridge concerned himself in any way with the typographical practice of either printer.

Although authors have frequently shown no care for such *minutiae,* or "accidentals," as Dr. Greg calls them, they are of some concern to the editor, and his treatment of them will in large measure be determined by the nature of the edition he is preparing. For our purposes we may distinguish between three classes of editions. (1) the modern-spelling edition, (2) the old-spelling edition; and (3) the facsimile edition, sometimes called the diplomatic edition.[7]

There will always be, one hopes, editions in modern spelling of the major English authors since Spenser. Chaucer can only be modernized by altering his language, and Spenser, with his deliberately cultivated archaisms, is also separated from us by a linguistic gulf, narrow and easily crossed, but none the less real. But if ever the day comes when no modernized editions of Shakespeare and Donne and Milton are available to the general reader, our cultural heritage will be in a sad state. The responsibility of the editor of a text in modern spelling is no less than that of him who edits in the old spelling; if anything, it is greater. Nor is the task any lighter; in fact, the editor of one such work, who had no modernized text already made for him, writes in his preface that the task of modernization had convinced him "that Elizabethan editors save themselves a vast deal of trouble and risk by adhering to the original spelling and punctuation."[8] Yet, in this particular case at least, the undertaking was well worth while, bringing as it did a great deal of otherwise inaccessible material within the range of the ordinary reader, who would have been easily repelled by the apparent remoteness and strangeness of the originals.

The aim of the facsimile reprint is to provide the most accurate substitute for a rare original that typography can supply. Those who contemplate the preparation of such a text will find the principles to be followed set out in the "Rules for Editors" drawn up for the Malone Society. But with the development of cheap photographic processes the facsimile reprint will be less and less in demand, except on those occasions where it is desirable to furnish a *literatim* transcript of a manuscript, either to preserve the peculiarities of an individual writer or to aid those unskilled in palaeography, as in a work like Greg's *English Literary Autographs, 1550–1650*.

⟨ The old-spelling text is of course requisite in any standard or definitive edition. After the copy-text has been chosen, the editor reproduces it faithfully except for such corrections as he finds it necessary to make. The copy-text will usually be either the first (authorized) edition, or the last to receive the author's revision; the editorial corrections will involve such matters as the elimination of misprints, the adjustment in poetry of faulty verse-lining, the correction of inadequate punctuation, the incorporation of manifestly superior (and authentic) readings from other editions, and the emendation of corrupt passages. The *rationale* of such editorial procedure has been fully discussed and set forth by McKerrow and Greg, and one can usually find in their writings a solution for one's difficulties.[9] ⟩

Thanks to these and to other scholars, current editorial practice is fairly clearly defined, but I should like to emphasize that many editors will sooner or later find themselves face to face with problems or with materials that demand treatment different from that worked out by classical scholars or even by editors of Shakespeare, and I propose briefly to survey some of these and indicate their consequence for an editor.

⟨In recent years it has become clear that in the seventeenth century certain authors cared sufficiently for textual accuracy not to rest content with printed errata slips, but had manuscript corrections made in as many copies of their works as possible.⟩ Such autograph corrections by Sir Thomas Browne and Izaak Walton are now well known, but they were by no means the only authors to resort to this device. Even the plays of such minor court dramatists as Sir William Berkeley and Sir William Lower are known to contain manuscript corrections by or at the instigation of the authors, and editors should constantly be on the watch for other instances. Obviously such corrections are of the highest textual importance.

Other classes of material throw light on the earlier history of a work, and no one,[10] I fancy, will dispute the fact that one of the functions of a definitive edition is to illuminate as much as possible the origin and development of the work edited. Every student of the Romantic Period, for instance, knows something of the fascinating struggle for artistic perfection revealed by Keats's manuscripts, or of the information about the development of Wordsworth's thought and art furnished by the new Oxford edition. Many writers, too, have constantly revised their writings after the first publication; sometimes the extent of revision can be shown by recording the readings of the successive editions, but often the revisions are so thorough that there is no alternative but to print all the versions or, if not all, at least the first and final ones. Examples that come to mind immediately are Whitman's *Leaves of Grass*, whose problems were discussed here several years ago,[11] or Fitzgerald's successive versions of *The Rubaiyat of Omar Khayyam*. But these are by no means solitary instances. Among the Elizabethans, Daniel and Drayton revised throughout their careers. In the eighteenth century Pope wrote *The Rape of the Lock* in two forms, and left two *Dunciads*. In the nineteenth century both Wordsworth and Tennyson completely rewrote some of their early poems, and Coleridge reworked *The Rime of the Ancient Mariner* from 1798 until his death. Nor are poets the only revisers. While English literature can scarcely furnish a parallel equal in interest and importance to the case of Montaigne's *Essays* in French, the two versions of Sidney's *Arcadia*, the successive editions of Burton's *Anatomy of Melancholy*, and of Walton's *Lives* involve problems scarcely less complex.

The bulk of authors' manuscripts, first drafts, and work sheets that has survived may sometimes be very considerable indeed. The most famous of such documents is of course the collection of Milton's manuscripts preserved at Trinity College, Cambridge. But there is scarcely a major author since the beginning of the eighteenth century of whose work some manuscripts have not survived. Such materials are not necessarily of primary textual authority, since they may consist of early drafts, or the author may have made his final revisions in proof; but they can be of utmost importance in correcting the text, as a simple example will make clear. The epigraph to the second chapter of *The Heart of Midlothian* consists of two stanzas from Prior's *The Thief and the Cordelier*. In the novel one of the lines reads

There the squire of the poet and knight of the post,

which is nonsense. It should be

There the squire of the pad and the knight of the post.

This example is unusual, because there is the possibility of a double check. Not only do the texts of Prior give the right reading, but Scott's manuscript, which is extant, shows that he quoted the passage correctly. Nevertheless this printer's error was repeated in all editions until 1948.[12]

Two other similar classes of material that have as yet been scarcely used by editors should also be noticed: printer's copy and author's proofs. Printer's copy and proof-sheets have both survived from as early as the fifteenth century; in neither of these instances, however, was the author involved. But even a brief enumeration of some of the surviving manuscripts which were sent by the authors to the press is an impressive one, including as it does Book I of Hooker's *Ecclesiastical Polity*, part of Sir John Harington's translation of Ariosto's *Orlando Furioso*, Book I of *Paradise Lost*, Pope's *Essay on Criticism*, the second edition of *Lyrical Ballads*, and Wordsworth's *Poems* of 1807. The Bodleian manuscript of Herbert's *Temple*, though not sent to the press, is the one bearing the *imprimatur* of the official licenser, and is therefore of textual authority at least equal to that of the first edition. Of author's proofs I know of no actual examples earlier than some of Dr. Johnson's in the R. B. Adam Collection, and the earliest I happen myself to have examined were of works by Hazlitt and Scott, but there must be many others in existence awaiting full examination by interested scholars.

A further class of material offering editorial problems of its own is to be found in those manuscripts, such as letters, diaries, and notebooks, which were never prepared for the press by the authors, and were never intended for the press. Editors, and especially biographer-editors, have allowed themselves a latitude in handling such materials that varies all the way from a naive desire to safeguard the hero's dignity to flagrant dishonesty. One of the earliest writers to suffer from such editorial ineptitude was Donne. His son in editing his letters not only showed extreme carelessness over dates and addresses but, it is now known, altered the names of those to whom the letters were written, presumably in order to suggest that he had access to a much greater volume of his father's correspondence than in fact he had.[13] Even Walton was not above tampering with Donne's letters, so that on one occasion he strung together excerpts from five different letters, clapped a date on the end, and presented the result as a single epistle.[14] My colleague Professor W. M. Sale tells me that Samuel Richardson's letters were similarly mishandled by Mrs. Barbauld, and other examples from eighteenth and nineteenth-century biographies could doubtless be found with little difficulty.

Many of these earlier editorial mutilations are explicable in terms of the standards of their age. Two of Donne's letters seem to have survived only in the opening and close; the intermediate news or business communication, or whatever it was, has been omitted.[15] His contemporaries were interested in the elegance of Donne's epistolary style and the ingenuity of his compliments more than in the details of his personal relations with his friends. Nineteenth-century taboos were responsible for a different kind of excision altogether; witness those, for instance, in the early editions of Lamb's letters. One recalls how Lamb wrote to Thomas Manning about the little book on honours and dignities which he had written for children,[16] and how in the course of it he had envisaged himself advancing through all the degrees of the peerage, concluding with "Duke Lamb."

> It would look like quibbling [he continued] to carry it on further ... otherwise I have sometimes in my dreams imagined myself still advancing, as 9th, King Lamb; 10th, Emperor Lamb; 11th, Pope Innocent, higher than which is nothing upon earth.

At least, that is what appeared in the nineteenth-century editions; what Lamb actually wrote was "higher than which is nothing but the Lamb of God."

Coleridge, who left behind him vast stores of marginalia, notes, scattered papers, and other *disjecta membra,* has given much trouble to his editors. Henry Nelson Coleridge, who edited the *Literary Remains,* did some very strange things with his uncle's writings, though he was attempting in all sincerity to impose some order on chaos, and to show his uncle to best advantage. Ernest Hartley Coleridge, in editing the series of extracts from the notebooks entitled *Anima Poetae,* had similar problems to face. Not only was the family still reluctant to reveal the extent of Coleridge's disagreement with his wife and his attachment for Sara Hutchinson (which entailed various excisions), but the compressed form of many of the notes, with their disregard for ordinary rules of syntax, to say nothing of their highly individual punctuation and capitalization, produced numerous additional difficulties. Here are two brief examples of E. H. Coleridge's editorial procedure. In each case the passage is transcribed as accurately as possible from the original, and then followed by the corresponding passage in *Anima Poetae.*

A new year—the old Wants/ The new from God, the old our own/ . . .

Time—3 fold—Future slow—Present swift—Past unmoveable—No impatience will quicken the Loiterer—no Terror, no delight rein in the Flyer—No Regret set in motion the Stationary—would'st be happy, take the Delayer for thy counsellor, do not choose the Flyer for thy Friend, nor the ever-remainer for thy Enemy—

(Notebook viii, p. 3)

The old world begins a new year. That is *ours,* but this is from God.

We may think of time as threefold. Slowly comes the Future, swift the Present passes by, but the Past is unmoveable. No impatience will quicken the loiterer; no terror, no delight rein in the flyer, and no regret set in motion the stationary. Wouldst be happy, take the delayer for thy counsellor; do not choose the flyer for thy friend, nor the ever-remainer for thine enemy.

(*Anima Poetae,* p. 22)

Reviewers resemble often the English Jury and the Italian Conclave, that they are incapable of eating till they have condemned or crowned—

Pope like an old Lark who tho' he leaves off soaring & singing in the height, yet has his *Spurs* grow longer & sharper, the older he grows.

(Notebook xvii, p. 167)

Reviewers resemble often the English jury and the Italian conclave, they are incapable of eating till they have condemned or craned.

The Pope [may be compared to] an old lark, who though he leaves off soaring and singing in the height, yet has his spurs grow longer and sharper the older he grows.

(*Anima Poetae*, p. 223)

In the first passage I suspect that E. H. Coleridge misread "Wants" as "world," as it is difficult otherwise to account for the rephrasing; in the second he was certainly baffled by "crowned," which he rendered by the unintelligible "craned." But the two notes in the second extract are interesting for another misconception, which would positively have delighted Coleridge, who was always fascinated by the workings of the principle of the association of ideas. In writing the first of the two notes Coleridge's mind went from the notion of juries condemning before eating to the line in *The Rape of the Lock*,

And wretches hang that juryman may dine,

and thence to its author, who became the subject of the next note; his grandson's mind, on the other hand, was caught by the phrase "Italian conclave," and he therefore interpreted the succeeding note as referring to the pontiff instead of the poet.

E. H. Coleridge was for many years a schoolmaster, and his procedure with the text of the notebooks resembles that of a conscientious instructor correcting a carelessly written schoolboy exercise. He believed, no doubt, that he was only doing what was needful to remove unnecessary stumbling blocks from the path of a reader, and he was preparing a book for the general reader rather than the scholar. But notions of editorial responsibility have changed within the last fifty years, and such manipulation of the text is contrary to modern standards. Editors of comparatively recent material will, no doubt, always have to make excisions out of regard to the susceptibilities of the family and friends of the author, but what they do print will be printed with scrupulous fidelity to the wording of the original, and there will be some statement as to the nature and extent of any necessary omissions. ⟨ The problem of fidelity to the minuter details of the author's text—to the "accidentals"—is a more difficult one and depends, in the last resort, on the editor's taste and judgment. It is worth bearing in mind, I think, that there is a real gain in consulting, wherever possible, the reader's convenience. Mr. Harold Williams, in his recent edition of Swift's Journal to Stella, reproduces faithfully Swift's "little language" from such of the letters as have survived in manuscript, with the exception that Swift's "th" and "te" become "the," "y" and "yo" becomes "you," and "yr" and "yrs" become "your" and "yours." The consequent gain in legibility is considerable, as may be seen by comparison with the edition which prints these forms as Swift wrote them. As Mr. Williams points out in his preface:

> In these days, when the art of photography has been enlisted in the student's service, the attempt to reproduce in print insignificant orthographical peculiarities has less meaning than it once had. The result can never be wholly satisfactory, and it may only repel or distract the reader.

Again, Professor Vinaver's edition of Malory, the most exciting piece of literary scholarship of the past decade, Is not least so because the editor has made Malory so much easier to read in the original text than ever before. Compare any page of this edition with the corresponding passage in Oskar Sommer's and the difference will be apparent at a glance. The paragraphing, the repunctuation, and the setting of the dialogue in the manner of the modern novel are all introduced without any compromising of editorial integrity, and the gain to the reader who is not primarily a mediaevalist is enormous.

A less successful solution of some of these problems is exemplified in the edition recently published of Melville's *Billy Budd*. Two pages of the original manuscript are reproduced, so that a measure of comparison with the printed text is possible. Melville's spelling, we are told, has been corrected "to modern American usage," and any editorial insertions in the text are enclosed within pointed brackets (instead of the more usual square ones). Thus the editor conceals the fact that Melville used such spellings as "Judgement," "fellow-man," "innocense," and "respectivly" (though the last two may have been mere slips of the pen), but if Melville neglected to close quotations marks or to add a period at the end of a paragraph, the fact is forcibly brought to our notice by means of pointed brackets. It would be of little value, no doubt, to record that the *um* of "circumstances" is two minims short, but Melville's characteristic spellings are not without interest, while his careless omission of occasional punctuation marks is of far less significance and their silent editorial correction would have been perfectly proper.

Further, the textual notes are insufficient to permit an adequate reconstruction of the original. One discovers, after some initial bewilderment, that what are referred to as "variants" are in fact words and phrases that have been deleted and on second thoughts replaced by others; words and phrases said to have been "omitted" are those which in revision were *added*, very often above a caret mark. Nor is there any attempt in the notes to distinguish the various stages of revision. In the phrase "he could never convert," "could" is above the line in ink over a caret mark, but the fact is not recorded; in the phrase "without first performing," "first" is above the line in ink over a caret mark, and here it is recorded as "*om.*" In the phrase "that hitherto has stood in human record," Melville first wrote in ink "that stands in human record," then altered it in pencil to "that hitherto has stood in authoritative record," but finally deleted "authoritative" and restored "human." The textual note here merely cites the phrase "that stands in authoritative record" as the "variant" of the final form, thus telescoping two steps in the process of revision into one. Thus an editor, however well intentioned, by departing from established conventions and inadequately describing the state of his original, can confuse more than he aids the reader, and a student wishing to make a close study of Melville's method of composition in this tale is still unable to do so without recourse to the original manuscript.

Though it is a function of the editor to aid the reader wherever he can, it is scarcely possible to condone the practice of the editors of *The Oxford Book of Seventeenth Century Verse:*

> Where words or lines might seem ugly to modern eyes [they write], or where a difference in usage might lead to ambiguity, we have substituted simpler forms, always taking care (we believe) that the substituted form *was actually in use during the seventeenth century.*

This, though the editors disavow it, is really normalization. One used to get Old English texts normalized to standard West Saxon of about 1000 A.D., and even normalized texts of Chaucer. But happily such a practice is out of favour nowadays, for editors know that not until the eighteenth century was normalization imposed on English orthography, and then by printers rather than authors.[17]

There is, however, a real difference between normalization and the expansion of contractions, or the attempt to reproduce in type scribal peculiarities outside the range of the printer's case. The value of the facsimile reprint, in other words, is strictly limited, and photographic aids are diminishing its usefulness. Hence, as a literary student—as distinct from the historian or the palaeographer—I deplore the over-meticulous habit of printing legal records and other old documents with all their contractions, or with the contractions expanded in italics. The silent expansion of contractions is but a courtesy to the reader. Actually, many of these documents ought merely to be described and summarized, with a few of the important phrases quoted; the class of document to which the example belongs may be indicated, if necessary, through reference to historical source books or to formularies.

Many of the processes in the preparation of a text, such as transcription, collation, and even proof-correction, involve, it must be admitted, much sheer drudgery, and unlike some other forms of drudgery they cannot be delegated. They are exacting, and they demand the unremitting concentration of a highly trained mind. But the less they show the better; the text's the thing, not the textual notes; and this is perhaps the final principle that an editor would do well to bear in mind. If he has been brought to his task by enthusiasm for an author or a book, he will wish above all things by his work to pass on that enthusiasm. We may fitly conclude with some other words of the classical scholar with whom we began:

> A man is led by some feeling of kinship for what is greater than himself to devote his life to the interpretation of a poet, philosopher, or historian, to the elucidation of the language itself on its purely linguistic side, or to that of the art or institutions of antiquity. Such a man will freely give himself up to the most arid and laborious investigations. No erasure in a manuscript, no half-read scholium, no fragmentary inscription will seem unworthy of his attention; no grammatical nicety or stylistic peculiarity will be passed by as too trivial for his patient study. All these things will live in his hands; for they are all transformed by his faith in something to which he can hardly give a name, but which, to him, is more real than anything else.[18]

NOTES

1. John Burnet, *Essays and Addresses*, p. 36.
2. R. W. Chapman, *Three Centuries of Johnsonian Scholarship*, pp. 28–29.
3. *TLS*, May 20, 1949, p. 329.
4. G. B. Harrison, *Shakespeare, Twenty-Three Plays and Sonnets;* O. J. Campbell, *The Living Shakespeare.*
5. M. J. Quinlan, *Victorian Prelude*, p. 246.
6. W. Hale White, *A Description of the Wordsworth and Coleridge Manuscripts in the Possession of Mr. T. Norton Longman*, plates i and iii.
7. The term "diplomatic edition" is so loosely employed that, pending more precise definition and agreement on its meaning, its use is better avoided. It has been employed to cover anything from an edition which consistently adopts the readings of a single text or manuscript to one which reproduces a particular text with extreme scrupulosity, down to every contraction and error, even, in the case of printed texts, to turned letters and irregular spacing.

In the discussion following the reading of this paper it was suggested that whereas a facsimile reprint was a page-for-page and line-for-line reprint, a diplomatic edition was not, but I cannot feel certain that this distinction can be made to hold.
8. J. Dover Wilson, Preface to *Life in Shakespeare's England.*

9. R. B. McKerrow, *Prolegomena for the Oxford Shakespeare* and W. W. Greg, *The Editorial Problem in Shakespeare*. See also Greg's "Rationale of Copy-Text" in the present volume.

10. With the possible exception of Messrs. Wellek and Warren, who state that "if we examine drafts, rejections, exclusions, and cuts, we conclude them not, finally, necessary to an understanding of the finished work or to a judgment upon it. Their interest is that of any alternative, i.e., they may set into relief the qualities of the final text. But the same end may very well be achieved by devising for ourselves alternatives, whether or not they have actually passed through the author's mind." (*Theory of Literature*, p. 86).

11. Sculley Bradley, "The Problem of a Variorum Edition of Whitman's *Leaves of Grass*," *English Institute Annual, 1941*, pp. 129–57.

12. H. J. C. Grierson, *Sir Walter Scott, Bart.*, p. 164, n. I am indebted for this example to my colleague, Professor David Daiches.

13. I. A. Shapiro, "The Text of Donne's *Letters to Several Persons of Honour*," *Review of English Studies*, VII (1931), 291–301.

14. R. E. Bennett, "Walton's Use of Donne's Letters," *Philological Quarterly*, XVI (1937), 30–34.

15. Evelyn M. Simpson, *A Study of the Prose Works of John Donne*, chapter 12, letters 23 and 25.

16. Letter of January 2, 1810.

17. For the argument against normalization, see W. W. Greg, *The Editorial Problem in Shakespeare*, p. 11.

18. Burnet, p. 34.

FREDSON BOWERS

Some Principles for Scholarly Editions of

Nineteenth-Century American Authors

FREDSON BOWERS *offers both a call to action and a guide to duty. Drawing particularly upon his experience with the Hawthorne Centenary Edition, Bowers argues that because "commonly esteemed editions" of classic American writers are untrustworthy, new editors of these texts must take care to "bring to their task the careful effort that has been established as necessary for English Renaissance texts." Only then will the editing of such texts "become a respectable occupation at long last and not a piece of hack work for the paperbacks." Bowers also outlines the exact procedures necessary to establish a critical text and describes the elements of an apparatus that will enable the reader to understand what the editor has done and why. By and large these procedures and desiderata have been adopted by the Modern Language Association's Center for Editions of American Authors and incorporated into its* Statement of Editorial Principles *. . . (New York, 1967).*

T HE FIRST PROBLEM that faces any editor of a text from the nineteenth century, or earlier, is whether to modernize. For nineteenth-century American books there is only one answer: no gain results from modernizing, and much is lost that is characteristic of the author. One may safely say that nothing in the spelling, punctu-

Reprinted from *Studies in Bibliography*, XVII (1964), 223–28, with the permission of the author and the Bibliographical Society of the University of Virginia.

ation, capitalization, word-division, or paragraphing of nineteenth-century books is likely to cause a presentday reader any difficulty, whereas an attempt at modernization is certain to destroy a number of the values of the original. Every reason exists to preserve these classic texts in as close a form as possible to the authors' intentions, to the extent that the surviving documents for each individual work permit of such reconstruction. Indeed, one may flatly assert that any text that is modernized can never pretend to be scholarly, no matter at what audience it is aimed.

The second problem is whether to edit the text critically or to content oneself with a reprint of some single document. Again, an argument cannot really exist in favor of a mere reprint, no matter how neatly such a procedure enables an editor to dodge his basic responsibility. It is probably safe to say that no nineteenth-century text of any length exists that is not in need of some correction, and possibly even of revisory emendation. Once an editor tinkers in any way with his original, he has entered upon the province of critical editing; and he had better go the whole way and be consistent than dip his big toe in the water and then draw back in alarm lest he suddenly find himself out of his depth.

⟨ The first step in critical editing is the so-called establishment of the text. The first step in *this* process is the determination of the exact forms of the early documents in which the text is preserved and of the facts about their relationship to one another. That is, the early editions within an author's lifetime, and within a sufficient time after his death to give the opportunity for testamentary documents to be produced, must be collated and the authoritative editions isolated. An authoritative edition is one set directly from manuscript, or a later edition that contains corrections or revisions that proceeded from the author.⟩ Authority divides itself between the words as meaningful units (i.e., the substantives) and the accidentals, that is, the forms that the words take in respect to spelling, punctuation, capitalization, and division. In this question the theory of copy-text proposed by Sir Walter Greg rules supreme. Greg distinguished between the authority of the substantives and of the forms, or accidentals, assumed by these substantives. If only the first edition, set from manuscript, has authority, as being the closest in each of these two respects to the author's lost manuscript, then both authorities are combined in one edition. On the other hand, a revised edition may alter the authority of some of the substantives; but the transmission of the author's accidentals through the hands, and mind, of still another compositor destroys the authority of these features of the first edition, set from manuscript. An eclectic text must be constructed which combines the superior authority of most of the words in the revised edition with the superior authority of the forms of words in the first edition.

The determination of authority is not always easy in a later edition. For example, in Hawthorne's *Scarlet Letter* three editions (i.e., three different typesettings) were made during his lifetime. In the second edition, set and printed in 1850 within two months of the first, 226 pages were completely reset, but 96 pages were printed from the standing type of the first edition. In the 226 pages of the resetting occur 62 variants from the first edition, of which three are corrections of first-edition typographical errors and four are typographical errors in the second edition. Twelve different words (i.e., variant substantive readings) appear in these pages, and there are 43 changes in spelling, capitalization, and word-division.

Of more import, in the 96 pages of standing type, someone ordered eight variants, of which three are spelling, four are punctuation, and one is division. Here if anywhere the author's intentions would be visible if he had ordered these changes in standing type; but an editor will find no clearcut authority in the changes, and indeed some evidence that at least two of them go contrary to Hawthorne's observed characteristics. Once these variants are rejected as non-authorial, therefore, the conclusion must be drawn that Hawthrone did not supervise the production of the second edition and hence no revisions can be accepted from the reset type-pages, although a few corrections will prove useful.

Nor does the third edition, the last in Hawthorne's lifetime, yield any readings other than a continuation of corruption, and some necessary but obvious correction. None of the 37 additional alterations in the words seems to have any chance of being an authorial revision, and most are clearly errors.

In these circumstances, the editor is forced back to the first edition as the sole authority. But the question then arises, what is the specific authority of each page of this first edition, for it is possible for copies to vary because of changes made during the course of printing. Mechanical collation on the Hinman Machine of eight copies of *The Scarlet Letter* discloses four differences in readings, but all of these seem to have resulted from type being loosened during the course of printing so that the progression is from correctness to error. However, unless an editor had established the correct readings where these errors exist, he would wrongly have imputed the errors to the first edition; and it is possible that he might have emended differently from the original reading. For example, because an exclamation point dropped out very early in the printing of page 228, no edition before the Centenary recovered this original authoritative punctuation, for all editors were content to follow the second-edition comma that the later compositor inserted when he came to the blank space in his copy.

The collation of multiple copies reveals other possibilities for variation. In *The Scarlet Letter*, interestingly enough, economy of printing led the printer of the first edition to typeset the last two text pages in duplicate. Fortunately no differences appear in these two settings, but the possibility of variation is always present. For example, the new Preface to the second edition was also set in duplicate, and here one typesetting has a comma that appears to be authoritative, whereas the other omits it. An editor who neglected to collate a number of copies might have reprinted arbitrarily from the wrong typesetting and thus, even though in a small matter, have departed from Hawthorne's intention.

Even if the first edition were printed from plates, machine collation is necessary to discover concealed printings within the so-called first edition, for the possibility exists that plates may be altered between impressions. For example, the Ticknor and Field cost books list four printings from plates in 1851 of *The House of the Seven Gables*, and one printing in 1852. Since no copy of an 1852 printing has turned up, it seems clear that one of the unidentified 1851 printings represents the fifth impression with a title-page date unchanged. No book collector or librarian has the least idea which printing his precious first-edition copy represents, but the Hinman Machine discloses the order by combining the evidence of type batter with the evidence for resetting of damaged plates as well as various mendings. It is pure luck that these extensive plate repairs were carried out without producing any changes in the text to baffle the non-bibliographical editor, and it is clear that Hawthorne (if he saw any errors) ordered no revisions between these printings.

But not all changes made in plates from printing to printing are so respectful of the text. For instance, the third edition of *The Scarlet Letter* was printed from plates in 1850 and these plates remained in use at least as late as 1886. In the course of the various repairs made in this interval, five different words got altered so that the text of the final printings from these plates differs from that of the initial printings in this respect as well as in dozens and dozens of punctuation marks worn off or quite altered by batter. These changes have no authority, but it is clear that Hawthorne himself made some alterations in the plates for one of the later printings of *The Marble Faun*, revisions of which an editor must take account if he knows about them.

⟨ When an author's manuscript is preserved, this has paramount authority, of course. Yet the fallacy is still maintained that since the first edition was proofread by the author, it must represent his final intentions and hence should be chosen as copy-text. Practical experience shows the contrary. When one collates the manuscript of *The House of the Seven Gables* against the first printed edition, one finds an average of ten to fifteen differences per page between the manuscript and the print, many of them consistent alterations from the manuscript system of punctuation, capitalization, spelling, and word-division. It would be ridiculous to argue that Hawthorne made approximately three to four thousand small changes in proof, and then wrote the manuscript of *The Blithedale Romance* according to the same system as the manuscript of the *Seven Gables*, a system that he had rejected in proof.

A close study of the several thousand variants in *Seven Gables* demonstrates that almost every one can be attributed to the printer. That Hawthorne passed them in proof is indisputable, but that they differ from what he wrote in the manuscript and manifestly preferred is also indisputable. Thus the editor must choose the manuscript as his major authority, correcting from the first edition only what are positive errors in the accidentals of the manuscript.

However, when words differ in the print from the manuscripts, as they do a certain number of times, the question of authority arises. Any difference in words can arise only by reason of printer's error that Hawthorne did not catch in proof, or by reason of changes that Hawthorne himself made in the lost proofsheets. Each variant, thus, becomes an editorial responsibility, to be adjudicated on the evidence available.) In *The Blithedale Romance* Hawthorne can be assigned twenty-four of the verbal proofchanges between manuscript and first edition. The printer is responsible, fairly clearly, for the remaining seven of the thirty-one differences in wording.

Here we encounter the theory of a critical edition. Obviously, an editor cannot simply reprint the manuscript, for he must substitute for its readings any words that he believes Hawthorne changed in proof. Once more, if one argues why not reprint the first edition and be done with it—then two questions of evidence are pertinent. First, in reprinting the first edition of *The Blithedale Romance,* one would be attributing to Hawthorne seven words that are actually printer's errors. Secondly, if an author's habits of expression go beyond words and into the forms that these take, together with the punctuation that helps to shape the relationships of these words, then one is foolish to prefer a printing-house style to the author's style. This distinction is not theory, but fact. Hawthorne's punctuation, for example, is much more meaningful in respect to emphasis and to delicate matters of parenthesis and subordination than is the printing-house style in which *Seven Gables* and *The Blithedale Romance* appeared. In each book, the real flavor of Hawthorne, cumulatively developing in several thousand small distinctions, can be found only in the manuscript.

Sometimes the Greg formula that authors' substantive revisions in later editions must always be followed, when identified, but that the best authority for the accidentals remains the edition set directly from manuscript, produces some complexity, and the result will agree in a number of details with no preserved document, even though it will represent the nearest approximation in every respect of the author's final intentions. An eclectic editor must be prepared for any eventuality.

⌐ Granted that an editor has established a critical text that will stand up under the most searching investigation of scholarship, then what will scholars want from his apparatus? First, a list of the internal variants in the first and in any other authoritative edition as revealed by the collation of a number of copies of each, preferably on the Hinman Machine. Secondly, a complete list of all editorial changes in the selected copy-text. These changes comprise corrections and revisions admitted from later editions as well as the editor's own alterations. For the sake of the record, the editor should list the earliest edition from which he draws any alteration. Textual notes should discuss briefly any arguable emendations, or failure to emend. >

⟨ The next item is the Historical Collation. This should contain all the substantive alterations from the established edited text found in a group of significant later editions. An edition is to be defined as any new typesetting. Obviously, any edition within the author's lifetime may be significant and must be collated. Thereafter the editor's discretion may enter. Usually it is important to select editions that have been influential in the formation of the text, or that have been commonly used by critics. For instance, the decision was made by the Centenary editors of Hawthorne to confine the Historical Collation largely to the Boston collected editions published in the Ticknor and Field line to Houghton Mifflin, as well as any separate editions published within the author's lifetime. For *The Scarlet Letter*, therefore, the Centenary Edition records the readings from the second edition of 1850, the third edition of 1850, the Little Classics edition of 1875, the Riverside of 1883, and ends with the Autograph of 1900. Included always are the first English editions in case any authoritative changes were made in the copy sent abroad, and usually any modern edition that has been freshly edited in fact instead of in theory.

To insure accuracy, the sets of plates are taken as representing the various editions, and the earliest and latest printings from each edition-set of plates have been collated on the Hinman Machine

and their variants recorded in the Centenary apparatus. All printings from plates within the author's lifetime have also been collated
whenever variants appeared between the first and last impressions
of any set of plates instituted before his death.

Although this Historical Collation is chiefly a record of the corruption of the text, it serves as a useful object lesson in the untrustworthy nature of various commonly esteemed editions. More
important, however, this list insures that all cards are on the table.
If any collated edition has authority not recognized by the editor,
the critic will find the record of its variants and all the evidence
on which, throughout, the editor made up his mind about the details of the text.

When a manuscript is preserved, an important separate list will
contain a record of all the rejected readings and revisions during
the process of inscription. Moreover, the variants in any preserved
proof-sheets should be recorded with the same scrupulousness
and for the same critical purpose.

So far as I know, a problem that no editor has faced concerns
the word-division whenever a compound in the copy-text is divided at the end of one line and the start of the next. The exact
form of all such compounds must be settled so that the edited text
will contain that one that is characteristic of the author. Since editorial judgment is sometimes involved in this process, a list of such
divided possible compounds should be provided. Correspondingly,
the modern printer will divide a number of compounds so that a
reader will not always know the exact form in the original. A
second section of the compound list should note the copy-text
reading in all such cases.

The amount of collating and checking in such an edition as has
been outlined is very heavy indeed; but only this editorial process
scrupulously carried out will produce editions of American classics
that will stand the test of time and, heaven willing, need never be
edited again from the ground up. When scholars editing American
literature will bring to their task the careful effort that has been
established as necessary for English Renaissance texts, say, then the
editing of American texts will become a respectable occupation at
long last, and not a piece of hack work for the paperbacks.

JAMES THORPE

The Aesthetics of Textual Criticism

JAMES THORPE *is concerned with the need for a "consistent set of aesthetic assumptions" as the basis for sound textual criticism, and explores three basic questions: "What is the aesthetic object with which textual criticism can deal? What constitutes the integrity of the work of art? When a literary work exists in several authorial versions, which is the real work of art?" Ranging widely and instructively over dozens of examples and illustrations, Thorpe calls attention to the "controlling importance" of the artist's intentions. Indeed, "while the textual critic should not neglect to carry out the more or less mechanical operations which his masters enjoin upon him, he must also undertake to discover all that he can, from whatever source, about the linguistic intentions of the artist." This sophisticated concern for all the evidence and its implications serves to make the textual critic's task more difficult, but more valuable.*

MANY PEOPLE on occasion prefer a textual error to an authentic reading. One mistake by a compositor of Melville's *White-Jacket*—setting "soiled fish of the sea" instead of "coiled fish of the sea"—achieved an adventitious fame some years ago. Various readers have since declared themselves in favor of the

---

Reprinted from *PMLA*, LXXX (1965), 465–82, with the permission of the author and the Modern Language Association of America.

error, on the grounds that "soiled fish" makes a richer, more interesting passage than the ordinary "coiled fish of the sea." In short, the error seems to them to create a better work.

The preference for one reading over another, the basic decision of textual criticism, is in this case being made on what are called aesthetic grounds. And the decision is made despite demonstrable proof that the preferred reading is a compositorial mistake. Most bibliographers, editors, and textual critics would at this point join in a chorus of denunciation of the person so ill-advised as to make such a preposterous decision.

On what grounds shall we decide which party to join? Does the wretch who hugs the error deserve denunciation because he decided on aesthetic rather than textual grounds? Because he put out the palace fire in Lilliput by improper means? Because we mistrust his taste? Because we fear lest the taste of any individual become the norm? Or because he contumaciously refused to prefer what the author wrote?

On the other hand, suppose we side with the man who chose the error. What is our reason? As a vote for value in a topsy-turvy world in which the worse is so often preferred? As a protest against those vile mechanics, the textual bibliographers, who claim that their findings alone are logical, scientific, and irrefutable because they involve infinite pains? As a forthright preference for the best works of art?

Some choose one way and some the other, A recent writer has suggested a rearrangement of Ben Jonson's eulogy on Shakespeare by transferring lines 51–54 to a point ten lines before the place that Jonson chose to put them. The passage "could seem less awkward following the lines just quoted than where it actually occurs." The transposed passage "forms with the lines preceding and succeeding it, a perfectly coherent unit." In short, "I think," the writer says, "a good case can be made that the change is an improvement."[1] The case rests on the greater literary merit of the resulting passage. The first flowering of William Empson's genius as an anatomist of language, his *Seven Types of Ambiguity*, included discussions of several passages in which he found the authorial readings inferior to revisions which he could make. In Rupert

Brooke's line about "The keen / Unpassioned beauty of a great machine," he considered "unpassioned" as "prosaic and intellectually shoddy" in comparison with his own word, "impassioned," which provided a daring and successful image. Similarly, his high evaluation of the playful dignity and rhythm of the line "Queen-lily June with a rose in her hair" depended on his misreading the first word as "Queen Lily" rather than as an adverb, which made the line (he thought) ebb away "into complacence and monotony."[2]

On the other hand, writers have suggested changes which resulted, they thought, in a text of less literary merit. In his edition of Shakespeare, Samuel Johnson replaced the passage in *Hamlet* which editors had been printing as "In private to inter him" with the original reading "In hugger mugger to inter him," which had apparently been considered inelegant. "That the words now replaced are better," Johnson observed, "I do not undertake to prove: it is sufficient that they are *Shakespeare's*." He went on to give his rationale for retaining the authorial reading in the face of a possible improvement. "If phraseology is to be changed as words grow uncouth by disuse, or gross by vulgarity, the history of every language will be lost; we shall no longer have the words of any authour; and, as these alterations will be often unskilfully made, we shall in time have very little of his meaning."[3] In wanting to conserve the past, his argument is basically historical.

Thus the choice in these cases seems to be between the better word and the words of the author. Such a choice was not likely to arise under an earlier view of textual study which assumed that the authorial version was always the "best" reading. If the power of a divine afflatus enabled the poet to create, he could hardly be improved upon. Shelley, for example, maintained in "A Defence of Poetry" that "poetry is indeed something divine" and that verse is "the echo of the eternal music." George Lyman Kittredge was horrified by the notion "that prompters and proofreaders can (or could) improve Shakespeare."[4] With a less romantic view of the act of artistic creation, one can face this possibility with equanimity: if you happen to believe that the compositor improved on Melville, the Great Chain of Being is not endangered.

Whether our preference lights on the better word or on the words of the author, and whatever reason we give for our decision, we have done more than make one elementary choice. For all textual decisions have an aesthetic basis or are built on an aesthetic assumption, and it is idle to try to dissociate textual grounds from aesthetic grounds as the reason for our choice. Consequently, to make one kind of textual decision is to commit oneself, in principle at least, to a whole series of related decisions. Before we realize what we have done, we may have decided who should be called the author of MacLeish's *J. B.*, whether the eighteenth-century emendations to *Comus* deserve to be incorporated into the text, and which one of the versions of Hardy's *The Return of the Native* is the "real" novel.

Before we make our choice, it might be useful to bring into the open at least the first aesthetic assumption which lies behind textual criticism, and to expose it to scrutiny. The basic questions are no different from those which one confronts in every form of literary study, and in the course of this essay I will discuss three assumptions about the work of art, assumptions which have a controlling effect on the practice of textual criticism. The most fundamental question is this: what is the phenomenon or aesthetic object with which textual criticism properly deals? The things which can be called aesthetic objects because they are capable of arousing an aesthetic response in us are (permit me to say) of three kinds: works of chance, works of nature, and works of art. Works of chance are any objects which are formed by random activity: a painting created when a can of paint is tipped over by the vibration of an electric fan and spills onto a canvas; a poem formed by combining an entry (selected by a throw of dice) in each column of a dictionary; a musical composition made by recording the sounds of traffic at a busy intersection; a sculpture consisting of a wastepaper basket into which an office worker has tossed the envelopes which brought the day's mail. Works of nature are any objects or effects which are formed by natural phenomena: a changing pattern of cumulus clouds against a blue sky, the sound of the wind whistling through the boughs of a tree, the smell of the blossoms of Viburnum carlesii. Since language is a human invention and not a natural phenomenon, literary works cannot by definition be works of nature. Works of art are any objects created by human agency for the purpose of arousing an aesthetic response. These are the works which satisfy our conventional ideas of the painting, the sculpture, the symphony, the poem, the play, the novel. Since the work of art is an intended aesthetic object, the idea of either a random or a natural work of art is self-contradictory. Human intelligence was purposefully engaged in the creation of the work of art, but it may not have been successful; the term "work of art" is thus descriptive rather than evaluative, and it includes failures as well as successes. The language of the literary work, whether judged a success or a failure, is a fulfillment of the author's intentions.

Having pushed all aesthetic objects into these three rooms, we cannot, however, very properly slam the doors and go on our way rejoicing. For every thing is an aesthetic object for somebody. The complex organization of some human beings will respond in aesthetic experience to the stimulus of any object, particularly if its usual scale is altered or its ordinary context is displaced. Moreover, memory stands ready, on the least hint, to supply the substance for aesthetic response. A classified ad describing a cottage for sale in Florida, with the beach on one side and an orange grove on the other, may create a response which is indistinguishable from that which derives from Marlowe's "Passionate Shepherd to His Love"; for a melancholic reader, however, the ad may be the poor man's "Dover Beach." Likewise, a random pile of beer cans may arouse a response similar to a sculpture, and so forth. These facts make the situation complicated, but we cannot simplify it by saying that people do not or should not have aesthetic experiences from such objects, or that they are all mad if they do; they do in fact have such experiences, and the invocation of madness may in these cases be the last defence of a bewildered man. Moreover, these examples do not represent clear types; there are innumerable objects which may be responded to as sculpture between the pile of beer cans on the one hand and the Pietà of Michelangelo on the other, and there is no convenient line that can be drawn which marks the limit of where the "normal" person "should" make an aesthetic response. It took "the wise men of the society of Salomon's House," in

Bacon's *New Atlantis,* to be able "to discern (as far as appertaineth to the generations of men) between divine miracles, works of nature, works of art, and impostures and illusions of all sorts."

The problems of criticism become immense, even intolerable, if every object must be taken seriously as a potential source of aesthetic experience, if criticism is invited to preside over all creation. So, in self-defence, we are always on the lookout for ways to cut the area of responsibility but never in search of less authority. In the last generation or two, one tendency in criticism has been to limit attention to the aesthetic object and to move away from the complex problems associated with the artist as unpredictable personality. We have been taught, by the French Symbolists and their followers at second and third hand, that the intentions of the artist are not to be trusted, that the intentions of the work of art are all-important, and that the task of the reader or critic is to understand the intentions of the work of art. Paul Valéry put the case sharply: *"There is no true meaning to a text*—no author's authority. Whatever he may have *wanted to say*, he has written what he has written. Once published, a text is like an apparatus that anyone may use as he will and according to his ability: it is not certain that the one who constructed it can use it better than another. Besides, if he knows well what he meant to do, this knowledge always disturbs his perception of what he has done."[5]

Though one may not like to think of art as gymnastic apparatus on which to exercise, the focus on the work of art seems manifestly sound as a way of trying to understand its intentions and its meaning. However, two secondary effects present themselves. First, we may be suspicious of anything that can be called authorial intention, for fear of committing the "intentional fallacy." Thus the authority of the author over the words which make up the text he wrote is subtly undermined by confusing it with the authority of the author over the meaning of his text. While the author cannot dictate the meaning of the text, he certainly has final authority over which words constitute the text of his literary work.

The other secondary effect is that of overturning the distinction between the aesthetic object (the genus) and the work of art (a species), of thinking that all automobiles are Fords. The fact that it generates an aesthetic response does not mean that it is a work of art. These two effects are interconnected, of course, at least under the definition I have given for the work of art, as an object created by human agency with the intention of arousing an aesthetic response. If the element of intention is minimized, the work of art tends to blend into, and be indistinguishable from, works of chance and works of nature. Indeed, these distinctions seem less important and less useful if commerce is restricted to the aesthetic object and to the general aesthetic response of the individual. The loss of these distinctions, however, leads to confusion and (ultimately) to abandoning conceptual thinking about works of art.

The difficulties which arise from these confusions are not merely visions of theoretical possibilities or of the ineluctable deviations from ideal purity. In every art one can point to aesthetic objects which in fact blend art, chance, and nature to a significant degree. Indeterminate music, for example, combines art and chance. The composer supplies blocks of music for the performers, who are to play the sections in whatever order they fancy on a given occasion; thus the composer incorporates in the work itself a variable governed by random chance. Examples of aesthetic objects which are not primarily works of art can be multiplied: the paintings of Beauty, the chimpanzee at the Cincinnati Zoo, for whose works there has been a ready commercial market; "happenings," or unstructured episodes with characters; self-destroying machines, which are designed to follow an unpredetermined course in destroying themselves. Let me say again that each of these examples will be the occasion for aesthetic response on the part of some people, perhaps a few and perhaps a great many, and no amount of laughing at them, of saying that they are being duped by frauds, will alter the fact that they are responding to aesthetic objects.

In the literary line, there are various current examples of aesthetic objects which depend on chance. The "novel" by Marc Saporta entitled *Composition No. 1*, published by Simon and Schuster in 1963, consists of loose printed pages which are to be shuffled before reading. Many poems have been written by computer. These examples may sound familiar in their resemblance to the language frame described in the Academy of Projectors in *Gulliver's Trav-*

els. That engine was actually a device to insure a random arrangement of words. All of the words in the language had been written on pieces of paper which were pasted on all the sides of bits of wood, which were linked together by wires. This device, twenty feet square, had forty iron handles on the sides which could be used to shake the frame and thus change the words which showed. Any groups of words which made part of a sentence were written into a book, and a rearrangement of those broken sentences was to produce the body of all arts and sciences. Swift's machine was a satire on modern learning; we are taking similar experiments in wise passiveness, perhaps because we are not sure of our grounds for responding otherwise.

The question of importance that these distinctions about aesthetic objects raise is whether criticism can deal with works of chance and nature as well as with works of art. I think that it can, but in very much more limited ways. It can give an account of affective qualities, and these reports may range from crude impressionism to elaborate psychological inquiry. It cannot ordinarily deal with those features on which criticism is most useful, matters of genre, tradition, and convention, without giving vent to a large amount of foolishness. Since textual criticism cannot traffic in works of nature, we need only distinguish between the kinds of authority it can have in dealing with works of chance and works of art. It is of course possible to establish a set of principles by which textual criticism could be applied to works of chance. In view of the random element in all works of chance, however, it is evident that an irrational variable of indefinite importance would always have to be included in the textual principles. Thus the operation of those principles would in the long run be little better than guesswork, and the results of a textual criticism established for works of chance would be about like pinning the tail on the donkey without peeking.

Let us return for a moment to the question of choosing between the "soiled fish of the sea" (the compositorial error) and the "coiled fish of the sea" (the authorial reading). What should our decision now be? Obviously we should choose the one which better fulfills our purposes. If we want to maximize our aesthetic experience by getting the biggest return from our attention, we are free to choose whichever reading satisfies that condition—with the error just as valid a choice as the authorial reading. Those readers who prefer the error—which is a simple example of a work of chance—can thus find perfectly logical grounds for their choice. It is a choice which repudiates the value of differentiating among classes of aesthetic objects, however, and the consistent application of it will, consequently, aid self-gratification on non-intellectual grounds. On the other hand, critics whose prime aesthetic interest is at that moment in works of art must choose the authorial reading whether they think it better or worse. Their main concern is to understand the literary production as a work of art, as an order of words created by the author; they cannot permit their attention to be pre-empted by any auxiliary effects, and they cannot properly set up in business as connoisseurs of all human experience. I certainly do not mean to suggest, however, that people should in general limit their aesthetic experience to works of art; it would be a sadly reduced world if we went about avoiding sunsets and other innocent forms of beauty. Only this: although one person may from time to time enjoy aesthetic experience from a wide variety of sources, he is not in a position to deal with works of nature and works of chance in his role as a textual critic; he is left, then, with literary works of art as the sole practicable subject for textual criticism.

II

Emily Dickinson's poem "I taste a liquor never brewed" was first printed, in May 1861, in the Springfield *Daily Republican*. The first stanza there reads as follows:

> I taste a liquor never brewed,
>   From tankards scooped in pearl;
> Not Frankfort berries yield the sense
>   Such a delicious whirl.

That was not, however, precisely what she had written. Her stanza had been more forthright and less delicate:

> I taste a liquor never brewed—
> From Tankards scooped in Pearl—
> Not all the Frankfort Berries
> Yield such an Alcohol!

The editor of the *Daily Republican* apparently thought that the stanza deserved a rhyme; he may well, like any sensible man, have objected to the logic of the third line. The version which he printed was a new stanza, produced under that power reserved by the editor to correct rhymes and alter figures of speech; he thought it (I feel sure) a notable improvement over Emily's crude work. Emily Dickinson was not at the time averse to publication; but she was, in the words of her distinguished modern editor, Thomas H. Johnson, concerned "how one can publish and at the same time preserve the integrity of one's art."[6] This is a topic which can lead into the central question, even paradox, relating to the creation of the work of art: whose intentions are being fulfilled, who can be properly called the author? The obvious answer in the present case —Emily Dickinson—is true enough, and it will serve perfectly for the manuscripts of those poems which she did not communicate to anyone. But once works of art are performed—even in elementary bardic song, or on the stage, or by a reader from copies reproduced from the author's inscription—then complex questions begin in time to arise.

In examining the nature of authorship, I am trying to inquire into what constitutes the integrity of the work of art. Whatever it is, it is apparently something which various classes of persons either do not respect or else define with such latitude that it includes their own efforts. On many magazines, for example, the editorial practice has been to alter the author's text to suit the policy or need of the magazine while retaining the author's name. The author is a tradesman, his work is a commodity which can be made more or less vendible, and the magazine is in a more favored position in the commercial hierarchy than is the author. A multitude of examples of the results can be gleaned from the pages of Frank Luther Mott's study of American magazines. When A. J. H. Duganne refused to furnish further chapters for his serial story, *The Atheist,* the editor of *Holden's* simply wrote the final chapters himself; Emerson's peculiarities were edited out of his contributions to the *Dial*.⁷ William Dean Howells acted the part of an "academic taskmaster freely blue-penciling the essays of his unhappy pupils," and he said that his proofreading "sometimes well-nigh took the character of original work, in that liberal *Atlantic* tradition of bettering the authors by editorial transposition and paraphrase, either in the form of suggestion or of absolute correction"; James Russell Lowell (the second president of the Modern Language Association) wrote to a contributor to the *North American Review* that "I shall take the liberty to make a verbal change here and there, such as I am sure you would agree to could we talk the matter over. I think, for example, you speak rather too well of young Lytton, whom I regard as both an imposter and as an antinomian heretic. Swinburne I must modify a little, as you will see, to make the *Review* consistent with itself. But you need not be afraid of not knowing your own child again."⁸ Edward Bok, the editor of the *Ladies' Home Journal*, once deleted a substantial portion of a story by Mark Twain; and the editor of *Collier's* modified a story by Julian Hawthorne about a seduced maiden by inserting a secret marriage and legitimizing the child.⁹ When extracts from *Huckleberry Finn* were printed in the *Century Magazine*, they were carefully altered by Richard Watson Gilder, the editor, with Twain's full consent, even though they had already been pruned both by Mrs. Clemens and by William Dean Howells; Gilder excised about a fifth of the extracts, including descriptive passages and those which (like "to be in a sweat") he thought too coarse or vulgar for his audience.¹⁰ Examples could be multiplied indefinitely. Sometimes the editor is a famous man of letters and the author a hack, and sometimes it is the other way around; sometimes a change seems to later critics to have been improvement, and sometimes debasement.

The reflection on these facts might be simple were it not that when authors publish their periodical contributions in book form, they very frequently retain the changes which have been introduced by the editors. Thus, by inference, they validate the changes and give them some kind of authority. Nathaniel Hawthorne, for example, retained the changes, despite his objection to editorial meddling; at least, in the case of the four short stories for which the manuscript is extant, he seems not to have restored the original readings when the editors altered his text, in punctuation, spelling, capitalization, and diction.[11] Similarly, when Thomas Nelson Page's stories were collected by Scribner's, he did not re-introduce the omitted passages (about drink, religion, and horror) nor the original Negro dialect; the changes made by the editors of the *Century Magazine* were largely allowed to stand.[12] Charles Reade objected strenuously to the editorial pressure from *Blackwood's* on *The Woman Hater*, but he then used the serial text as copy for the book, with only a few inconsequential changes in phrasing.[13]

On the other hand, occasionally authors have restored their original readings in book publication. When Thomas Hardy's novels were first published in periodicals, the texts were considerably changed at the urging of editors. Sometimes the alterations were verbal, as the change from "lewd" to "gross," "loose" to "wicked," and "bawdy" to "sinful" in *Far from the Madding Crowd*; sometimes they were more substantial, as the omission of the seduction scene from *Tess of the D'Urbervilles* and the substitution of a mock marriage. When Hardy got his manuscripts ready for book publication, however, he restored nearly everything that the magazine editors had made him change.[14] But not always, even with Hardy. Many editorial changes were made in his manuscript for the first serial appearance, in the *Atlantic Monthly*, of *Two on a Tower*. This edited text then served, with few changes, as copy text for the first London edition, and the edited version has continued in all later editions of Hardy.[15]

In cases of these kinds, there is generally some uncertainty as to the interpretation to be put on the author's actions. Often we cannot be sure whether he makes suggested changes because of a compliant nature, whether he allows editorial alterations to stand in later editions out of laziness, whether he reverts to earlier readings out of pertinacity, or whether there is reasoned conviction in support of his actions. Once another hand helps to prepare a work of art for dissemination, it is usually difficult to distinguish with certainty which part is not by the author.

One of the most common kinds of intervention in the publication of books is made by the publisher's editor—the person whose job it is to read material before publication, to recommend acceptance or rejection, to "house style" the text, to query anything which seems inaccurate, ineffective, or offensive, and to make or suggest any changes which appeal to the editor as desirable. I suppose that almost every writer—even the lowly scholar—has found his death-less prose altered by a publisher's editor, who is sometimes an eminent man of letters and sometimes a mere slip of a girl barely out of college. Some authors blanch at the thought of any alteration, some accept any change gratefully as an improvement. There appears to be a perennial joke among editors of "educational" publishers that they completely re-write the books of some authors, reducing the text to half of its original length, and the authors never realize that any changes have been made.

Probably the most celebrated editor of this century was Maxwell E. Perkins of Charles Scribner's Sons, editor for Fitzgerald, Wolfe, Hemingway, and a dozen other writers of consequence. Perkins was rather reluctant to offer any specific suggestions to authors except about legal or libellous matters. Frequently he sent long letters or memoranda of advice to "his" authors about their manuscripts; but his suggestions were general and undemanding. He was like a kindly parent, proud of his children, always encouraging them to fulfill their potentialities, ready to offer a guiding hand in time of need. It was only when an author called for help that he would be party to the making of important changes in a manuscript. The most significant revisions he ever made, presumably, were his extensive cuts in Wolfe's first two manuscripts, trying to bring order out of chaos.[16] The cuts were apparently made by Perkins with Wolfe's acquiescence, and they reduced *Look Homeward, Angel* (for example) by thirty percent.[17] To mention only one more of an almost unlimited number of instances, Theodore Dreiser had the advantage—however unlikely it seems—of several editors, notably Louise Campbell. She acted as literary assistant, revised eight of his books while preparing them for publication, and even wrote character sketches for publication under his name in *Esquire*.[18] What is called ghost writing, however, goes a little beyond the usual requirements of editing.[19]

[74]

Then there are some books the final form of which (it would be accurate to say) are not so much written as constructed. Mark Twain, for example, left *The Mysterious Stranger* unfinished; Albert Bigelow Paine put it together somewhat arbitrarily and added a last chapter found separately among the author's papers. Bernard de Fallois reconstructed Marcel Proust's *Jean Santeuil*, that first rough version of *Remembrance of Things Past*, by the use of seventy notebooks and several boxes of torn and detached pages made available to him after Proust's death by Madame Gérard Mante-Proust.[20] *More Stately Mansions* was made by Karl Ragner Gierow by shortening Eugene O'Neill's partly revised script.

Editors play an important role in the production of magazines and books, and they are often responsible for changes in the author's text. I am not trying to say whether these changes are or are not improvements, whether they are made willingly or reluctantly by the author, whether there should or should not be editors—only that textual changes for which an editor is responsible do in fact take place, frequently and regularly.

This editorial activity results in the embodiment of the editor's intentions in the work of art. In a complex way, the integrity of the work of art is thereby, in some measure, the effect of a juncture of intentions. Another major entanglement, this one mainly accidental in nature, occurs in the translation of the text from authorial to public form—the physical process of turning the author's dictated or typed or handwritten copy into print or (in earlier times) into scribal manuscript form. To speak only of printing, I suppose it is true to say that few if any books of any size have ever been printed without mistakes, even that "No book is completed until *Error* has crept in & affixed his sly Imprimatur." The usual assumption is that every printed book includes many errors, and it is easy to see why this must be: a page of type may contain from one to five thousand characters; there is only one way of getting each of them right, and many ways of getting each one wrong. No matter how experienced the compositor, he will make changes, the proofreader will fail to notice some of them, and every change is an error. The editors of the Centenary Hawthorne have sought to minimize this state of nature by having *all* proofs "read at least five times and by three or more editors."[21]

Proofreading by authors was not usual before the eighteenth century; indeed, early proofreading normally consisted of a reading (by the master printer or his assistant) of one of the first sheets printed off, without recourse to the copy, and marking any apparent errors for correction; in the meantime, of course, a certain number of uncorrected sheets would have already been printed. The fact that proof sheets were later run off, and given to the author for correction, is certainly no guarantee that all the mistakes were caught. Careless proofreading is not uncommon, and writers differ in their interest and skill in handling such details. It has been said that F. Scott Fitzgerald's *This Side of Paradise* is an "inexcusably sloppy job, and that the blame must be distributed between author and publisher"; the first edition contained a large number of misspellings, inconsistencies, and other examples of carelessness which neither the author nor the publisher corrected —indeed, some of the errors noted by the reviewers in 1920 have not yet been corrected.[22] Even when the author and publisher both take care, there are still errors. Sinclair Lewis, for example, wrote as follows to his publisher after he had seen a list of errors and inconsistencies observed by Mr. Louis Feipel in the published version of *Babbitt*: "J. Henry! This man Feipel is a wonder—to catch all these after rather unusually careful proofreading not only by myself and my wife but also by two or three professionals!"[23] Sometimes misprints become, in effect, a permanent part of the text.[24]

Sometimes an author prefers the mistakes to his own work. Richard Ellmann has described such a preference on the part of James Joyce. It occurred while Joyce was dictating *Finnegans Wake* to Samuel Beckett. "There was a knock on the door and Joyce said, 'Come in.' Beckett, who hadn't heard the knock, by mistake wrote down 'Come in' as part of the dictated text. Afterwards he read it back to Joyce who said, 'What's that "Come in"?' 'That's what you dictated,' Beckett replied. Joyce thought for a moment, realizing that Beckett hadn't heard the knock; then he said, 'Let it stand'."[25]

Perhaps the play is the form of literary art in which the principles associated with the integrity of the work and the identity of the author are most visible. If the playwright wants his play to find its way onto the stage, he must accommodate his text to the financial claims of the producer, the presentational claims of the director and actors, and the undefined claims of the theatre-going public. William Gibson has given a detailed account of his struggles in revising and re-writing *Two for the Seesaw*. From the time that the first draft was completed until it opened in New York, Gibson re-wrote the entire play several times and re-cast some parts of it as many as five times. These changes were made in trying to meet objections and accommodate the text to the various claims made on it. For example, the male star did not like the character which he was to portray, and the changes made for his benefit covered a wide range: from the deletion of those speeches in which the character talked aloud to himself (since the actor "personally did not talk aloud to himself") all the way to the assurance that he would not "go onstage with one line unrewritten that he felt uncomfortable or untruthful with."

Gibson came to feel that the play as it was produced was not quite his: his collaborators had made a new play. It was a successful play, one which was (he thought) much better and more effective because of the revisions which had been forced on the writer. But not quite his. He told of visiting the studio of a painter and envying her because "she was working in a medium where she alone could ruin it. This seemed to me a definition of art." When Gibson turned over a text to his publisher, he could not bear to put his name to the final version: so he rewrote once more, using much of the stage version, restoring much of what had been surrendered, writing new bits, and ending with a composite of several versions.[26]

The rewriting of plays to meet the demands of performance has for some time been typical of theatrical practice. Oscar Wilde, for example, wrote "The Importance of Being Earnest" as a four-act play, and he did not submit it until it had passed through three stages of composition; when Sir George Alexander (the manager of St. James's Theatre) told him to re-cast it into three acts and to reduce the length in order to allow time for a curtain raiser,

Wilde complied. It is only a few writers of strong will, fierce independence, and eminence—such as G. B. Shaw and Eugene O'Neill —who have been able to see their work performed in accordance with their own intentions, and they have had to fight for their convictions.[27] For the most part, Moss Hart's description in *Act One* (New York, 1959) of the birth of *Once in a Lifetime* is more characteristic: throughout rehearsals and try-outs the author is busily engaged in re-writing the text, adjusting it to the realities of performance, trying to make it into a show which will be a public success.

This process is by no means limited to the work of commercial experts. The conversion of Archibald MacLeish's *J. B.* is an instructive—if rather sad—example. MacLeish spent four years writing the play, which was published by Houghton Mifflin in book form in March 1958 and produced in the Yale University Theatre the next month. Alfred de Liagre, Jr., bought the play, engaged Elia Kazan as director, and brought Kazan and MacLeish together. Kazan thought the play "needed important changes for professional production," gave detailed directions, and MacLeish enthusiastically agreed. The story of the revision of the play, from July through December 1958, is one filled with demands for changes by Kazan and agreement by MacLeish. "You are right to want something from Nickles at the end of Act 1," says MacLeish. "Hell, you are always right. Why should I mention it? Here is what I propose." After the Washington opening, Kazan told MacLeish that the play needed a "recognition scene," and he outlined where and why it should take place. MacLeish agreed, and in two days supplied the scene.[28]

It appears likely that the production of plays has always occasioned considerable modification of the text. Undoubtedly a few dramatists at any given time have been able to stand their ground in the running battle with actors, directors, producers, and public; but usually the writer seems to have thought of his words as variable in the process of converting a text to a finished performance.[29] Thus there are, in theory at least and often in practice, two or more versions of every produced play. In Elizabethan times, the author's foul papers represent a non-produced version and the prompt book a produced version.[30] For *J. B.*, the Houghton Mifflin edition (1958) is a non-produced version, while a produced version was printed in *Theatre Arts* (February 1960) and by Samuel French, Inc.; the versions are naturally different.

In dramatic performances, collaboration on the text is greater as the non-verbal effects become more important. In a musical, for example, the author is less in control of his text than in a play, while in a musical revue the identical show is not usually repeated for two performances in succession. In the production of movies, the writer ordinarily has little control over his text, must supply changes upon demand, and may be properly listed in the credits among the chief cameraman, electrician, and sound man. In the production of "Cleopatra" (released by Twentieth Century Fox in 1963), the valuable properties were the female star and the assignational publicity, not the text. Three distinguished writers were successively employed to provide a scenario, and most of their work was scrapped.

It can be claimed that nearly every person involved in the transmission of literary works helps, in some sense, to shape the effect that a work will have on a reader. The designer, for example, can in some measure make the experience of reading the book a little more pleasant or easy or irritating by the appropriateness of the format, paper, binding, font and size of type. His work is not usually observed consciously. In order to realize something of the range of his effect, however, one has only to imagine reading *Tom Jones* in black letter throughout, on coated art paper, with the sheets printed alternately in red and black, in a tight binding with no inner margin, with illustrations by Willem de Kooning. On the other hand, influences which shape the intentions of the artist are sometimes advantageous. Few regret, I suppose, that James T. Fields (the publisher) was successful in persuading Hawthorne to make *The Scarlet Letter* into a full-length novel rather than finishing it (as Hawthorne had planned) as a long story for publication with half a dozen shorter ones.

So far, this discussion about the integrity of the work of art has emphasized its creation and the agents who are then at work in modifying the intentions of the artist. In fact, the work of art is also subject to alteration long afterwards. For nine plays by Euripides, the earliest manuscript—and the only one with any authority—is of the thirteenth-fourteenth centuries; thus any changes made in the text in the course of that transcription, some 1,750 years after the plays were composed, would have definitively altered the intentions of the author so far as the modern reader is concerned.

Emendation may be taken as an example of that range of editorial effort which modifies the works of the past in the hope of purging corrupt readings from them. Boswell tells of Johnson confronting him with a textual problem that required an emendation for its solution. "On the 65 page of the first volume of Sir George Mackenzie's folio edition. Mr. Johnson pointed out a paragraph beginning with *Aristotle*, and told me there was an error in the text which he bid me try to discover. I hit it at once. It stands that the devil answers *even* in *engines*. I corrected it to *ever* in *enigmas*. 'Sir,' said he, 'you're a good critic. This would have been a great thing to do in the text of an ancient author'."[31] Boswell here casts himself in the role of the clever schoolboy responding to the questions of the schoolmaster, who knows all the answers. In real life, however, nobody knows the answers, and it is impossible to say "I hit it at once."

As an expression of editorial preference, emendation is the exercise of textual decision. The corrupted readings in most of the manuscripts of the authors of Greek and Latin antiquity have made their works the happy hunting ground for ingenious editors. Since any plausible reading is preferred to one which is obviously corrupt, and since there is usually no way to validate conjectural emendations beyond the tests of meter and sense, our received texts are peppered with editorial guesses which have silently become indistinguishable from what textual scholars have agreed to consider the author's intentions.

This process of reconstruction by emendation has by no means been limited to writers of classical antiquity. Even such newcomers as English and American authors have also had these benefits conferred on them. The emendations suggested by some eighteenth-century editors and critics to two lines in Milton are instructive. In the 1645 edition of Milton's *Poems*, lines 631–635 of *Comus* (the beginning of the "Haemony" passage) appear as follows:

> The leaf was darkish, and had prickles on it,
> But in another Countrey, as he said,
> Bore a bright golden flowre, but not in this soyl:
> Unknown, and like esteem'd, and the dull swayn
> Treads on it daily with his clouted shoon. . . .

It is the third and fourth of these lines that were thought to require emendation. Hurd said that "the passage before us is certainly corrupt, or, at least, inaccurate; and had better, I think, been given thus . . . 'Bore a bright golden flower, *not* in this soil / Unknown, *though light* esteem'd'." Seward proposed "*but* in this soil / Unknown and *light* esteem'd." Newton suggested that no change be made beyond the omission of either "but" or "not"; thus the reading could be "*but* in this soil / Unknown and like esteem'd" or else "*not* in this soil: / Unknown, and like esteem'd." Fenton printed "*little* esteem'd" rather than "*like* esteem'd," while Warburton proposed "*light* esteem'd" as the only change.[32] No one of these emendations is now accepted. The weight of the testimony in favor of the reading with which we began is apparently so overwhelming that no one now thinks to suggest any alternative. The same reading (minor variants in orthography and punctuation aside) is to be found in the Trinity College Manuscript (in Milton's hand), in the first (1637) edition of *Comus* (which derived from the Trinity College Manuscript), in the corrected copy of the 1637 *Comus* which Milton presented to the Earl of Bridgewater, and in the 1645 *Poems;* moreover, there is no shred of evidence elsewhere that Milton's intentions were not carried out in this passage, which he reviewed so many times while he still had his sight. Each of the editorial emendations was thus (we may conclude) a temporary substitution of the intention of the editor for that of the author.

Very frequently, emendations are made in cases where there is not enough external testimony to confirm or reject them with any feeling of confidence. Sometimes they slide into the text and become the objects of our veneration on the principle that whatever is printed is right.[33] Such is the case in an indefinite number of passages in the works of writers of the past.

Emendation offers the appeal of a puzzle and the release of creation. "The allurements of emendation are scarcely resistible," Samuel Johnson wrote. "Conjecture has all the joy and all the pride of invention, and he that has once started a happy change, is too much delighted to consider what objections may rise against it." Johnson offered a great many emendations to Shakespeare, most of them pure guesses sanctified by the supposition that Shakespeare wrote them. Unlike many critics and readers, however, he came to be aware that his own textual conjectures were likely to be mistaken; and he believed that the best any person can do is produce one of many plausible readings. He trusted conjecture less and less, and he congratulated himself on including none of his own emendations in the plays of Shakespeare that he latterly edited.[34]

Johnson put a high value on the creative aspect of emendation. He described one change by Bishop Warburton as "a noble emendation, which almost sets the critic on a level with the author."[35] One can go further than Johnson: without praising either Warburton or the emendation, one can say that the critic who adopts an emendation of his own creation, without a genuine basis for showing it to be a recovery of what the author intended to write, has indeed become co-author of this portion of the work of art— he has in fact been set on a level with the author.

This brings us to a major point about the nature of authorship and of the integrity of the work of art. The literary work is frequently the result, in a pure sense, of composite authorship. We do not have to meddle with the unconscious, the preconscious, or the race consciousness in order to hold this view. In a quite literal sense, the literary work is often guided or directed or controlled by other people while the author is in the process of trying to make it take shape, and it is subject to a variety of alterations throughout its history. The intentions of the person we call the author thus become entangled with the intentions of all the others who have a stake in the outcome, which is the work of art. And yet we agree to say simply "*Two for the Seesaw*, by William Gibson." Not "*Two for the Seesaw*, by William Gibson, Henry Fonda, Fred Coe,

Arthur Penn, Anne Bancroft, the elevator boy, wives, friends, and others." "*Jean Santeuil*, by Marcel Proust," not "by Marcel Proust and Bernard de Fallois." "*Look Homeward, Angel*, by Thomas Wolfe," not "by Wolfe and Perkins." "*J. B.*, by MacLeish," not "by MacLeish and Kazan." Our identification of the author is partly a convention for the sake of simplicity, partly a case of the Boss being given credit, whether he wants it or not, for all the work that the office (including volunteer workers) turns out.

Whatever complexities we agree to ignore in our daily encounters with works of art, it remains a fact that the literary work is a mingling of human intentions about which distinctions should be made. Its status as a work of art is not affected by whether these intentions all belong to the titular author; even collaborative authorship does not alter that status, however much it may endanger friendships. On the other hand, the integrity of the work of art depends very much on the work being limited to those intentions which are the author's, together with those others of which he approves or in which he acquiesces. When these intentions have been fulfilled, the work of art has its final integrity or completeness. It may be aesthetically imperfect or unfinished, and it is altogether possible that an indefinite number of people may be capable of improving it. But in the authorial sense it is already finished, it is already complete, it already has that final integrity which should be the object of the critic's chief attention. This is the final integrity which it is the business of the textual critic to identify as an order of words in fulfillment of the authorial intention, the business of the literary critic to understand as an order of words in the context of all literature.

We commenced this discussion with the question, put in the mouth of Emily Dickinson, as to how one can publish and still preserve the integrity of one's art. In a pure sense it is probably impossible, but anyone who is concerned enough to ask the question will undoubtedly realize that a good deal depends on the exercise of will: one must fulfill one's own intentions rather than the conflicting intentions of others, however valuable and well-meaning. Their desire to help is praiseworthy, and altruism is all the more appealing when it is self-effacing; but the dedication of such help to the improvement of others' works of art dissipates the integrity of those works.

III

In the conclusion to *Great Expectations*, Charles Dickens thought it necessary to have a final confrontation between the hero, Pip, and the greatest of his lost expectations, Estella. They meet casually in London. Estella has married a Shropshire doctor after the death of her first husband, the cruel Drummle. She sees Pip walk by on the street while she is sitting in her carriage. They shake hands, she wrongly assumes that the boy with him is his own child, he perceives that suffering has given her an understanding heart, and the book ends. This is the "unhappy," or at least unromantic ending; in less than three hundred words these ships pass one last time, saluting each other gravely all the while. Bulwer Lytton was dissatisfied with this ending, and at his urging Dickens wrote another. This time Estella is free: she has been a widow for two years and has not remarried. They meet, not in impersonal London, but in memory's lane itself—the site of Miss Havisham's house, where they had first met, which neither has visited for some thirteen years. A silvery mist is rising, the stars are shining, and the first rays of the moon illumine the tears that course from Estella's eyes. They are full of forgiveness for one another, and understanding; they emerge from the ruins holding hands, and there is no shadow of another parting. This is the "happy," the romantic ending, accomplished in a thousand pulsing words. The ending which you read must to some degree affect your understanding of the entire novel. Which is the real *Great Expectations?*

The collection of W. H. Auden's sonnets and verse commentary which he entitled "In Time of War" concludes with these lines:

> Till they construct at last a human justice,
> The contribution of our star, within the shadow
> Of which uplifting, loving, and constraining power
> All other reasons may rejoice and operate.

It is an eloquent plea for men of good will to join together and "construct" a "human justice" for the benefit of all mankind. So the passage appeared in its first publication in 1939, in *Journey to a War*. Within a few years Auden's ideas about the right way to attain human justice—as well as his ideas about many other subjects —had changed markedly. When he came to reprint "In Time of War" in his *Collected Poetry* of 1945, he altered the concluding passage of the commentary as follows:

> Till, as the contribution of our star, we follow
> The clear instructions of that Justice, in the shadow
> Of Whose uplifting, loving, and constraining power
> All human reasons do rejoice and operate.

Instead of constructing human justice, man is now enjoined to follow Divine Justice.[36] Which is the real "In Time of War"?

Thomas Hardy printed four different versions of *The Return of the Native*, from 1878 to 1912. Between the first and second versions he made some 700 changes (of which 40 are major revisions), between the second and third about 350 changes, and between the third and fourth about 115. These changes substantially altered the characterization and plot. In his first manuscript version, Hardy envisioned Eustacia Vye as a literal witch, a demon; by the time he had finished his revisions, she had become a passionate, unconventional beauty with a surprisingly rigid sense of morality. An example of the change in plot may be found in Eustacia's plan to run away from her husband, Clym Yeobright. In the early versions, her moral problem was whether it was right to accept assistance and financial help from Wildeve since each was married to another; in the later versions, with Wildeve more forward, her problem was whether she could avail herself of his services or whether she also had to accept him as her lover and go away with him.[37] Which is the real *Return of the Native?*

I have asked this kind of question three different times, partly because the three situations are somewhat different, partly to suggest that the problem which I am now to treat is very widespread. That problem is the existence of the work of art in multiple versions, each created by the author. The principle which is involved touches the nature of composition: the work in process, the work in completion, the work in re-completion. Familiar examples of authorial revision abound in all periods: there are two distinct versions of *Piers Plowman*, two of Chaucer's Prologue to *The Legend of Good Women* and two (possibly three) of *Troilus and Criseyde*, five of Gower's *Confessio Amantis*, two major versions of Sidney's *Arcadia*, two of Ben Jonson's *Every Man in His Humour*, several versions of Browne's *Religio Medici* and Walton's *Life of Donne*, two of Pope's *Rape of the Lock* and of *The Dunciad*, two of Keats's "La Belle Dame Sans Merci," four of Fitz-Gerald's *Rubáiyát of Omar Khayyám*, seven of Whitman's *Leaves of Grass*, from two to five for each of Arnold's major prose works, and so on and so forth.

These are all familiar instances. To add a few other writers who have been notable revisers, within the limits (say) of nineteenth-century poetry, one might first mention Wordsworth, who spent forty-five years in tinkering with *The Prelude*, making the 1850 version in many ways a quite different poem from the 1805 version.[38] Or Tennyson, who was a devoted, continual, and minute reviser: he worked over his manuscripts (sometimes in as many as six versions), he altered the texts in the proofs for the first and later editions, and he made marginal changes in the printed editions. Sometimes there are as many as fifteen texts, all different, each armed with the poet's authority.[39] Or Emily Dickinson, who had second and third and fourth thoughts about what she wrote, and who sometimes could not decide which was the final form of a poem. For "Blazing in Gold and quenching in Purple," in the three fair copies she sent to friends, each time one line was different in the supposed final version; "the Otter's Window" in one is "the kitchen window" in another, which is "the oriel window" in a third. She wrote them all and meant each of them to be the poem.[40]

Recent scholarly investigations have revealed that authorial revision is embodied in multiple printed versions to an extent which seems to be almost limitless. I can at least hint at the spread of these findings through the mere mention of a sampling of the subjects, naming only those to whom I have not already alluded. For the twentieth century, Joyce, Faulkner, Yeats, Conrad, Lewis, Dos Passos, Lindsay, Cozzens, and West. For the nineteenth century, James, Twain, Crane, Pater, Clough, Hawthorne, Poe, Emerson,

Thoreau, Longfellow, De Quincey, Blake, and Coleridge. For the eighteenth century, Swift, Fielding, and Johnson. For the seventeenth and latter sixteenth centuries, Shakespeare, Drayton, Daniel, Burton, Crashaw, Lee, Rochester, and Dryden. The prize for revision should probably be awarded to Philip James Bailey. He wrote seven different versions of his poem *Festus*, which was, or were, published in thirteen British (and at least forty American) editions between 1839 and 1903. In the process it grew from a modest 8,103 lines (a little shorter than *Paradise Lost*) to a monstrous 39,159 lines.[41]

The more of these scholarly studies one reads, the more one is impressed by the likelihood of authorial revision in any literary work where the writer had an opportunity to alter his work before communicating it to his public yet another time. What the scholar seems to need in order to demonstrate authorial revision in these cases is simply the good fortune to find that the evidence has not been destroyed. It seems logical to assume that revision may have taken place in other cases, wherever there was occasion for it, even though the editions, manuscripts, or letters to prove it are no longer extant.[42]

I am trying to make it clear that the examples with which I began, of works by Dickens, Auden, and Hardy, are by no means instances of authorial revision which can be dismissed because they are rare freaks. On the contrary, they seem to be examples of a fairly common phenomenon. The matters of principle which they raise will have widespread application.

When people write about literary works which exist in multiple versions, the question they commonly address is "Which is the best version?" About *Great Expectations*, for example, J. Hillis Miller writes that "the second ending is, in my opinion, the best. Not only was it, after all, the one Dickens published (would he really have acceded to Mrs. Grundy in the mask of Bulwer-Lytton without reasons of his own?), but, it seems to me, the second ending, in joining Pip and Estella, is much truer to the real direction of the story."[43] On the other hand, Edgar Johnson is somewhat contemptuous of the second ending as a "tacked-on addition of a belated marriage to Estella." "Both as art and as psychology," he informs us, "it was poor counsel that Lytton gave in urging that the shaping of a lifetime in Estella be miraculously undone. Save for this, though, *Great Expectations* is the most perfectly constructed and perfectly written of all Dickens's works." Johnson then proceeds to outline a third ending, of his own imagining, which he prefers to either of those that Dickens wrote. "It should close with that misty moonlight scene in Miss Havisham's ruined garden," but the final action should be that of Pip and Estella "bidding each other a chastened farewell."[44] Personally, I do not feel greatly assisted by any of these answers. The making of a choice between the versions may seem to be of a high order because it involves the exercise of taste; but it is not the first question to ask, and it turns out to be more of an innocently curious quest than a serious critical inquiry.

The first problem is to identify the work of art. The basic proposition which I submit about works created by authorial revision is that each version is, either potentially or actually, another work of art. It remains a "potential" work of art—it is in process, it is becoming—so long as the author is still giving it shape, in his mind or in successive drafts or interlineations or in whatever manner he suspends those works which he is not yet ready to release to his usual public. On the other hand, the "actual" work of art is a version in which the author feels that his intentions have been sufficiently fulfilled to communicate it to the public, as his response to whatever kinds of pressure bear on him, from within or from without, to release his work into a public domain. The distinction which I am offering is a practical (rather than idealistic) way of separating the potential from the actual, the work of art which is becoming from the work of art which is. The distinction thus turns on the intentions of the artist: the work can have only such integrity, or completeness, as the author chooses to give it, and our only reasonable test of when the work has achieved integrity is his willingness to release it to his usual public. His judgment may not always be good, and he may release it too soon or too late or when (we think) he never should have; but it is his judgment not ours, his intention not ours, his work of art which he makes ours.

The nature of the public differs for different writers. For Dickens—as for most writers since the invention of printing—it was the readers of a periodical or of a book issued by publishers to whom he had turned over a text. For Emily Dickinson, however, her usual public might be her sister-in-law, Susan Dickinson, or Thomas Wentworth Higginson, or Helen Hunt Jackson. If she sent a fair copy of a poem to one of them, this action—as the equivalent of voluntary publication—can be taken as evidence that the work had achieved its integrity. For William Blake, the usual public might be anyone in the small circle of friends and kindly benefactors who accepted or purchased a copy of one of his books —written, designed, engraved, colored, and bound by Blake, with the assistance of his wife. >

The application of this test is sometimes difficult, mainly when the evidence leaves obscure the question as to whether the artist intended to release the work to his public in the form in which we have it. Books which are published piratically or circulated surreptitiously are examples. Sir Thomas Browne "at leisurable houres composed" *Religio Medici*, as he says in his address "To the Reader," "for my private exercise and satisfaction"; "being communicated unto one, it became common unto many, and was by transcription successively corrupted untill it arrived in a most depraved copy at the presse. He that shall peruse that worke, and shall take notice of sundry particularities and personall expressions therein, will easily discerne *the intention was not publik*." (I use italics to call attention to the key phrase.) There were two unauthorized editions issued anonymously in 1642, but Browne then proceeded to supply—to the same bookseller who had pirated his work—text for an authorized edition; he used a copy of one of the pirated editions, correcting some 650 errors (while overlooking many others), and adding four new sections, a dozen new passages, and many new errors.[45] However hasty and careless his alterations, *Religio Medici* was then a public work. With some writers, pirated (or even manipulated) publication has been used as an excuse to issue works (like Pope's publication of his own letters) which it might otherwise seem immodest to release to the usual public. Sometimes a writer feels that publication puts an end to his freedom to revise. Guillaume De Guileville told, in the prologue to his *Pèlerinage de la vie humaine,* of a wonderful dream he had in the year 1330 and of writing it down hastily "that I myht after, by leyser, / Correcte hyt when the day were cler." But before he had finished mending it, it was stolen from him and published abroad, "a-geyn my wyl & my plesaunce." Up to that time, he says, "fredam I hadde / To putte away, and eke to adde, / What that me lyst, lyk as I wende"; but after publication he lost that freedom. It was only after the passage of twenty-five years that he made a new version, by thorough revision, and was ready to send it forth into the world to replace the incomplete version which he had not wished published.[46]

The revisions which a writer makes while a work is in process—that is, before it becomes a version which he chooses to make public—constitute an intimate and complex view of that writer at work. "The minute changes made in their compositions by eminent writers are," in Edmond Malone's blunt dictum, "always a matter of both curiosity & instruction to literary men, however trifling and unimportant they may appear to blockheads."[47] The study of revisions can enlighten us, as Paul Valéry says, "about the secret discussion that takes place, at the time when the work is being done, between the temperament, ambition and foresight of the man, and, on the other hand, the excitements and the intellectual means of the moment. The strictness of the revisions, the number of solutions rejected, and possibilities denied, indicate the nature of the scruples, the degree of conscience, the quality of pride, and even the reserves and diverse fears that are felt in regard to the future judgment of the public." With a writer whose mind is reflective and rich in resonances, the work can only emerge "by a kind of accident which ejects it from the mind."[48] The taste for making endless revisions is, according to Valéry, an occupational disease; "in the eyes of these lovers of anxiety and perfection, a work is never *complete*—a word which to them is meaningless—but *abandoned.*"[49] Other writers have less difficulty with the creative process, and some find greater satisfaction in the results they obtain.[50]

In any event, the several verbal forms in which the literary work exists while it is being written are in the private province of the writer as part of his interior dialogue with himself. When extant documents preserve these variant forms, we must remember that they provide glimpses into the creative process and not a final form. Dickens never used the first ("unhappy") ending of *Great Expectations*; he wrote it, sent it to the printer, had it set in type, and read the proofs. But he allowed his mind to be changed and wrote the second ending, which he used in the serial and book editions of the novel. The first ending was preserved by his friend and biographer, John Forster; it was never printed as part of the novel until 1937, when it was used in the Limited Editions Club version, which carried the imprimatur of an introduction by George Bernard Shaw. The Rinehart Edition prints both endings, as if each reader could choose the one he preferred. As I read the evidence, the first ending never became an integral part of the novel in a public version; only the second ending—no matter whether you think it better or worse—attained that status, and the only "real" *Great Expectations* by Charles Dickens is the one with that ending. Edgar Johnson's "third" ending, being of his own construction, could have status only if Johnson were considered a co-author of the novel. The work of art cannot be judged by loading it with hypotheses of what it might have been or of what it could be made to be: the work of art has a radical integrity, and we must take that integrity, once discovered, as it is. The tactic of posing self-made alternatives is one which involves tremendous risks for a doubtful advantage.

When the literary work emerges as a public version it then has the integrity of its unique authorial form. Our suspicions about the sheer decency of contemplating more than one public version of a single literary work may be allayed if we think of the versions as separated in time, with something like five years between the two versions of Auden's "In Time of War," with about thirty-four years for insulation between the first and the last *Return of the Native*.

"I cannot go back over anything I have written," said Valéry, "without thinking that I should now make something quite different of it."[51] If we consider the theory and practice of William Butler Yeats and Henry James, the status of multiple versions of a work of art will perhaps be clearer. Yeats understood, with the utmost clarity, his drive to revise. When friends objected to his habit of returning again and again to his old poems and altering them each time, he replied with these lines:

> The friends that have it I do wrong
> When ever I remake a song,
> Should know what issue is at stake:
> It is myself that I remake.[52]

Yeats was an inveterate reviser because he was, quite simply, always trying to make his poems contemporaneous with his self as a changing human being. "This volume contains what is, I hope, the final text of the poems of my youth," he wrote in the Preface of January 1927 to the thirteenth reprinting and revision of his *Poems* of 1895; "and yet it may not be," he added, "seeing that in it are not only the revisions from my 'Early Poems and Stories,' published last year, but quite new revisions on which my heart is greatly set." To read his prefaces to the various editions of "The Countess Cathleen," for example, is to see more clearly what is involved in the making of a new public version of a literary work.

Yeats was always re-reading his earlier poems, and always making new versions to issue to his public. He did not scruple to keep re-writing any of his previous work. Henry James, on the other hand, approached the revision of his earlier novels with anxiety, as a job that bristled with difficulties.[53] He had been at pains to dismiss his earlier work, to put it behind him, to become unacquainted with it. He was disinclined to exhume it, and very loath to start tidying it up for fear that he would become involved in expensive renovations. He had been accustomed all of his life to revising his work, it is true, to changing the periodical version for book publication, to altering the text from one edition to another; but those revisions were made in warm blood while the original vision of the story was still with him. What has made his revisions of special interest was this task that he approached with such reluctance, for the Definitive New York edition. The gulf of time which separated him from most of the novels to be included made him think of the idea of re-writing them as so difficult, or even so absurd, as to be impossible; it would not be a mere matter of expression, but of somehow harmonizing the man he then was and the man he used to be.

James resolved his dilemma by discarding the idea of re-writing altogether and by taking the task of revision in its etymological sense—to see again, to look over, to re-peruse. Thus he never thought of himself as re-writing a novel, but of seeing it again and recording the results of that re-vision in so many close notes that the pages were made to flower. James respected his novels and their characters as having an independent existence of their own, and he wanted to keep his hands off of them. By his own application of the term "revision," he made himself believe that he had done so. I take his argument to be an innocent but necessary piece of deception to avoid facing the fact of rewriting. However James looked on his job, the revisions for the New York edition resulted in new versions of the works. He made, for example, more than two thousand revisions in *The Reverberator*.[54] Voices rise and fall as to whether James improved or debased his novels by revision, as to whether his later style is more tortuous and labored or clearer and more expressive, even as to whether the revision of a given novel makes a radical or minimal change in the effect of a certain character, like Newman in *The American*. The unarguable fact is that James supplied multiple versions of the novels which he revised.

The literary critic can afford enough detachment to observe the work of art as an historical phenomenon, as a part of the past from the moment of its creation. But few writers are able to take this view; for many of them the work continues, as for a possessive parent, a part of the self, as a child whose hair must be brushed into submission, as an adult who must be nagged into wearing more stylish clothes.

I suggested that our suspicion of multiple versions of the work of art may be allayed if we think of them as separated by long periods of time. Time is, however, only a practical convenience in envisioning why multiple versions may or must exist. No clock can measure the rate at which a man becomes different, a little, a lot. Enough might happen in a day or even in a flash to require that the man rediscover his self and make a poem over in a new way.

We come back again to the questions with which we began this discussion. The problem of identifying the "real" *Great Expectations*, we found, was simplified when we insisted on respecting the public version to which Dickens gave authorial integrity. The application of this basic test will not select one or the other of Auden's "In Time of War," however, since each is a fulfillment of his intentions, and each was communicated to his usual public. From our review of what takes place in revision for private and public versions, I hope it is clear that the two versions of the Auden collection are equally "real." They stand, side by side, as two separate works, and each has every bit of the dignity and integrity with which an author can endow any work of art. So it is with Hardy, with Yeats, with James, with all multiple versions of works of art where each was given authorial integrity and communicated to the usual public.

This embarrassment of riches may make us restless to distinguish. Hence the critic asks "which is the best?" And the editor asks "which shall I print?" And the student asks "which shall I read?" Usually these three questions are the same, the latter two being applications of the first.

There is a conventional answer, made smooth by constant use. "It is generally accepted that the most authoritative edition is the last published in the author's lifetime." "The book collector may prefer to possess a first edition, however faulty the text, but an author's last revision must, as a rule, claim precedence in literature." This answer can be duplicated from the writings of most of the famous bibliographers and textual authorities, and it is also the password when one is explaining one's terms in a footnote to a textual study: "By 'best text' I mean the text that represents the poet's own final choice among variants of the poem."[55]

It is a bit puzzling to know why this dictum should for so long have passed unchallenged. For it is much like saying that an author's last poem (or novel, or play) is, as a general rule, his best one; it may be, and it may not be. This rule of thumb—whether applied to the choice among multiple versions of a work of art or among works of an author in general—is a desperate substitute for the whole process of critical understanding, which is the only sensible way of trying to arrive at a sound evaluation of any-thing.

IV

What is the aesthetic object with which textual criticism can deal? What constitutes the integrity of the work of art? When a literary work exists in several authorial versions, which is the real work of art?

These are the three questions which we have been addressing. The first invites us to consider the characteristics of the several types of phenomena which can be called aesthetic objects because they yield an aesthetic response. I have argued that the textual critic must limit himself to works of art: thus aesthetic objects which are the result of chance or nature are beyond his scope, however appealing or meritorious they may be, even if they improve the work of art. In being limited to the work of art, the textual critic is thereby limited to the linguistic intentions of the author. The basic goal of textual criticism is, therefore, the verification or recovery of the words which the author intended to constitute the literary work.

The second question asks us to explore the nature of authorship and of the literary works as an intricate entangling of intentions. Various forces are always at work thwarting or modifying the author's intentions. The process of preparing the work for dis-semination to a public (whether that process leads to publication in printed form or production in the theatre or preparation of scribal copies) puts the work in the hands of persons who are professionals in the execution of the process. Similarly, the effort to recover a work of the past puts it in the hands of professionals known as textual critics, or editors. In all of these cases, the process must be adapted to the work at hand, and the work to the process. Some-times through misunderstanding and sometimes through an effort to improve the work, these professionals substitute their own in-tentions for those of the author, who is frequently ignorant of their craft. Sometimes the author objects and sometimes not, some-times he is pleased, sometimes he acquiesces, and sometimes he does not notice what has happened. The work of art is thus always tend-ing toward a collaborative status, and the task of the textual critic is always to recover and preserve its integrity at that point where the authorial intentions seem to have been fulfilled.

The third question opens the nature of composition and seeks to define the authoritative quality of each work of art. Works which are in process can be called potential works of art, while the actual work of art is the one which fulfills the author's intentions. Our only practicable way of distinguishing is to observe whether the author does or does not communicate the work to his usual public. When the author provides us with multiple actual versions of what we commonly think of as a single literary work, he has in fact written separate works, among which there is no simple way to choose the best.

Throughout this discussion, the intentions of the artist have occupied a central position. It is his intentions which distinguish the work of art as an order within the class of aesthetic objects, which must be protected in order to preserve the work from becoming a collaborative enterprise, which give the integrity of completeness to the actual work of art. The inference for the textual critic is that the intentions of the artist are of controlling importance over textual work. While the textual critic should not neglect to carry out the more or less mechanical operations which his masters enjoin upon him, he must also undertake to discover all that he can, from whatever source, about the linguistic intentions of the artist. It is his interpretation of this evidence, within a consistent aesthetic, which plays the crucial role in giving his work value.

I would not wish to argue that these inferences simplify the task of the textual critic, nor that they supply him with a ready formula for solving hard cases, nor that they qualify him as a seer. They do, in fact, make his work more difficult. Whenever we deal with human motives and the operation of human intentions, we soon reach the point—if we do not have the advantage of being the omniscient author—beyond which the best we can suggest is probability, then possibility, then uncertainty. Whenever these stages are reached, the incidence of error is necessarily high. The main merit of establishing textual criticism on a consistent set of aesthetic assumptions is (I think) that it brings the real problems into the open and provides a fairer chance of producing results which will be fundamentally sound.

N O T E S

1. Wesley Trimpi, *Ben Jonson's Poems: A Study of the Plain Style* (Stanford, 1962), p. 151.

2. London, 1930, pp. 260–261, 83; see also p. 34. These examples were retained in the revised edition (London, 1947).

3. Notes to *Hamlet* (IV.iv.84 in modern editions, IV.v in Johnson's edition).

4. Ed., *The Tragedy of Hamlet* (Boston, 1939), p. viii.

5. "Concerning *Le Cimetière marin*" (1933), in Paul Valéry, *The Art of Poetry* (New York, 1958), p. 152.

6. *The Poems of Emily Dickinson* (Cambridge, Mass., 1955), I, xxvi.

7. *A History of American Magazines 1741–1850* (New York, 1930), p. 504.

8. *A History of American Magazines 1865–1885* (Cambridge, Mass., 1938), p. 21.

9. *A History of American Magazines 1885–1905* (Cambridge, Mass., 1957), p. 37.

10. Arthur L. Scott, "The *Century Magazine* Edits *Huckleberry Finn*, 1884–1885," *AL*, XXVII (1955), 356–362.

11. Seymour L. Gross and Alfred J. Levy, "Some Remarks on the Extant Manuscripts of Hawthorne's Short Stories," *SB*, XIV (1961), 254–257.

12. John R. Roberson, "The Manuscript of Page's 'Marse Chan'," *SB*, IX (1957), 259–262.

13. Royal A. Gettman, "Henry James's Revision of *The American*," *AL*, XVI (1945), 295.

14. Oscar Maurer, " 'My Squeamish Public': Some Problems of Victorian Magazine Publishers and Editors," *SB*, XII (1958), 21–40.

15. Carl J. Weber, "The Manuscript of Hardy's *Two on a Tower*," *PBSA*, XL (1946), 1–21.

16. *Editor to Author: The Letters of Maxwell E. Perkins*, ed. John Hall Wheelock (New York, 1950), pp. 171–174, 175–180, 286–294, 227–230, 98–102.

17. Francis E. Skipp, "The Editing of *Look Homeward, Angel*," *PBSA*, LVII (1963), 1–13. On the basis of analyzing the material cut, Skipp is of the opinion that the changes improved the work.

18. Robert H. Elias, rev. of *Letters to Louise: Theodore Dreiser's Letters to Louise Campbell* (Philadelphia, 1959), *AL* XXXIII (1961), 90–91.

19. For an interesting account by a noted editor (of O'Neill and Faulkner, for example) who had been a prolific ghost writer, see Saxe Commins, "Confessions of a Ghost," *PULC*, XXII (1960), 26–35.

20. Marcel Proust, *Jean Santeuil* (London, 1955), pp. ix, xxi–xxii.

21. *The Scarlet Letter* (Columbus, Ohio, 1962), p. xlvii.

22. Matthew J. Bruccoli, "A Collation of F. Scott Fitzgerald's *This Side of Paradise*," *SB*, IX (1957), 263–265.

23. Matthew J. Bruccoli, "Textual Variants in Sinclair Lewis's *Babbitt*," *SB*, XI (1958), 263–268.

24. M. R. Ridley, "The Perpetuated Misprint," *TLS*, 28 August 1959, p. 495.

25. "The Backgrounds of *Ulysses*," *KR*, XVI (1954), 359–360. I have heard it said that Joyce retained some of the printer's errors in *Ulysses* because he preferred them to what he had written, but I have been unable to find any evidence for this claim.

26. William Gibson, *The Seesaw Log: A Chronicle of the Stage Production, with the Text, of "Two for the Seesaw"* (New York, 1959), pp. 32, 37, 101, 43, 140.

27. "Often then the rehearsals of an O'Neill play would degenerate into a series of running battles between the playwright and the producer, the director, and the actors. Invariably, O'Neill was able to stand his ground against them all." Croswell Bowen, "Rehearsing *The Iceman Cometh*," in *O'Neill and His Plays: Four Decades of Criticism*, ed. Oscar Cargill and others (New York, 1961), p. 460.

28. "The Staging of a Play," *Esquire*, LI (May 1959), 144–158.

29. There is considerable evidence in Shakespeare's plays, for example, of revision for production. "All of the texts of the First Folio of 1623 for which there are documents for comparison show stage alteration in varying degrees, and in that fact there is a proof of the universality of stage influence on acted plays. . . . One may say that stage alteration appears in all plays that have been acted on the stage." Hardin Craig, "Textual Degeneration of Elizabethan and Stuart Plays: An Examination of Plays in Manuscript," *Rice Institute Pamphlets*, Vol. XLVI, No. 4 (1960), p. 74. See also Craig's *A New Look at Shakespeare's Quartos* (Stanford, 1961).

30. A vast amount of modern Shakespearean scholarship has been concerned with trying to infer which of these was the basis for the first

printed edition of a given play. There seems to be a tacit assumption among some scholars that the earliest editors of Shakespeare were most interested in printing the words that he wrote. Alice Walker (with whom one fears to disagree) believes that Heminge and Condell "may have known that the *Lear* prompt-book better represented what Shakespeare wrote than the *Hamlet* prompt-book" (*Textual Problems of the First Folio*, Cambridge, Eng., 1953, p. 136). It seems a more plausible assumption that men of the theatre like Heminge and Condell would (unlike many modern scholars) have preferred the text which better represented the play in a good production.

31. *Boswell's Journal of A Tour to the Hebrides With Samuel Johnson, LL.D.*, ed. Frederick A. Pottle and Charles H. Bennett (New York, 1936), p. 173. Entry for Wednesday, 15 September 1773.

32. These various emendations are recorded in the notes to Henry John Todd's edition of Milton's poetical works (London, 1801, and many later editions). The most elaborate and extensive of all unnecessary emendations to Milton were undoubtedly those made by the great classical scholar Richard Bentley in his edition of *Paradise Lost* (1732).

33. See, for example, the history of the reading "mid-May" in Keats's "The Fall of Hyperion," l. 92.

34. "Preface to Shakespeare," *The Works of Samuel Johnson, LL.D.* (Oxford, 1825), v, 151, 150, 149.

35. This is the "god kissing carrion" passage in *Hamlet*: "For if the sun breed maggots in a dead dog, being a god kissing carrion—Have you a daughter?" (ii.ii.181–183). The folios and quartos concur in the reading "good," which Warburton emended (without any external evidence) to "god"—a reading which has been pretty generally accepted, although W. W. Greg objected, a little primly: "It is facile and plausible, but I think unnecessary. Hamlet's fancies are not always as nice as editors would have them" (*Principles of Emendation in Shakespeare*, London, 1928, p. 68). Johnson's observation appears in his edition of Shakespeare at the conclusion of his reprinting of Warburton's note to the passage.

36. For an account of the very numerous revisions, excisions, and eliminations which Auden silently made in preparing his text for the *Collected Poetry* (New York, 1945) and *Collected Shorter Poems* (London, 1950), see Joseph Warren Beach, *The Making of the Auden Canon* (Minneapolis, 1957); his remarks on "In Time of War" are on pp. 5–10. Auden has continued to revise: the unsuspecting reader may be surprised to discover that there is a strong possibility of a significant change in any given poem reprinted in one of the "collected" volumes.

37. See Otis B. Wheeler, "Four Versions of *The Return of the Native*," *NCF*, xiv (1959), 27–44. See also John Paterson, *The Making of*

"*The Return of The Native*" (Berkeley, Calif., 1960), particularly for Hardy's first intentions.

38. See Helen Darbishire's revision of Ernest de Selincourt's edition (Oxford, 1959), pp. liv–lxxiv.

39. See, for example, Edgar F. Shannon, Jr., "The History of A Poem: Tennyson's *Ode on the Death of the Duke of Wellington*," SB, XIII (1960), 149–177; or Shannon, "The Proofs of *Gareth and Lynette* in the Widener Collection," *PBSA*, XLI (1947), 321–340; or W. D. Paden, "A Note on the Variants of *In Memoriam* and *Lucretius*," *Library*, 5th ser., VIII (1953), 259–273.

40. See Thomas H. Johnson, "Emily Dickinson: Creating the Poems," *Harvard Library Bulletin*, VII (1953), 257–270; or, more comprehensively, *The Poems of Emily Dickinson*, ed. Johnson (Cambridge, Mass., 1955), esp. I, xxxiii–xxxviii and 163–165.

41. Morse Peckham, "English Editions of Philip James Bailey's *Festus*," *PBSA*, XLIV (1950), 55–58.

42. The consideration of this possibility will, of course, complicate the reasoning of the textual critic. On the whole, it is a possibility which has usually been disregarded unless the evidence to demonstrate the fact of revision has been overwhelming.

43. *Charles Dickens: The World of His Novels* (Cambridge, Mass., 1958), p. 278.

44. *Charles Dickens: His Tragedy and Triumph* (New York, 1952), II, 988, 992–993.

45. Jean-Jacques Denonain, ed., *Religio Medici* (Cambridge, Eng., 1953), pp. xxiv–xxviii.

46. EETS (Extra Series), LXXVII (1899), 6–8. (The Lydgate translation.)

47. Quoted by James M. Osborn, *John Dryden: Some Biographical Facts and Problems* (New York, 1940), p. 131.

48. "On Mallarmé" in *Selected Writings* (New York, 1950), pp. 217, 216.

49. "Concerning *Le Cimetière marin*" in *The Art of Poetry* (New York, 1958), pp. 140–141.

50. For discussion and examples of authorial revision of work in progress, see *Poets at Work*, ed. Charles D. Abbott (New York, 1948), and Robert H. Taylor and H. W. Liebert, *Authors at Work* (New York, 1957).

51. "Concerning *Le Cimetière marin*" in *The Art of Poetry*, p. 144.

52. Untitled poem *ss*, in *The Variorum Edition of the Poems of W. B. Yeats*, ed. Peter Allt and Russell K. Alspach (New York, 1957), p. 778. (This poem is not included in the "definitive" edition.)

53. The Prefaces to *Roderick Hudson* and *The Golden Bowl* (Vols.

i and xxiii, respectively, in the New York edition) set forth James's central ideas on revision. In the collection of his Prefaces called *The Art of the Novel*, with an introduction by Richard P. Blackmur (New York, 1934), the passage about revision in the Preface to *Roderick Hudson* is on pp. 10–12 and the one in the Preface to *The Golden Bowl* on pp. 335–340. My exposition of James's views is based mainly on the latter passage and includes close paraphrase of what I take to be the major issues.

54. See Sister Mary Brian Durkin, "Henry James's Revisions of the Style of *The Reverberator*," *AL*, xxxiii (1961), 330–349. There has been, I dare say, more extensive scholarly investigation, in books and articles and theses, of the revisions by James for the New York edition than of those by any other writer on any occasion. The three novels in which the revisions have so far been examined the most thoroughly are, probably, *The American*, *The Portrait of a Lady*, and *The Ambassadors*. Such fertile fields are attractive to the husbandman, and we can expect every last one of the twenty-four volumes to be harrowed in each direction.

55. The first quotation is from R. W. Chapman, "The Textual Criticism of English Classics," in *English Critical Essays: Twentieth Century*, ed. Phyllis M. Jones (London, 1933), p. 274. The second is from Sir Harold Williams, *The Text of "Gulliver's Travels"* (Cambridge, Eng., 1952), p. 36. The third is from Zahava Karl Dorinson, " 'I Taste a Liquor Never Brewed': A Problem in Editing," *AL*, xxxv (1963), 363, n. 1.

DAVID M. VIETH

A Textual Paradox: Rochester's

"To a Lady in a Letter"

DAVID M. VIETH *offers in his essay and addendum one of the neatest and intrinsically most interesting studies of the text of a single poem. Vieth applies logic and plain sense with uncommon clarity and grace in charting the growth and change of Rochester's lyric in manuscript, and in exposing the subsequent castration and garbling of the poem in print; the modernized, critical text he gives us makes quite clear how much we owe to textual editors who are patient, careful, inventive, and sensitive.*

THE TEXT OF THE SONG by John Wilmot, Earl of Rochester, usually known as "To a Lady in a Letter" is significant for several reasons. To the general reader, this poem is interesting as one of Rochester's cleverest lyrics and one of the finest songs of the late seventeenth century. For Rochester's editors and biographers, it provides the best example yet discovered showing his methods of revising his poetry—indeed it proves, contrary to

Reprinted from *Papers of the Bibliographical Society of America*, LIV (1960), 147–62; addendum, LV (1961),130–33; with the permission of the author.

the still-prevalent popular notion, that he *did* revise his work. To the textual critic with no special concern for Rochester, it offers an intriguing puzzle which is classic in its clarity and capable of almost complete solution.

If the *textus receptus* of a literary work should be the last complete draft from its author's hands, then the textual traditions of "To a Lady in a Letter" are a bundle of paradoxes. The early texts of the poem readily divide into three groups, which in this discussion will be termed "versions" and designated A, B, and C. At first glance, version B might seem the logical candidate for *textus receptus* because it is preserved in a draft in Rochester's own handwriting. Actually, it is an intermediate state in process of revision and therefore less satisfactory than either version A or version C, both of which probably represent final drafts even though neither is known to exist in a holograph manuscript. Version A might also seem a likely choice, since it was printed in 1680 in the first collected edition of Rochester's works, a volume that provides the best extant texts for many of his poems and served as an ultimate source for almost all later Rochester editions. This version, however, was apparently the earliest of the three to be written and is therefore least representative of Rochester's final intentions.

Version C, the version an editor should adopt, presents further paradoxes. Jacob Tonson's edition of 1691, which frequently derives its texts from those of 1680, nevertheless uses some manuscript source for this poem and prints version C. Unlike the earliest texts of versions A and B, however, Tonson's text is seriously bowdlerized—or "castrated," as Rochester's contemporaries would have said. Though version C was evidently the last to be written, it was the first to be published, appearing in a miscellany dated 1676. But even this text is bowdlerized, albeit less thoroughly than in Tonson's edition.

The paradoxes of the seventeenth-century textual history of the poem have continued to haunt its treatment by Rochester's numerous twentieth-century editors, none of whom has examined the problem exhaustively or distinguished the three versions one from another. Although most editors—including John Hayward, Quilter Johns, Harry Levin, Ronald Duncan, and Vivian de Sola

Pinto—have rightly selected version c, they have reprinted Tonson's text, which is the most fully bowdlerized, and some have used later Tonson editions instead of the first edition of 1691. Hayward also classified version A (which he printed in a deteriorated text) as spurious and termed version c "the original version"—conclusions, I suggest, quite opposite to the real situation. Though Pinto chose version c for his edition, in his earlier biography of Rochester he printed the uncompleted holograph text of version B as if it were a final draft. James Thorpe was the first editor to perceive that Tonson's text is bowdlerized, but his resulting generalization that the edition of 1680, which gives version A, "presents the most reliable text of the core of the Rochester canon" is too sweeping and does not, in particular, apply to this poem.[1]

Among the early printed texts of "To a Lady in a Letter," the only one not favored by Rochester's editors is that of 1676, which the evidence shows to be closer than any other to his final intentions. Moreover, the finest text of all, extant in a manuscript, is the only known text of any importance that has never before appeared in print.

II

Investigation of the early texts of "To a Lady in a Letter" must begin with a separate examination of each of the three versions.

Version A, consisting of six four-line stanzas, exists in two independently derived texts that are verbally identical. Text A₁ occurs (p. 146) in a large manuscript miscellany, compiled in spring or summer of 1680, which is located in the Yale University Library and has been designated the Yale MS. Text A₂ was printed in Rochester's *Poems on Several Occasions*, 1680, the first collected edition of his works. The verbal congruence of texts A₁ and A₂ is not surprising, for the Yale MS. and the edition of 1680 bear a close collateral relationship to each other, both being descended independently from a no longer extant manuscript archetype; evidence in support of this conclusion has been presented in detail elsewhere.[2] Text A₁ is here reproduced; A₂ is easily accessible in Thorpe's volume (p. 68).

Song

How happy Cloris (were they free)
    Might our Enjoyments prove,
But you w^(th) formall Jealousie
    Are still tormenting Love.

[5]   Let us (since Witt instructs us how)
    Raise pleasures to ye topp,
If Rivall Bottle you'll allow,
    I'll suffer Rivall Fopp.

There's not a briske insipid Sparke,
[10]   That flutters in ye Town,
But w^(th) your wanton Eyes you marke,
    the Coxcomb for your owne.

You never thinke it worth your care,
    How empty nor how dull,
[15]   The heads of your Admirers are,
    Soe that their Codds be full.

All this you freely may confesse,
    Yet we'll not disagree;
For did you love your pleasure lesse,
[20]   You were not fit for me

While I, my Passion to pursue
    Am whole Nights takeing in
The lusty Juice of Grapes, take you
    The lusty Juice of Men.

Version B, consisting of eight stanzas, is found in two manuscript texts, the first in Rochester's handwriting and the second derived from the first. Text B1 is preserved at the University of Nottingham in a collection known as the Portland MS. (fol. 1^r), where it appears together with eight other poems and a short prose piece in Rochester's autograph; this manuscript also includes seven poems in the hand of Rochester's wife and one poem in a hand not yet identified. Text B2 occurs in British Museum Harleian MS. 7316 (fol. 21^v) as one of six poetical texts which almost certainly descend from the Portland ms. and are probably direct copies. The derivation of these six poems is indicated by evidence too extensive to consider here.[3]

In the holograph text B1, the last two stanzas are preceded by a symbol consisting of a long horizontal line twice looped back on itself. Between the second and third stanzas is another symbol probably formed in similar fashion but looking like a long horizontal line with a dot at its center surrounded by a small circle. The last two stanzas are plainly out of place in their present position, as the scribe of B2 recognized by leaving a wide space to separate them from the rest of the poem. Evidently Rochester intended to insert the last two stanzas between the second and third; this conclusion is supported by additional circumstances to be discussed shortly.

Since text B2 provides no information not available in its source, only B1 need be reproduced.[4] In two instances where B1 has readings deleted and then rewritten in altered form above the line, B2 adopts the revised reading. In line 19, B2 repairs Rochester's inadvertent omission of the last letter of "your," but in line 10 it does not correct his similar omission of the last letter of "flutters." In all other readings B2 is verbally identical with B1.

[no title]

perfect
How ~~happy~~ Cloris, & how free
   Would these enjoyments prouve,
But you wth formall jealousy
   Are still tormenting Love

[5]   Lett us (since witt instructs us how)
   Raise pleasure to the topp,
If Rivall bottle you'l allow
   I'le suffer rivall fopp,

[symbol]

Ther's not a brisk insipid sparke
[10]   That flutter in the Towne
But wth y^r wanton eyes you marke
   Him out to be y^r owne

You never thinke it worth y^r care
How empty nor how dull
[15] The heads of y^r admirers are

backs
Soe that their   bee full.

purse

All this you freely may confess
Yett wee'l not disagree
For did you love you pleasures less
[20] You were not fitt for mee

Whilst I my passion to persue
Am whole nights taking in

Lusty juice of
The ~~juice of Lusty~~ grapes, take you
The juice of Lusty Men—

[symbol]

[25] Upraide mee not that I designe
Tricks to delude y^r charmes
When running after mirth & wine
I leave y^r Longing Armes

For wine (whose power alone can raise
[30] Our thoughts soe farr above)
Affords Idea's fitt to praise
What wee thinke fitt to Love

Version c, in eight stanzas, exists in four texts, each deriving at
least one reading from sources not known to be extant. Text c₁,
here reproduced as base copy, appears in Harvard ms. Eng. 636F
(p. 8), a large manuscript miscellany assembled during the early
1680's which is familiar to Restoration scholars. Text c₂ was printed
in *A New Collection of the Choicest Songs*, 1676 (sig. A₄ʳ), and
text c₃ in *The Last and Best Edition of New Songs*, 1677 (sig. D₈ʳ).
Text c₄ is found in Rochester's *Poems, &c. on Several Occasions*,
1691 (p. 36), published by Tonson. In the apparatus following the
base copy, variants in spelling, capitalization, and punctuation are
ignored.⁵

To A Lady, in A Letter

1

Such perfect Blisse faire Chloris, wee
  In our Enjoyment prove
'Tis pitty restless Jealiousy
  Should Mingle with our Love.

2

[5]   Lett us (since witt has taught us how)
  Raise pleasure to the Topp
You Rivall Bottle must allow
  I'le suffer Rivall Fopp.

3

Thinke not in this, that I designe
[10]   A Treason 'gainst Loves Charmes
When following yᵉ God of Wine
  I Leave my Chloris armes.

4

Since you have that for all your hast
  Att which I'le ne're repine
[15]   Will take his Likour of as fast
  As I can take of mine.

5

There's not A brisk insipid Sparke
  That Flutters in yᵉ Towne
But with your wanton eyes, you marke
[20]   Him out to be your owne.

6

Nor doe you thinke it worth your care
  How empty and how dull
The heads of yoᶠ Admirers are
  Soe that their Codds be full.

[25] All this you freely may Confesse
    Yett wee nere disagree
   For did you love your pleasure lesse
   You were noe Match for mee.

8

   Whilst I my pleasure to pursue
[30] Whole nights am takeing in,
   The Lusty Juice of Grapes, take you
   The Juice of Lusty Men:

Heading] Against jealousie. C₂, C₃
Stanza numbers om. C₂, C₃
2 Enjoyment] enjoyments C₂, C₃
8 I'le] I C₂, C₃
10 A Treason 'gainst] treason against C₂, C₃
15 Will take his Likour of] Will take its ------- off C₂; Will take its
  liquor off C₃; Its Pleasure can repeat C₄
16 can take of mine] do take off mine C₂, C₃; the Joys of Wine C₄
24 Codds] bags C₂, C₃; Veins C₄
26 wee] we'd C₂, C₃
28 Match] mate C₂, C₃
28 mee.] me, &c. C₂, C₃
29–32 *om.* C₂, C₃, C₄

  Texts C₂ C₃, and C₄ are rather obviously bowdlerized. C₂ and C₃
omit the last stanza but include after line 28 the sign "&c.," implying
that another stanza originally followed. In line 24, the vague and
ambiguous "bags" of C₂ and C₃ seems to replace an obscene word,
probably "Codds" as in C₁. In line 15, C₂ omits an objectionable
word, probably "liquor" as in C₃ and C₁. It is not unusual to find the
process of castration carried even further in C₄ than in C₂ and C₃,
since the edition of 1691 normally bowdlerizes all obscene or blas-
phemous poems by alteration or omission. C₄ omits the last stanza,
replaces the obscene word in line 24 with "Veins," and verbally alters lines 15 and 16 even while retaining more or less their original
sense. Though C₂, C₃, and C₄ agree in omitting the last stanza, the

bowdlerization of c_4 is probably independent of that in c_2 and c_3; there is no evidence that the edition of 1691 was influenced in other instances by the miscellanies of 1676 and 1677.

Texts c_2 and c_3 are reducible to a hyparchetype c_2–c_3. Indeed, except for the single word "liquor" in line 15, c_3 is a verbally identical reprint of c_2. The miscellanies of 1676 and 1677 were both published by Philip Brooksby, and they appeared within a few months of each other: *A New Collection* was licensed on 28 Apr. 1676 and advertised in the *Term Catalogues* on 12 June, while *The Last and Best Edition* was licensed on 20 Nov. 1676 and advertised in the *Term Catalogues* on 22 Nov. Aside from the word "liquor," c_3 slavishly follows c_2 even in accidentals; the only deviations are the insertion of one comma, capitalization of the initial letter in four words, and a single-letter spelling change. Since the word "liquor" appears in c_1 as well as c_3, it was almost certainly the reading of the manuscript copy-text of c_2. After the publication of c_2, Brooksby doubtless decided that "liquor" was not too offensive and restored it from his manuscript when c_3 was printed. Clearly, the hyparchetype c_2–c_3 is this manuscript, whose readings we must reconstruct as best we can from its two direct descendants and the other two texts of version c. c_2–c_3 will therefore consist of the text of c_2 with "liquor" inserted in line 15, and—lacking evidence to contradict—with "Codds" substituted for "bags" in line 24 and an eighth stanza identical with that in c_1. These last two decisions are further supported by the appearance of "Codds" in version a and the inclusion of an equivalent stanza in both a and b.[6]

Similarly, c_1 and c_4 can be resolved into a hyparchetype c_1–c_4. Aside from readings altered by bowdlerization, c_1 and c_4 invariably agree with each other against c_2–c_3. It is true that in line 15, where the third word is "his" in c_1 and "its" in c_2–c_3, the first word in c_4 is "Its"; but this reading of c_4 may well have resulted from the bowdlerization of lines 15 and 16 and should be disregarded. Thus the evidence sufficiently demonstrates that the state of the text represented by c_2–c_3 is in no sense intermediary between c_1 and c_4. Moreover, since c_4 varies from c_1 only in its bowdlerized readings, we must assume that the hyparchetype c_1–c_4, so far as the available evidence can show, is verbally identical with c_1. c_4 is probably not derived from c_1, however, for there is no other indication that the edition of 1691 depends upon Harvard MS. Eng. 636F. Nor is there reason to suspect that c_4 was influenced by the readings of A_2, even though many texts in the edition of 1691 are partially or wholly derived from one of the editions of 1680.

The foregoing conclusions narrow the possible relationships between c_1–c_4 and c_2–c_3 to three general types: (1) one state may descend from the other; (2) both may descend independently from an authorial draft or an archetype which is descended from an authorial draft; (3) each may descend from a different authorial draft. Before these three possibilities can be explored, however, it is necessary to establish the relationships among versions A, B, and C.

III

Close comparison of the three versions of "To a Lady in a Letter" leaves little doubt that version A is the earliest, version B an intermediate draft in process of revision, and version C the product of this revision. The total variational pattern is enough to suggest that version B is intermediary between A and C. Though B agrees extensively with A against C and with C against A, in only three substantive readings do A and C agree against B. Each of these three readings affects only a single word, and all are special cases: one, which may be a slip of Rochester's pen, is a difference between singular and plural (line 27 of C), another is an obscene term (line 24 of C), and the third is part of a larger variant which does not support the agreement of A and C against B (line 2). This evidence is stronger than may appear, since it is not uncommon for an author to adopt one reading in his first draft, substitute another in a second draft, and then return in a third draft to his original choice. More important, however, three major sets of variants indicate not only that B is intermediary between A and C but that the direction of change is from A through B to C. These variants must be examined in detail.

(1) In the holograph text B_1, as noted earlier, the symbols appearing between stanzas 2 and 3 and between stanzas 6 and 7 evidently indicate that the last two stanzas, which are out of place at the end of the poem, were to be inserted after the second stanza.

Comparison with versions A and C confirms this conclusion. Except for variants involving less than one line each, the first six stanzas of text B₁ correspond exactly to the full six stanzas of version A. Also, two stanzas corresponding to the last two in text B₁ actually appear after the second stanza in version C. Though version C exhibits considerable variation in these added lines, it retains the rhyme-words of B₁ in the first of the two stanzas, and in both stanzas its general sense is recognizably similar.

Apparently Rochester's intention in adding the two stanzas was to reinforce and extend the poem's wittily outrageous plea for separate but equal debauchery. Like a Metaphysical poem, his song turns on the conceit that though the speaker and his mistress pursue their separate pleasures of wine and love, they are united by their common hedonism. This designedly specious argument culminates in an ironic echo of Lovelace's famous lines:

> For did you love your pleasure lesse
> You were noe Match for mee.

In version A, as Rochester may have felt, the opposed interests of Bacchus and Venus give the impression of being yoked by too much violence; the force pushing them apart seems greater than the force striving to hold them in tension. In version B, the two added stanzas strengthen the linkage by introducing the idea that only wine can inspire love-poetry. In version C, this idea is discarded in favor of a parallel between the respective "liquors" of wine and love.

(2) In the initial line of text B₁, the canceled reading "happy" is that of version A, whereas the preferred reading "perfect" is found in version C. Rochester's revisions of the first two lines of the poem seem aimed at greater verbal exactness. In version A he wrote "How happy Cloris (were they free) | Might our Enjoyments prove." In text B₁ he altered this to "How happy Cloris, & how free | Would these enjoyments prouve"—which is scarcely any better. Then, however, he struck out "happy" and substituted the more precise word "perfect." In version C, his final draft, he adopted the syntactically tighter "Such perfect Blisse faire Chloris, wee | In our Enjoyment(s) prove."

(3) A similar deletion and correction occurs in text B_1 at line 23. The last two lines of version A are a parallel between "The lusty Juice of Grapes" and "The lusty Juice of Men." The parallel in ideas is so obvious, however, that the complete rhetorical parallelism is rather wooden, nor does it exploit the richer effects attainable through such devices as chiasmus. Accordingly, in text B_1 Rochester tried altering the first phrase to "The juice of Lusty grapes." Since the revised reading is not very satisfactory, he struck it out, wrote the original reading above it, and altered the second phrase to "The juice of Lusty Men." These are the readings of version C.

A detailed list of the variants separating versions A, B, and C should be given both to document clearly the conclusions reached in preceding paragraphs and to show the nature of Rochester's revisions. Included are all important variants of the hyparchetypes C_1–C_4 and C_2–C_3, since we have not yet determined which of these readings are authoritative. The line-numbering follows version C.

Song $A \rightarrow$ *no title* $B \rightarrow$ To A Lady, in A Letter C_1–C_4; Against jealousie C_2–C_3

1 How happy Cloris (were they free) $A \rightarrow$ How happy Cloris, & how free $B \rightarrow$ How perfect Cloris, & how free $B \rightarrow$ Such perfect Blisse faire Chloris, wee C

2 Might our Enjoyments $A \rightarrow$ Would these enjoyments $B \rightarrow$ In our Enjoyment C_1–C_4; in our enjoyments C_2–C_3

3 But you wth formall $A, B \rightarrow$ 'Tis pitty restless C

4 Are still tormenting $A, B \rightarrow$ Should Mingle with our C

5 instructs $A, B \rightarrow$ has taught C

7 If Rivall Bottle you'll $A, B \rightarrow$ You Rivall Bottle must C

8 I'll A, B, C_1–C_4; I C_2–C_3

9–16 *added* B, C

9 Upraide mee not $B \rightarrow$ Thinke not in this C

10 Tricks to delude y^r $B \rightarrow$ A Treason 'gainst Loves C_1–C_4; treason against love's C_2–C_3

11 running after mirth & $B \rightarrow$ following y^e God of C

12 y^r Longing $B \rightarrow$ my Chloris C

13 For wine (whose power alone can raise $B \rightarrow$ Since you have that for all your hast C

14 Our thoughts soe farr above) $B \rightarrow$ Att which I'le ne're repine C

15 Affords Idea's fitt to praise $B \rightarrow$ Will take his Likour of as fast C_1–C_4; Will take its liquor off as fast C_2–C_3

16 What wee thinke fitt to Love $B \rightarrow$ As I can take of mine C_1–C_4; as
    I do take off mine C_2–C_3

20 The Coxcomb for $A \rightarrow$ Him out to be B, C

21 You never $A, B \rightarrow$ Nor doe you C

22 nor $A, B \rightarrow$ and C

24 Codds $A \rightarrow \dfrac{\text{backs}}{\text{purse}}\ B \rightarrow$ Codds C

26 we'll not $A, B \rightarrow$ wee nere C_1–C_4; we'd ne'r C_2–C_3

27 pleasure $A \rightarrow$ pleasures $B \rightarrow$ pleasure C

28 not fit $A, B \rightarrow$ noe Match C_1–C_4; no mate C_2–C_3

29 While $A \rightarrow$ Whilst B, C

29 Passion $A, B \rightarrow$ pleasure C

30 Am whole Nights $A, B \rightarrow$ Whole nights am C

31 lusty Juice of $A \rightarrow$ juice of Lusty $B \rightarrow$ Lusty juice of B, C

32 lusty Juice of $A \rightarrow$ juice of Lusty B, C

This list of revisions prompts at least one further observation which might, to be sure, have been gathered from Rochester's other works: as a poet, he is noteworthy for his discriminating ear and his sure touch. Though many of his revised readings will seem, to the average ear, neither better nor worse than the words he canceled, they must have appealed to his superior sensitivity to language. Also, the list reveals very few instances in which Rochester altered a reading, then returned later to his original thought. Evidently he possessed rare facility in finding exactly the words he wanted to body forth his conceptions.

IV

The final paradox of the early texts of "To a Lady in a Letter" is a frustrating joke on Rochester's editors: version c, which an editor is bound to adopt, is the only one of the three versions whose variants cannot be resolved with full confidence. The evidence fails to indicate clearly whether the states represented by the two hyparchetypes are descended one from the other, related collaterally through an archetype, or descended separately from different authorial drafts. Since editors must render decisions in such matters, however, there is no choice but to consider the available arguments, inconclusive though they may be.

In the absence of better data, the relationship of version c to versions B and A offers a makeshift test that may help to identify corrupt variants in the two hyparchetypes. Wherever c_1–c_4 and c_2–c_3 differ in their readings, the variant which agrees with version B or with both B and A is probably authentic, whereas the other variant may be corrupt. Unfortunately, a peculiar circumstance reduces the usefulness of this test, for six of the eight unresolved pairs of variants occur in places where neither c_1–c_4 nor c_2–c_3 agrees with versions B and A. The remaining two cases, however, yield reasonably clear results. In line 2, the reading "enjoyments" in c_2–c_3 agrees with both B and A, whereas "Enjoyment" in c_1–c_4 does not. In line 8, "I'll" in c_1–c_4 agrees with B and A, whereas "I" in c_2–c_3 is unsupported. The readings "I" and "Enjoyment" are *prima facie* corruptions. Line 2 refers to the twin pleasures of love and wine, so that the plural form "enjoyments" is almost mandatory. "I'll" in line 8 gives a closer parallelism with the preceding line, and a more natural sequence of tenses.

These two pairs of variants also suggest that the states represented by the hyparchetypes do not descend one from the other, since one corruption occurs in c_1–c_4 and the second in c_2–c_3. Normally, in determining manuscript stemmas, such minor variants should carry little weight; these, in particular, seem to result from inadvertent omissions of letters which could easily be resupplied by any number of later copyists working independently. On the other hand, the close relationship of c_4 to c_1 and of c_3 to c_2, together with the notable lack of any other texts of version C, argues that this version was not copied extensively and that the two pairs of variants may therefore be significant. Furthermore, if the states represented by the hyparchetypes were ancestor and descendant, all variants in the descendant would be corruptions, and some of them, at least, should be obviously incorrect. This condition does not obtain, for in each of the six unresolved pairs of variants, the readings of c_1–c_4 and c_2–c_3 are both plausible.

Again, if the hyparchetypes descend independently either from a single authorial draft or from an archetype descended in its turn from an authorial draft, the variants in both c_1–c_4 and c_2–c_3 should ordinarily include some evident corruptions. This, we have seen, is true only of the readings "I" and "Enjoyment." Even these two incorrect readings may have been present in separate drafts from Rochester's own hand. In the holograph text B_1, Rochester similarly drops the final letters of "flutters" (line 10) and "your" (line 19). Possibly he was prone to this type of error, at least during the interval when he was transcribing "To a Lady in a Letter." Moreover, the occurrence of so many unresolved pairs of variants at places where version c differs from versions b and a may hold some significance: these are exactly the places where Rochester, having revised the readings of b, is most likely to have continued revising after he completed his earliest draft of c. On the whole, then, the evidence slightly favors the conclusion that c_1-c_4 and c_2-c_3 descend from separate authorial drafts, and consequently that we possess not just three, but four authoritative versions of the poem.

Fortunately, a sort of *deus ex machina* rescues an editor at this point, for special circumstances virtually require him to adopt hyparchetype c_1-c_4 as preserved in text c_1, altering it only by correcting "Enjoyment" to a plural. Three arguments support this procedure.

(1) Since c_1-c_4 and c_2-c_3 may descend from separate authorial drafts, one of the two should be chosen and its readings followed consistently; an editor should not attempt to combine readings which may stem from different holograph texts. This decision has the additional advantage of avoiding the risks of eclecticism. Readings from one of the two hyparchetypes should not be substituted in the other unless, as with "I" and "Enjoyment," the rejected reading is apparently a corruption whose origin is explicable in terms of the preferred reading.

(2) Since both extant descendants of c_2-c_3 lack the last stanza and probably bowdlerize at least one more word, c_1-c_4 is by far the better choice as *textus receptus*, other considerations being equal.

(3) Subjective criteria appear to favor the readings of c_1-c_4. Though the variants in c_2-c_3 may be authoritative, those in c_1-c_4 are in all instances just as good, and in some instances better; possibly they are later revisions. In line 28, "Match" (c_1-c_4) expresses the sense more precisely than "mate" (c_2-c_3). In line 26, "wee"

(c_1–c_4) gives a better sequence of tenses than "we'd" (c_2–c_3). In line 16, "do" (c_2–c_3) is a weak expletive, whereas "can" (c_1–c_4) is functional. In line 15, "its" (c_2–c_3) is ambiguous, since it might refer to "that" in line 13; the implied antecedent of "his" (c_1–c_4), as Rochester probably intended, is the god of love in line 10. In line 10, "treason against" (c_2–c_3) involves a trochaic substitution which would be unusual in this song; "A Treason 'gainst" preserves the regularity of the meter. The inclusion or omission of stanza numbers is immaterial, and the choice of titles is perhaps indifferent —though the heading in c_1–c_4 may indicate that Rochester actually sent this version in a letter to one of his mistresses.

For reasons too complex to outline here, full modernization of accidentals seems the least unsatisfactory form for a twentieth-century edition of Rochester's poetry. The following text of his song, one hopes, prints its substantive readings for the first time in their pristine impurity.

To a Lady in a Letter

Such perfect bliss, fair Chloris, we
    In our enjoyments prove,
'Tis pity restless jealousy
    Should mingle with our love.

Let us, since wit has taught us how,
    Raise pleasure to the top:
You rival bottle must allow;
    I'll suffer rival fop.

Think not in this that I design
    A treason 'gainst love's charms,
When following the god of wine
    I leave my Chloris' arms,

Since you have that, for all your haste
    (At which I'll ne'er repine),
Will take his liquor off as fast
    As I can take off mine.

There's not a brisk, insipid spark
    That flutters in the town,

But with your wanton eyes you mark
  Him out to be your own;

Nor do you think it worth your care
  How empty and how dull
The heads of your admirers are,
  So that their cods be full.

All this you freely may confess,
  Yet we ne'er disagree,
For did you love your pleasure less,
  You were no match for me.

Whilst I, my pleasure to pursue,
  Whole nights am taking in
The lusty juice of grapes, take you
  The juice of lusty men.

N O T E S

1. John Hayward, *Collected Works of John Wilmot, Earl of Rochester* (1926), pp. 15, 313, 351. Quilter Johns, *The Poetical Works of John Wilmot, Earl of Rochester* (1933), p. 25. Harry Levin, *A Satire against Mankind and Other Poems by John Wilmot, Earl of Rochester* (1942), p. 14. Ronald Duncan, *Selected Lyrics and Satires of John Wilmot, 2nd Earl of Rochester* (1948), p. 51; *Rochester* (1959), p. 20. Vivian de Sola Pinto, *Rochester: Portrait of a Restoration Poet* (1935), p. 40; *Poems by John Wilmot, Earl of Rochester* (1953), p. 22. James Thorpe, *Rochester's Poems on Several Occasions* (1950), pp. [v], xxxvi.

2. In my article, "The Text of Rochester and the Editions of 1680," *PBSA* L (1956), 243–63. See Thorpe for full bibliographical information on the first and later editions of 1680. Text A1, which has no known descendants, is reproduced with the kind permission of the officials of the Yale University Library. Text A2 was reprinted in the other editions of 1680 and in later editions in the same series published in 1685, 1701, 1713, and 1731. From the edition of 1685 it was reprinted in *The Triumph of Wit*, 1688 and 1692. From some edition of this miscellany it was again reprinted in the second volume of *The Hive*, 1724.

3. This evidence is analyzed in my *Attribution in Restoration Poetry: A Study of Rochester's "Poems" of 1680* (1963), pp. 227–29.

4. In reproducing B_1, I have normalized Rochester's erratic indention of lines. Besides the symbols separating stanzas 2 and 3 and stanzas 6 and 7, B_1 includes a short horizontal line between stanzas 1 and 2, 3 and 4, 5 and 6, and 7 and 8. Stanzas 4 and 5 are not separated by one of these lines because stanza 4 occurs at the bottom of a page. B_1 has no known descendants except B_2. B_1 has twice been printed by Pinto, once in his biography (p. 40) and again in his edition (p. 167). Both of Pinto's texts omit the symbols after the second and sixth stanzas, give the first two words of line 13 wrongly as "Nor ever" instead of "You never," and reproduce accidentals rather carelessly. In his edition (pp. 166–67), Pinto mistakenly groups the text in Harvard MS. Eng. 636F with those representing version A and describes it as "not so full" as B_1.

5. I am grateful to the officials of the Houghton Library of Harvard University for permission to print text C_1; its sometimes erratic indention of lines has been normalized. C_1 has no known descendants, and C_2 has none except C_3. C_4 was reprinted in the later Tonson editions of 1696, 1705, 1714, and 1732, and in piracies dated 1710 and 1718.

6. My procedure in determining these two readings of C_2–C_3 entails some risks, since, as we shall see, C_2–C_3 and C_1–C_4 possibly descend from different authorial drafts. The risks are minor, however, because I base no further conclusions on these hypothetical readings and do not choose C_2–C_3 as *textus receptus*.

ADDENDUM:
AN UNSUSPECTED CANCEL IN
TONSON'S 1691 "ROCHESTER"

A copy of Jacob Tonson's 1691 edition of Rochester's *Poems, &c. on Several Occasions*, which I have recently acquired through Percy Dobell and Son from the collection of the late Colonel C. H. Wilkinson, has directed attention to new information that supplements the evidence and arguments in my article on the text of Rochester's lyric "To a Lady in a Letter." In the Wilkinson copy, leaf D_3, containing all but the title and first two stanzas of Rochester's song, is plainly a cancel—a fact not readily apparent in the copy of Tonson's edition used in preparing my article and not, of course, discernible from microfilms of other copies preserving the canceled state. A quick search has identified one copy, in the Henry E. Huntington Library, which gives D_3 in the uncanceled state.[1]

The uncanceled leaf reveals an unusually interesting situation which explains the reason for the cancellation. The cancelland preserves an *unexpurgated* text of Rochester's song, whereas the text of the cancellans, printed from an entirely different setting of type, is rather heavily expurgated by alteration and omission of obscene readings.[2] This circumstance should answer once and for all those students of Rochester who have continued to doubt that Tonson's edition is bowdlerized.

As was shown in my article, the early texts of "To a Lady in a Letter" divide into three well-defined groups A, B, and C, with B comprising a version intermediate between the earliest version A and the final version C. Version A survives in two independently descended texts A_1 and A_2. Version B exists in two manuscripts, a holograph text B_1 in process of revision and a later transcript B_2 which almost certainly descends from B_1. The newly discovered cancel, which belongs to version C, has no direct bearing on versions A and B, nor does it affect the conclusions previously formulated concerning the relationships among the three versions.

Prior to the discovery of the cancel in Tonson's edition, version C was known to exist in four variant texts. Texts C_1 (Harvard MS. Eng. 636F) and C_4 (the canceled state of Tonson's edition) descend independently from a manuscript hyparchetype C_1-C_4 which appeared, from the data originally available, to be verbally identical with C_1.[3] Likewise, texts C_2 and C_3 (in printed miscellanies dated 1676 and 1677) are reducible to a hyparchetype C_2-C_3; C_3 was printed from C_2, but an obscene word omitted in C_2 was apparently restored in C_3 from the manuscript source of C_2. The evidence slightly favors the assumption that the two hyparchetypes descend, not from an archetype, but from separate drafts in Rochester's own hand. For several reasons, C_1-C_4 seems to offer a better basis than C_2-C_3 for the *textus receptus* of the poem.

The readings of Tonson's uncanceled leaf D_3 require augmentation of four sets of variants in the collation of version C printed on page 109 of my article. The cancelland and cancellans will be designated C_4a and C_4b respectively; elsewhere in the collation, the siglum C_4 may stand for both C_4a and C_4b.[4] In lines 16 and 29–32, C_4a is verbally identical with the base copy C_1.

15 Will take his Likour of] Will take its ——— off C_2; Will take its
  liquor off C_3, C_4a; Its Pleasure can repeat C_4b
16 can take of mine] do take off mine C_2, C_3; the Joys of Wine C_4b
24 Codds] bags C_2, C_3, C_4a; Veins C_4b
29–32 *om.* C_2, C_3, C_4b

These variants immediately suggest an important conclusion.
Since C_4a and C_4b agree against C_1, and C_4a and C_1 against C_4b, but
never C_4b and C_1 against C_4a, C_4a may be intermediary between C_4b
and C_1. In all likelihood, therefore, C_4b was printed from C_4a without
any apparent consultation of the manuscript source of C_4a. The resulting relationships among the surviving texts of version c should
be diagramed for the sake of clarity:

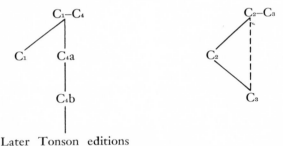

Later Tonson editions

In the main, the uncanceled state of leaf D_3 confirms the conjectures ventured in my earlier article regarding the readings of the
hyparchetype C_1–C_4. In C_4a, all four lines of the eighth stanza (ll.
29–32), which is omitted in C_4b, are verbally identical with those in
C_1. Similarly, except for one word, lines 15 and 16 in C_4a and C_1 are
verbally identical. Only two single-word variants between C_4a and
C_1 call for qualification of earlier conclusions concerning the readings of C_1–C_4 and thus of the *textus receptus*:[5]
    (1) In line 15, C_4a reads "it's" where C_1 reads "his." Since the hyp-
archetype C_2–C_3 also has "its," this may well have been the reading
of C_1–C_4. Consequently, in spite of the subjective argument offered
in favor of "his" (p. 117), the *textus receptus* should probably be
altered to read "its" (p. 117). At the time when "To a Lady in a
Letter" was composed, "its" and "his" were easily interchangeable
forms of the neuter singular possessive pronoun.

(2) In line 24, c_{4a} reads "Bags" where c_1 reads "Codds." Since c_2 and c_3 also have "bags," this variant is probably not a bowdlerization of an obscene word in c_2–c_3, as formerly conjectured (pp. 109, 110), but an authoritative reading. For the same reason, "Bags" may have been the reading of c_1–c_4. On the other hand, "Codds," the reading of c_1, appears in version A (l. 16) and may therefore be authoritative too. Possibly Rochester provided alternative readings here, as he did at the corresponding point in the holograph text B_1 (l. 16). Under the circumstances, a clear choice between "Codds" and "Bags" in the *textus receptus* does not seem feasible, though subjective considerations (p. 109) may still favor "Codds."[6]

N O T E S

1. Call number 132762. I am indebted to the staff of the Huntington Library for verifying that D_3 in this copy of Tonson's edition is not a cancel. A second copy in the Huntington, call number 148508, preserves the canceled state of D_3.

2. A similar situation occurs with leaf D_7, which is a cancel in the Wilkinson copy but appears in the uncanceled state in Huntington copy 132762. The cancellans, representing an entirely separate setting of type, omits the last stanza of Rochester's lyric beginning "Love a Woman! you're an Ass." The cancelland prints this stanza as follows:

4.

Then give me Health, Wealth, and Wine;
  And, if busie love intrenches,
There's a soft young Page of mine,
  Does the trick worth forty Wenches.

3. In my article as originally published, the term "hyparchetype" was erroneously given as "hyperarchetype." The term is taken from Paul Maas, *Textual Criticism*, trans. Barbara Flower (1958), p. 6.

4. There are also some variants in accidentals between c_{4a} and c_{4b}. In c_{4a}, moreover, the recto of leaf D_3 contains stanzas 3, 4, 5, and the first two lines of stanza 6, with the rest of this stanza and all of stanzas 7 and 8 printed on the verso. In c_{4b}, which omits stanza 8, the recto of D_3

contains only stanzas 3, 4, and 5, with stanzas 6 and 7 appearing on the verso.

5. These two sets of variants also require adjustments at ll. 15 and 24 in the table printed on pp. 113–14 of my earlier article.

6. For the resulting text, see my edition, *The Complete Poems of John Wilmot, Earl of Rochester* (1968), pp. 83–85.

ROBERT HALSBAND

Editing the Letters of Letter-Writers

ROBERT HALSBAND *considers without polemic the social and literary justifications of editions of collected letters, reflects on the criteria for their selection and the options for their arrangement, and speaks to many aspects of their textual presentation, annotation, and indexing. Though he proposes to be less rigorously faithful to manuscript than some editors have been, and although he does not cover all the problems that beset editors of letters, Halsband offers a suggestive survey of the topic. His title suggests a preoccupation with literary letters like those of Lady Mary Wortley Montagu, but Halsband's essay is instructive for editing letters of any kind.*

D URING THE LAST FEW DECADES so many new editions of letters have been produced that any editor contemplating still another must pause and take his bearings. In the edition of Lady Mary Wortley Montagu's letters which I am now preparing I hope to be guided by the virtues and warned by the faults of others before me. But if in my remarks here I raise questions which I do

Reprinted from *Studies in Bibliography*, XI (1958), 25–37, with the permission of the author and the Bibliographical Society of the University of Virginia.

not answer with definite conviction, it is because my editorial resolutions are still somewhat flexible.

Certainly it is easy enough to criticize nineteenth-century editors of letters. We are often impatient with their methods—their casual attitude toward accuracy of text, their skimpy and superficial annotations, their partisan attitudes, and their diligence in excising any word or passage that might bring a blush to a maiden's cheek or a blot to a family escutcheon. Perhaps we can regard them more kindly if we recall what they conceived their function to be. They intended their editions to be enjoyed by a reading public interested in genuine literature but intolerant of pedantry and dullness. These editors did not require patronage or subsidies—from either well-endowed angels or universities; they prepared their handy volumes for a reading public who bought and read.

It is inconceivable, for example, that—aside from the indelicacy of publishing a living writer's complete letters—there could have been produced in the nineteenth century such a work as Professor Haight's recent seven-volume edition of the George Eliot letters. Let me say immediately that this edition is admirable as an editorial job; its only fault, reviewers have agreed, is that the letters are terribly dull. Although it is a useful work for the study of nineteenth-century literature, and will no doubt prove its value to students of George Eliot, of the novel, of literary economics, of German influence, of medical history, its warmest defenders will hardly allege that it will be read by any one whose interests are unconfined by any of these special subjects.

Here, I believe, is the prime difference between letter-editing in the nineteenth century and today. In our view letters have become "documents"; and the editor, instead of presenting a literary work, is setting up an archive. The long shelves of books are no longer meant to be read but only to be referred to. Is this not corroborated by the proliferation of indexes in recent editions? Professor Haight has been temperate in allowing himself one uncomplicated index; what are we to think of Dr. Chapman's three-volume edition of Johnson's letters with its seven immense indexes? If index-learning turns no student pale, how fortunate is the student who holds the eel of science by seven tails!

Our editions differ from the nineteenth century's in another related way: our tendency to "monumentalize" editions of letters, to provide—as Dr. Chapman's reviewer in the *Times Literary Supplement* writes—"an edition which shall be, humanly speaking, definitive and final." The sceptic may well wonder how definitive and final this edition can be when each volume has a section of addenda, and there is even a last minute inclusion in the preliminary leaves of Volume I. Our concept of definitive editions—which nineteenth-century editors did not try to produce—is perhaps related to the advertisements one sees by beauty parlors which offer *permanent* waves "guaranteed for three months." Our desire to make these editions all inclusive leads us to throw into them every scrap of writing by, to, and about the writer, every collateral and associated reference however remote; and so annotations grow in length and appendixes in number.

Besides differing from us in their attitude toward readability and toward completeness, nineteenth-century editors necessarily reflected the genteel tone and taboos of their time. Thus in 1861 when Moy Thomas edited Lady Mary Wortley Montagu's letters he was confronted in one of her gossipy ones with a scandalous anecdote, and rather than discard it—for it makes a clever, vivid episode—he dropped it into a footnote and labeled it an excerpt from an anonymous friend's letter to her. Of course, following the editorial practice of his time, he corrected her grammar and usage like a fussy governess; and he emasculated or omitted her frank expressions and racy anecdotes. Today, fortunately, Victorian prudishness has given way to plain frankness. No word is too crude for the editors of Walpole's correspondence to transcribe or translate. The editor of Hart Crane's letters, a few years ago, published the full record of that poet's neurotic existence—only twenty years after his death. There can be no difference of opinion as to the desirability of transcription without bowdlerizing; for in an age when four-letter words unabashedly litter our fiction, and Freudian theory has passed into everyday lingo, the editor need not be a verbal or moral censor.

Before discussing specific questions of text and annotation, I should like to discriminate between what we may consider the letters written by writers who are noted for their other writings and the letters by writers noted mainly for their letters. This distinction, I believe, has some bearing on the form of the edition. For the eighteenth century—which I am primarily concerned with—we may consider as letter-writers Lord Chesterfield, whose letters were last edited by Bonamy Dobrée in 1932; Horace Walpole, whose correspondence under the urbane general-editorship of Mr. Lewis has been in progress since 1937; and Lady Mary Wortley Montagu, whose letters, last edited in 1861, still await complete publication. For these three writers, letters are their main claim to a place in literary history; hence they can be classified as letter-writers rather than mere writers of letters. The letter as a *genre* was exceptionally congenial to their talents, and they expended on it all their self-conscious, disciplined craft. In contrast, there are the mere writers of letters—Addison, edited in 1951; Steele, edited by Professor Blanchard in 1941; and Pope, whose correspondence has recently been edited by Professor Sherburn. Unquestionably these letters are important in literary history, but it is at least debatable whether they are themselves literature. To Addison and to Steele letters were a functional means of transacting business or sending messages. Addison's letters smell of the Public Record Office, where many of them indeed lie; and doesn't one become a little tired of the repetitive "Dear Prue" notes of Steele?

Between these two categories—letter-writers and writers of letters—fall Thomas Gray, edited in 1935, and Johnson, edited by Dr. Chapman in 1952. Neither Gray's nor Johnson's stature comes from their letters alone, but it is raised by them. Gray's scintillate with the lively intimacy repressed in his external life; and Johnson's display the drama of a combative many-sided personality. Many readers, no doubt, go to these letters not for any particular fact but for the enjoyment of reading.

And now to the editor's problems—to his "job of work." He must first decide what to include in his edition. This problem is, today, less obvious than it would seem. All of us agree that every letter *by* the writer should be included, whether it survives in manuscript or only in a printed copy. The headaches that afflict editors of printed works in deciding on a correct copy-text are spared the letter editor: the manuscript has prime authority, and where it does not survive, then the printed text closest to it. In printing every letter, the editor may have to welcome brief and inconsequential notes. It is Robert Browning's recent editor, I believe, who was confronted by scores of postal cards on which the poet had merely accepted or declined dinner invitations. Fortunately eighteenth-century letter-writers did not bother to write letters unless they had something to say in them. Johnson remarked to an old friend, "I find myself very unwilling to take up a pen only to tell my friends that I am well." And where only brief notes survive, they are valuable for filling in sparsely documented biography.

If most editors print all the letters *by* their writers, there is some disagreement in the matter of printing letters *to* or even *about* them. Professor Haight calls his edition *The George Eliot Letters*, yet only two-thirds of the letters come from her pen. The editions of Gray and of Walpole, called correspondences, print letters to and from these writers; so does Professor Sherburn, although since he also prints letters by Pope's friends to each other, his edition may be called "Pope and His Circle." A more extreme example of this tendency is Theodore Besterman's edition of Voltaire's correspondence, now in progress; and that collection, one may observe, is not so much an edition of letters as a collection of materials toward Voltaire's biography.

The practice of giving both sides of a correspondence—as we see in the Walpole edition—has obvious advantages; it also has the disadvantage of swelling the volumes with a great mass of material which is dull and only of oblique literary interest. Horace Mann's letters to Walpole illustrate this; and his editors even print the long official documents which Mann occasionally enclosed. If this correspondence is intended to be a political history of the eighteenth century, the plan is sound; but it is difficult to see its literary justification. Mr. Lewis admits as much, when he writes (in *Collector's Progress*), "From the first the *Yale Walpole* has been planned as an encyclopedia of eighteenth century life and thought."

Any decision as to what to print rests ultimately on two factors: what is the edition's purpose and what materials are available. If I may discuss, for the moment, my own concern with Lady Mary's letters, this is how it works out: I wish to present, essentially, her own writings—not because they are a source of historical, literary, social, or biographical information, but because they have value as literature. (I need not take time now to say why they can be considered so; we can accept the sanction of critical opinion since her own time.) In round numbers I have about 800 letters written by Lady Mary, more than twice the number printed by her last editor. Of these 800, about 650 survive in manuscript—which will give my text a solid and reliable basis.

What of the surviving letters written to her? Should they be printed in the text? I have about 90 from her husband, and about 60 drafts of letters sent to her by the Countess of Oxford. These two series are so dry and dull that they would, if printed, infect the book with a deadly tedium. I plan instead to quote from them, only where relevant, in my annotations. Lady Mary's correspondence with Pope presents a different problem. There are about 20 of his letters to her; and although they illustrate Pope's inflamed imagination and one of his epistolary styles, they tell us very little about Lady Mary's lost letters to him. Since Professor Sherburn has carefully printed from manuscript this series of letters from Pope, there is no point in my duplicating the text. The only surviving letters from Lady Mary to Pope are two very brief notes sent after his effusive friendship and correspondence had abated. These two will appear in my text, in accordance with my rule that all of her letters deserve a place there.

Her correspondence with Lord Hervey raises still a different problem. For over twenty years they maintained a lively friendship, usually sympathetic but sometimes malicious. (Lady Mary is responsible for the epigram that there are three sexes: men, women, and Herveys.) After his death his son courteously sealed up all of Lady Mary's letters and returned them to her. Not a single one has come down to us. But of Hervey's letters to her, I have his manuscript copies of 43 which have never been printed. Many of them are direct replies to those she sent him, and so they tell us something of her lost letters; they are, besides, of great interest in their own right, displaying the copious talent and skill that make his

Memoirs of the Reign of George II such a brilliant document. I plan to print them as part of my text; or, if I lose heart at thus flouting my own rule, I can assign them to an appendix.

Having decided, in general, that only Lady Mary's own letters belong in the text, and that those to her belong in the annotations, I must next decide how to arrange them: in a single chronological sequence or in separate correspondences. Mr. Lewis's edition of Walpole and the Nichol Smith-Cleanth Brooks edition of Bishop Percy's letters follow the latter arrangement. Mr. Lewis's defense of it for his edition seems to me persuasive for two special reasons: that both sides of the Walpole correspondences are very fully printed, and that Walpole channeled his four main interests among particular friends— so that each series has an inherent unity. But editors of both letter-writers and writers of letters generally prefer the single sequence. The fascination of reading these collections comes from seeing the gradual unfolding of their writers' lives and ideas, as well as their coherent comments on topics which caught their interest.

If editors agree on the arrangement of their letters, they diverge sharply in the matter of how to present their texts. The root of the divergence is the fact that the copy-text is a manuscript. The editor must decide, essentially, whether he wishes to put the letter into the reader's hands as a manuscript or as a printed text. Dr. Chapman writes in his introduction: "I have aimed at reproducing my manuscripts as closely as typography admits." But does he? I notice, for example, that he does not reproduce Johnson's long *s*. I believe, perhaps naïvely, that the exact reproduction of a manuscript is impossible. Even if we used a photo-process, we should then begin to worry about the color of the ink, the quality of the paper, the manner of folding the sheet, and so on. When we decide to reproduce it by means of typography, we have made a great concession; and once having made it we need not be stingy as to its extent. No reader of the book will be fooled into thinking he has a manuscript in his hand.

Dr. Chapman, of course, is neither the innovator of this point of view, nor even its most extreme champion. The Toynbee-Whibley edition of Gray prints long *s*'s, abbreviations, and raised letters; it is fussy and finicky about every detail of the manuscript. It does not indent, so that we sometimes come up against a tight-packed, full page of dense type without a crack in the text to allow us a breath. As a reference work this edition is excellent, but who reads it? At the other extreme of textual style—that of normalizing—stand the newest editions of Walpole and Chesterfield. Mr. Lewis's practice is to retain Walpole's spelling of proper names and (careful) punctuation, but to normalize other spellings and capitalization. Professor Dobrée also normalizes spelling and capitalization. His object, he writes in his preface, has been "to make the text as pleasurable as possible to the reader of today, while altering as little as possible." As a general principle this makes good sense.

It seems paradoxical that political and social historians—who, one would think, are sticklers for exactness—should prefer normalized texts, whereas literary historians strive for exact transcription. I can only conjecture why this is so: the former group want the letters set forth as factually exact as possible but without any distracting irrelevances because to them the facts are paramount; literary historians believe that they will lose the nuances of style if the text is normalized, and that these small details convey the flavor of the writer's personality and milieu. Between these extremes there are other sensible styles. Nichol Smith writes in his edition of the Burnet-Ducket letters: "It has been found desirable to expand the simpler contractions and to add occasionally to the punctuation"; but in his Swift-Ford letters (twenty-one years later), although he expands contractions he retains raised letters for titles—a confusing procedure when footnote numerals are also raised. (One would think a title like Lord or Duchess simple enough to expand.) Professor Tinker in his 1924 edition of Boswell's letters has normalized except for spelling; and it is only necessary to glance at his page to see how much is gained and how little lost.

What kind of text—to come to my own job—do I plan to use for Lady Mary's letters? I am fairly certain that I do not want a facsimile manuscript reproduction. Nor do I want the letters to look as though they had appeared in this morning's *Times*. My solution, a compromise, comes from these factors: that the edition will be published by a university press, and so must be scholarly and reasonably complete; that as a great letter-writer Lady Mary will attract readers beyond the ranks of eighteenth-century students and scholars; and that her letters, as manuscripts, raise several peculiar problems.

I have therefore decided on the following style. I shall reproduce her exact spelling and capitalization. The range of her spelling—extending over more than fifty years of her activity as a letter-writer—illustrates the gradual evolution of her writing from that of a girl haphazardly and self-educated to that of a poised woman of letters. Her spelling of family and place names is historically useful. Her use of capitals for nouns, though unsystematic, was often her way of achieving emphasis. These differences (in spelling and capitalization) from twentieth-century norms do not impede the reader, for he finds them in the printed texts of the eighteenth century. In regard to capitalization, Mr. Lewis states that it is often not possible to be sure when the writer intended a capital; but an editor, who is presumably best qualified to read the manuscript, is least likely to make this error in transcription.

With all abbreviations (including the ampersand) and with raised letters I intend to be pitiless: the contractions and abbreviations will be expanded in full, and the raised letters lowered to the plane where they belong. (Proper names will be expanded within square brackets.) These niceties are of no more importance, it seems to me, than an extra flourish of the pen or the placing of a date on the left or right hand side of the manuscript page. It may be objected that abbreviations are significant in showing the degree of familiarity or of formality in a letter, for letter-writers tended to avoid abbreviations in their formal notes. But surely we judge the tone of a letter by its actual words and ideas and not by its flourishes and shorthand. As the reader picks his way through stenographic symbols like D^s for *Duchess* or y^m for *them*, he may forget the thought. Even Dr. Chapman, so faithful to his manuscripts, does not reproduce Johnson's "displayed" conclusions because he believes they would waste space and offend the eye. Professor Sherburn, with more precision, uses vertical lines (as in the bibliographical description of title pages) to set forth the conclusions of Pope's letters; but it is difficult to see any advantage beyond mere exactness. Nor do I see any benefit in indicating the pages of the manuscript letter, as the editors of Percy's letters do by printing marginal glosses. As a result their page is disfigured, and the reader is burdened with useless information about the physical condition of the manuscript.

How should the editor treat the writer's erasures (assuming he can read them) and inadvertent errors like repeated or omitted small words and syllables? Dr. Chapman neglects Johnson's erasures but preserves his inadvertences "partly because they furnish some indication of his state of health or his state of mind, partly because they show the sort of error to which he was prone. . . ." As good or even a better case can be made for preserving the one and neglecting the other; for the erasures show us the writer's literal intention, whereas his inadvertences provide an incalculable number of speculative possibilities. When Johnson repeats a syllable in carrying a divided word over to a new page, what does that signify? Perhaps merely that a fly alighted on his nose and distracted his attention. For both types of lapses the editor need not set himself any rigid rules. In many instances he can avail himself of square brackets to insert what the reader does need, and common sense to omit what the reader clearly does not.

My most radical treatment of the text is this: I shall add punctuation where the sense demands it, and I shall capitalize the first word of every sentence. Lady Mary's custom in these two respects is rather cavalier; its exact reproduction would be meaningless. I have noticed that when I read a text exactly reproduced from manuscript, a sentence ending without a period or a sentence beginning with a lower-case letter stops me in my tracks, and my eye swings forward and back to catch hold of the sense. Careful analysis of the clauses usually determines the sentence sense; and if the editor does this first, then the reader can read without interruption.

The exact typographical copy of a manuscript has this ironic effect (as Mr. Lewis shrewdly remarks); it "imparts an air of quaintness to a text which was not apparent to the correspondents themselves." For their letters printed in their own day do not challenge the modern eye, as we can see in any eighteenth-century collection. The text-style I have chosen, then, is a compromise, but I believe a sensible one—something between eighteenth-century printed and manuscript styles and at the same time hospitable to the modern reader. So much for my text. These matters of spelling, capitalization, abbreviations, and punctuation are relatively trivial compared to the fact that every word written by Lady Mary in her letters will be clearly reproduced.

A manuscript letter contains more than simply the writer's message; and the editor must decide how to deal with this other material. The recipient's name and the date of the letter, although they may not appear on the letter (and are hence editorial intrusions) are obviously a necessary adjunct to the letter if it is to be intelligible. The postmark, if any, should be recorded, for it is evidence that the letter was actually sent, and may have some bearing on the letter's date of composition and of transmission. But I see no reason why it should be with the text when it can be dropped into a footnote. The endorsement, since it is also part of the letter, should also appear on the page—under the text, if by the writer; as a footnote, if by the recipient. Most of Lady Mary's letters to her husband were endorsed by him with a date and a summary of their contents, and this information is often clarifying.

Does the editor have to record which passages in a letter have been struck out by the recipient or subsequent owners of the manuscript? Here his own judgment takes precedence over definite rules. Of course he will always decipher and print the passages. Any mutilation of the manuscript likely to mislead a later user can be noted at the foot of the page. This editorial problem does not exist in Lady Mary's letters, for her heirs, instead of using scissors or india ink, more effectively censored the letters which they disapproved of by burning them. Fanny Burney censored her father's letters, Mr. James Osborn tells us; there is good literary justification for an editor's noting her editorial treatment. The recent owners of Boswell's manuscripts censored before selling; and to record their attempts at suppression may illustrate Victorian prudery, but nothing is thus added to Boswell's letters. Mr. Lewis's edition of Walpole points out what has been omitted in previous printed editions. Although this unwittingly focusses the reader's attention on the scandalous and off-color anecdotes, it adds nothing to the letters. Any reader interested in what earlier editions have omitted can simply collate the printed texts.

With a manuscript letter in his hand the editor can disregard a previously printed copy. But if he cannot find the manuscript and must depend on a printed text, he must be grateful—and very cautious. In my own work on Lady Mary's letters I have had a variety of illuminating experiences. Moy Thomas printed a letter from Lady Mary to her daughter, but he could not find the original among the Wortley Manuscripts, and so he took his text from Dallaway, Lady Mary's first acknowledged editor (in 1803). The letter contains an elaborate anecdote about William Pitt's ministry, and Thomas footnotes it thus: "It is remarkable that Lady Mary herself appears to have appropriated the passage from a letter of her friend, Miss Tichborne"; and he then quotes the identical passage from the friend's (manuscript) letter. But the truth of the matter is that Lady Mary's letter—which exists among the Wortley Manuscripts, though Thomas could not find it—does not contain the anecdote. Dallaway had simply transferred it from the friend's to Lary Mary's letter. Thomas should have been on guard, particularly since in his preface he accuses Dallaway of flagrant tampering.

Of greater importance than this kind of conflation—which an editor can discover by carefully checking his manuscripts—are those letters which exist only in printed form and without clear authority. The editor of Lady Mary's letters must deal with this situation: her Embassy Letters were published posthumously and without her family's permission, but their authenticity is beyond doubt since her own manuscript still exists. Four years later the same publisher issued an *Additional Volume* containing six letters, of which one had been published long before (in 1719). The other five, I do not doubt, are spurious, yet they have since then been printed among Lady Mary's letters. Moy Thomas put them in his text, labeled as of doubtful authenticity, but that has not prevented careless literary historians and anthologists from using them as examples of Lady Mary's epistolary art. How shall I treat them in my edition? Probably consign them to the purgatory of an appendix.

What of each letter's provenience as a manuscript and its bibliographical history? Most modern editors put these facts at the head of the letters. I believe that this information, although interesting and perhaps important, is primarily antiquarian; and so instead of cluttering the text to the reader's distraction, it can be neatly dropped into the footnotes.

Having set up the text of his letters the editor must then wrestle with his annotations. In this bout he will find even less agreement than in textual style. "It is impossible," wrote Dr. Johnson, "for an expositor not to write too little for some, and too much for others." Mr. Lewis's Walpole annotations are considered by many to err on the side of generosity; and in England one hears quips about the full genealogies attached to everyone mentioned in the text. This tendency to annotate Walpole widely and deeply has become more pronounced in the Mann correspondence, so that the volumes are becoming not a source for political history but a veritable reference collection. Whether or not one agrees with this objection, there can be no doubt as to the balance, tact, and efficient accuracy of these annotations.

Although the editor may set up formulas to determine what requires elucidation, he must actually judge each instance individually. When Lady Mary writes of *Gulliver's Travels*: ". . . and very wonderful it is, God knows!" should the reader be referred to the Bible *passim* or to Sir Harold Williams' bibliographical study? But if she refers to an obscure politician, the reader should be told his identity and referred to the *DNB*. If you will recall my initial premise—that the reader wishes to read the letters— then the annotations must remain subservient. They must not be tantalizingly brief lest they generate their own puzzles. Nor should the editor disregard a name or quotation or allusion in a letter because—he may rationalize—his main job was to present the text.

It would be easy, but not really necessary, to quote examples of faulty annotations. Let me instead give a couple of samples of how I intend to deal with this. In a letter from Avignon, Lady Mary writes to Lady Oxford in October 1744 that she supposes the slowness of the mails is "occasioned by the cessation of correspondence between Dover and Calais." My footnote reads: "War between England and France had broken out on 15 March 1744." Merely that. It is not necessary to give the causes or battles of the war, the organization of the post office, or a survey of postal routes in 1744. In the same letter Lady Mary sends her opinion of Pope's will; and in my footnote I quote the few sentences from Lady Oxford's letter which had told Lady Mary the news. I doubt that more is required, for this is not a biography of Pope or a study of his reputation; it is a letter by Lady Mary.

Should passages in foreign languages be translated in the footnotes? Most editors have conceded that the reader of even scholarly editions needs to have Latin translated for him. (Professor Sherburn's edition of Pope does not make this concession.) The relatively few Latin quotations in Lady Mary's letters will be translated in the footnotes. And like all these other editors I do not intend to translate French passages. To the reader unfamiliar with that language, about twenty newly discovered letters in French by Lady Mary will have to remain buried in the obscurity of a modern language.

I hope Dr. Chapman's extensive use of abbreviations in his letterheads and footnotes does not win many imitators. (So far, Miss Norton, in her edition of Gibbon's letters, has imitated.) The reader must fight his way through an alphabetical thicket, for he is forced to expand initials into names so frequently that reading gives way to mnemonics. The elaboration of short cuts can reach a point of diminishing returns. I also confess myself irritated by Dr. Chapman's abbreviated year dates—'74 for 1774. Only one space is saved, and again the reader's attention is distracted by having to fill in what has been omitted. The editor's job, after all, is to remove obstacles, not to create new ones. For my own abbreviations: since I have such mouth- and line-filling names for Lady Mary and for her husband, I designate them as M and as W. But there I draw the line. Where sensible and useful, the editor can use short cuts. The letters, for example, can be assigned numbers, and these can then be used for cross references. If the letter-numbers are printed as shoulder-notes on each page, they can easily be found by the reader.

The freedom and elasticity of footnotes are a great temptation to a vivacious editor. He can fill them with materials for his autobiography as a scholar, telling us how and where he has searched, whom solicited, why failed, when succeeded, and so on. His acknowledgments belong in the prefatory material; after page one the reader is concerned not with the editor but with the letter-writer. A simple rule for avoiding editorial exhibitionism is to avoid the first person pronoun. Besides cozy footnote chats, the editor will be tempted into sly quips and oblique jokes; and this should also be resisted. The editor, in short, should practise the most extreme self-effacement in favor of the letter-writer.

I hope I do not seem to be in favor of erasing the editor. I wish, on the contrary, to restore to him the function stated in Dr. Johnson's definition: "he that revises or prepares any work for publication." The editor, as I see him, should be discriminating as to what goes into the edition and also as to what belongs in the text and in the annotations. He should prepare his text in such a way as to make it faithful to his manuscript and at the same time serviceable to his readers; he should arrange his annotations and apparatus in a simple, lucid form.

Earlier in this paper I made a distinction between letter-writers and writers of letters. Perhaps this gap can be narrowed if we print more letters as though they were worth reading for their own sake. Unless we print letters in such a form as to allow them to be read as widely as possible and with ease and pleasure we are in danger of creating a coterie scholarship, when we will only read each other's footnotes; and the ranks of monumental editions will, in truth, be only monuments.

If I seem reactionary in advocating a return to the nineteenth-century concept of readable editions, I hope it is still progress—on a spiral, so to speak; for we can also make our texts accurate and our annotations full and scholarly.

Is this possible? you may well ask. I hold here the first volume of the new edition, in the Pléiade series, of Madame de Sévigné's letters. In several respects it is more radical than I have outlined:

the notes, of exemplary brevity and directness, are in the back of the volume, and the spelling, punctuation, and capitalization are normalized. (The text is for the most part based not on the writer's own manuscripts, which do not survive, but on a later transcript.) While it is both scholarly and complete, it is at the same time attractively made and invitingly readable.

"Mon cousin," she once wrote to Bussy-Rabutin, "s'il vous prend fantaisie un jour de publier mes lettres, je vous prie de les corriger." He answered, "Ma cousine, on ne corrige pas le Titien." (But he did.) If today we do not believe in correcting our Titians, we as editors should at least clean, frame, and light them for all to see and enjoy.

THOMAS H. JOHNSON

Establishing a Text:

The Emily Dickinson Papers

THOMAS H. JOHNSON *devotes himself chiefly to the "pre-editorial" problems of texts of a special if not unique kind—texts of undated letters and poems mostly unpublished in the author's lifetime and inadequately edited posthumously. To establish a reliable chronology for the poems and letters, Johnson discusses the significance of paper and handwriting, drawing particular attention to the inferred relationship between Emily Dickinson's hand and health.*

IT WAS FIFTEEN YEARS AGO this month that I first saw the manuscript volume which Edward Taylor had assembled during his long life as pastor in Westfield, Massachusetts. He had labeled it his "Poetical Works," and bequeathed it at the time of his death in 1729 to his descendants with the injunction that the poems should never be published. At the time, I thought the problems ahead were very challenging. And so, no doubt, they were. First of all, would scholars and lay critics share my belief that Taylor deserved to be published? Would the Corporation of Yale University—the

Reprinted from *Studies in Bibliography*, V (1952–53), 21–32, with the permission of the author and the Bibliographical Society of the University of Virginia.

legal heirs—grant permission in the light of Taylor's prohibition? Could one learn to read Taylor's handwriting? Most important, would the pattern of a poet emerge? As I say, this was several years ago, and seems at this remove, when all the questions are answered, a simple story. For there was but one heir: a notable institution that seeks advancement of learning. There was but one manuscript: a 400-page volume assembled by the author in orderly fashion. The handwriting was never, or almost never, an obstacle. And there was no copyright problem at all.

With Emily Dickinson I again feel challenged, and all the problems seem even more complicated. Perhaps they are. Or perhaps I'm beginning again. In either event, I accept the challenge and enjoy the fun. Though Dickinson never requested that her poetry remain unpublished, the fact is that at the time of her death in 1886 her poems were still in manuscript. The mere handful published before then either were issued surreptitiously or were anonymous. She bequeathed them, along with her other effects, to her sister Lavinia, who with passionate singleness of purpose determined that they should be known, since to her, at least, Emily was a poet. Had the poems been left untouched until 1950, then to be transferred intact to a learned institution, the parallel with Taylor would be reasonably obvious. At this point the analogy breaks down.

All who have had access to material touching upon Emily Dickinson's life and writing agree—I think without exception—that she knew during her twenties that she was uncommonly gifted; that by the time she was thirty-one, when she sought advice from Thomas Wentworth Higginson in the now famous letters written in April, 1862, she did indeed crave assurance regarding a talent which at times literally overwhelmed her. "Alone I cannot be," she wrote at this time in a remarkable poem:

> Alone I cannot be;
> The hosts do visit me,
> Recordless company
> Who baffle key.

How was this gift to be shared? She must have been somewhat prepared to accept Higginson's hesitation to advise publication, for it matched the opinion of other writers and critics whom she knew and respected, gentlemen who knew something of her writing, notably Samuel Bowles and Josiah Gilbert Holland. She should delay submitting any letters to the world, they all told her in effect, until she had learned "control." Since she could no more "control" the quality of the hosts who visited her than she could alter her wren-like size, she must therefore, in her own lifetime at any rate, sublimate her desire for public recognition, however compelling the wish for it may have been. That the longing was present seems beyond doubt. In the first place, it was within the months just preceding her first letter to Higginson that she began to make copies of her poems, presumably from original drafts that were then destroyed. These early original drafts do not now exist and there is no record that they survived her. Perhaps she disposed of them as, one by one, she transcribed them into packets or fascicles.

Written fair, these assemblages of anywhere from ten to twenty transcribed verses are the gatherings, threaded loosely at the spine, which she laid away in her cherry bureau. The number of poems so transcribed during the years 1861-62-63 is very large indeed. On the evidence of stationery and of handwriting—and much will be said about both later—this large body of verse, fully half of all her extant poems, belongs in these three years. A packet or two may have been completed as early as 1858, but there are none at all for the years preceding. In fact there is not to my knowledge a single poem which in its present transcription can be safely assigned an earlier date.

The conclusion therefore is inevitable either that she wrote verses at white heat for a period of three or four years at the turn of the decade as she passed her thirtieth year, or that the packets assembled at that time represent fair copies made from drafts which had been accumulating for the previous eight or ten years, roughly from the time she was twenty. Unless the originals, which certainly must have existed, are recoverable—and there is no reason to think they are—the issue can never be resolved by direct evidence. It is outside the province of this paper to try conclusions, and the process of editing the Dickinson papers has not yet advanced to the point where final speculations are warranted. I cite the problem, however, as a major example of the nature of the work involved in establishing a provenance of Emily Dickinson's poetry and the order of its composition. The task is further complicated by the fact that she seems to have had no discoverable design in the order of the packets or of the poems within a packet, and that since her death the packets have been handled, separated, and reassembled by several hands. The possibility of confusing the original order— if one did in fact exist—has been multiplied by each handling. If these packets represent Emily Dickinson's copying of her earlier drafts, and if the earlier drafts are irrecoverable, then an exact chronology of actual composition can never be established. A *terminus ad quem* date must therefore, certainly for the most part, be all that we can expect for the poems which we conjecture she composed in her twenties.

So far I have emphasized Emily Dickinson's compulsion to write poetry and to preserve it as she wrote it, with its half-rimes, broken stanzas, unexpected figures, even though the advisers she con-sulted counseled greater smoothness and regularity, with fewer oddities of thought. I have pointed out the difficulties that beset an editor of her poems who attempts to establish chronology, at least down to 1863 when she seems to have been convinced that publication in her own lifetime was out of the question. At about this time she began to develop a new medium for her verse, and a way of sharing it with her friends. She incorporated whole poems or parts of them in almost every letter she wrote. Such had not been markedly true earlier. She had always been a notable letter writer, from the time that her earliest extant letter, written to her brother Austin when she was eleven, shadowed forth the sensi-tive perceptiveness and originality which are her special genius. By the time she was thirty her contact with the world, except for the few members of her immediate family, was almost solely through correspondence. This she now freighted with poetry. Complete poems might thus be conveyed. Or it might be but two lines, or a quatrain from some longer poem recently transcribed into a packet, but here adapted by the change of a pronoun to apply to a particular recipient or situation. Sometimes the poems are archly disguised as prose.

From an editorial point of view such readings must be treated as variants. Often a letter is solely a poem; it usually is without salutation, but is signed "Emily." The text of one such was recently acquired by the Library of Congress. It consists of two quatrains, and the handwriting as well as the content suggest that it was inspired by a homesick mood during her enforced stay in Cambridge where in 1864 she underwent eye treatment. It is written in pencil, because during these months the physician forbade her to use a pen.

Away from Home are Some and I—
An Emigrant to be
In a Metropolis of Homes
Is easy, possibly—

The Habit of a Foreign Sky
We—difficult—acquire
As Children, who remain in Face
The more their Feet retire.

Emily

The poem was first published in the 1894 edition of the *Letters* among those, Mrs. Todd notes, "sent to the Hollands at various times." Presumably all the Holland letters published in 1894 were returned to Mrs. Holland and subsequently destroyed, but the poem as it appears in the 1931 edition of the *Letters* is printed as two quatrains (not as in 1894 as a single eight-line stanza), and offers an alternative reading for the fourth line. Presumably therefore Mrs. Todd had seen another version before she brought out the 1931 edition.

She sent this letter-poem to some member of her family in Amherst, probably to Sue, her brother Austin's wife. It presents a textual problem that is not unusual, and one that is especially interesting because it may never be satisfactorily solved. The Library of Congress holograph is the only manuscript version I know to be extant. It differs from the published versions chiefly in its fourth line which reads "Is easy, possibly." ("An Emigrant to be / In a Metropolis of Homes / Is easy, possibly"—not "Is common possibility.") And it offers no alternative reading.

At this point an editorial footnote is demanded, and unless further information alters the conclusion, it will go something like this: "The letters to Dr. and Mrs. J. G. Holland, published in 1894, were returned to Mrs. Holland after they were transcribed, and presumably were destroyed. Access to a second manuscript, with an alternate reading offered for the fourth line, must have occurred before 1931. The single-stanza version Dickinson sent the Hollands probably substituted *common* for *easy*, and may have shown no stanza division. Such variants in wording and stanzaic form are not exceptional when the same letter-poem is written to more than one correspondent. Unless the hypothetical second manuscript proves to be extant, and can confirm the reading of the 1931 text, one queries the substitution of *possibility* for *possibly*. Is it a copyist's or printer's error? It renders the line meaningless and destroys the meter."

The purpose of any editorial task is to establish as definitive a text as possible, and to give it a chronology. For Emily Dickinson, it will be to edit all poems and letters known to exist, to give them order, and to place in context, as far as possible, those which, once published, were ultimately destroyed. Of the near 2000 poems known to have been written—most of them already published— a very large number exist in holograph. Of the some 1200 letters, a much greater percentage are still unpublished; and of those in print, a great many were lost or destroyed subsequent to publication. For example, Emily Dickinson's correspondence with her cousins, Fanny and Lou Norcross, was fairly voluminous. It covered many years and was particularly intimate on a domestic level. The spinster cousins, shy by nature, permitted use of the letters for the 1894 edition with the proviso that every personal allusion to them or to others be deleted. On that basis the letters appeared, so blue-penciled as at times to be fairly uninterpretable. They were then returned to the sisters, and in the manner deemed proper for families of their status, were destroyed at the time of their death. Much that would help interpret other letters, or give better insight into Emily herself, is thus irrecoverable. The Norcross letters, and others which suffered a like fate, will continue to tantalize, never explain. But the large number of letters that do still exist are not only intrinsically important (for Emily Dickinson takes rank as a letter writer) but are of tremendous importance in understanding her verse and helping to give it a chronology.

Probably no part of the editing of the Dickinson papers is more exacting than that which involves establishing chronology. Emily dated nothing after 1850, and after her death Lavinia with characteristic thoroughness burned all letters written *to* Emily. Three possibilities are open for assigning dates to the letters. First there is internal evidence. If it is direct, it is conclusive: "Father died a year ago today." But it often is circumstantial. "Perhaps the flowers wilted," she says in a letter written presumably in late summer, 1880, "because they did not like the Pelham water." The Amherst water supply was first piped in from Pelham earlier in that summer. Second, there is the handwriting. And finally there is the paper that she used. The degree to which these latter two possibilities can be effective is proportionate to the mass of manuscripts which can be studied. For Dickinson the volume is large. I do not hesitate to conjecture that her manuscripts can be dated within a twelve-month, when the handwriting is checked against the evidence of the paper groups. I will shortly discuss paper groups. Let me say something here about Emily Dickinson's handwriting.

A scholar's first reaction to placing dependence upon handwriting as a guide to dating a manuscript is apprehensive skepticism. Of course handwriting changes, but can the changes be interpreted in a chronology? I knew at the start that I would be compelled to seek an answer to the question, but I began with no assurance I would be led to conclusions which could be accepted. There are too many human factors. People are subject to moods which handwriting reflects. You write one way when you are rested, or another when you are in haste. The size of letters may vary with the size of the sheet written on, depending on how much you wish to say in a given space. The form and shape of the characters depend also upon the implement you use, as well as the quality of the stationery. A sharp, stiff pen gives results very different from those formed by a stubby pencil. A glossy ledger sheet permits a movement of arm, hand, and fingers that rough, resistant linen will not allow. Absorbent foolscap is something different still. Finally, I thought, let anyone allow a manuscript of his own, which he has no recollection of ever writing, to be placed before him for dating solely on the basis of the calligraphy; how close can he come? Within five years? within ten? Perhaps not even that. And if not, the use of handwriting will be more of a hazard than a help in attempting to establish a chronology for a poet, where the purpose is no less than to discover the growth of an artist.

Yet when I had begun the task, which I knew was necessary to undertake even though the results after many tedious and discouraging hours might only lead into a blind alley, I found trustworthy patterns emerging. And now, after a year of intensive study of the Dickinson handwriting, covering the span of her years, I feel confident that great reliability can be placed upon a chronology that derives from it. Bear in mind that we are not working in a vacuum. Though no poem is ever dated, and no letter dated after 1850, there are many, many letters that can be assigned exact dates, either on a given day, or within a week or a month. For our purposes, that must be considered as close as we can ever get. Next, there is always the check we can apply by arranging manuscripts into paper groups. For the undated documents these three forms of evidence are the only possible ones which can be used. In many instances, that is, where no internal evidence is possible and where the paper is unidentifiable, the handwriting alone must furnish the clue. In such cases the degree of reliability is lessened. Yet it often happens that a poem, identifiable only by handwriting, is exactly duplicated in another manuscript that can be precisely dated. These cross-checks appear with enough frequency to buttress the confidence I have in our procedure. Let me now explain the way the Dickinson handwriting can be made to tell its story.

First of all, I repeat that the effectiveness with which any handwriting can be used is proportionate to the mass and coverage available. We have both here. And obviously one proceeds from the known to the unknown. Setting the poetry aside to begin with, let us consider only the letters to which dates can be assigned through internal evidence. (And here may I digress long enough to say that photostatic reproductions for such work are essential. They are expendable. They can be handled, arranged, cut, and pasted onto charts for purposes of comparing formation of letter, line slants, the length of ascenders and descenders of g's, f's, p's, and so on; and in Emily Dickinson's case they tellingly reveal the story of her linked and unlinked letters.)

My preliminary conclusion, reached after a tentative examination of all datable letters, is one I still hold: That it will be possible to assign a given year to any manuscript of sufficient length from evidence of handwriting alone. Such a calendar year must be assumed to extend a few months backward or forward. But with those reservations in mind, a chronology is possible within fairly limited periods in which manuscripts—and this is important—may be given their *relative association*. The second conclusion was that all writing in ink could be judged by commonly applicable rules, but that another set of rules applies to the writing in pencil. I prepared a loose-leaf notebook which would allow incorporation of specimens of four pieces of writing from each year of undated material—from 1850 to 1886. The plan was to place a photostat of two handwriting samples in ink and two in pencil, each representative of different periods in each year, chosen always from manuscripts that could be dated by internal evidence. The more samples per page the better, for thus one could determine whether variations were trivial or significant. Some pages still remain blank. For instance, there are several samples in pencil of writing in the latter part of the year 1864 and early 1865, but none in ink. Since these are the months she was under orders not to use a pen, it is unlikely that she would have done so. By extension, and because I believe she followed her doctor's orders, I doubt whether any document in ink will be found in that period. Similarly for the period after 1878. Why this abrupt adaptation?

One cannot pursue a study of the handwriting without considering the problem of her eyes and the general state of her health. Why did the character of the letters balloon so in the 'seventies, and the letters unlink? Emily Dickinson's death was due to some form of nephritis. It may never be possible to establish the exact nature of the affliction, though it was then diagnosed simply as Bright's disease. But there are hypotheses that cannot be overlooked, even though they may ultimately remain suggestive only, for lack of sufficient proof. One not uncommon cause of a fatal nephritis is now known to be a deepseated streptococcic infection that becomes recurrent. The evidence for such in Emily Dickinson's case is striking. She was withdrawn from Mount Holyoke very suddenly and against her wish in the spring of 1848 by her parents, who sent Austin to fetch her home quite unceremoniously. They had heard indirectly that she was suffering from a severe throat infection that her letters home had tried to belittle. The recurrences were so continual through the next spring and summer that the family effectively prevailed in their demand that she give up thought of returning to the seminary. The letters she wrote during the 'fifties indicate her susceptibility to nose and throat colds. Injury to the kidneys was perhaps begun, though probably not known. It happens that this could have a great deal to do with her handwriting.

Such organic injury, where it does exist, can in its early stages produce a partial blindness or periods of visual aberration that doom the victim to impaired sight. With Emily Dickinson it certainly had progressed far enough by 1864 to compel her trips to Boston, to doctor's orders that she use a soft pencil in place of a fine-pointed pen, and to an acceptance—later modified—of darkened rooms. As years pass, her neuroticism becomes clear enough, but the degree of its basis in a physical handicap is not clear and may never be established. By 1867 her writing certainly has increased in size and the letters within words are broken to a point that one reckons, not in terms of linked words or syllables, but in terms of those that are unlinked, so general has become the separation of letters. The process was so steadily continuous that by 1875 only an occasional *of*, *th*, or *Mr.* remained fastened. She was still writing most of her letters in ink, however. In this year the size of the letters she formed with her pen reached a maximum. By 1878 she evidently found it necessary to forego ink altogether, and no part of any word is linked after that year. But the size of letter decreased when she used only a pencil. From her nervous collapse in the early 'eighties till her death in 1886 the progressive changes become increasingly marked.

I have inquired of physicians whether this increased size and gradual unlinking could have relationship to her vision and fatality. The evidence at the moment is inconclusive. But the bearing of her medical history upon the problem of her handwriting cannot be ignored, and the ultimate verdict will certainly include a study of her health.

There are two areas into which handwriting changes fall: the general and the particular. The general includes characteristics involving five to eight-year periods. During the 1850's all words are linked, the writing is small and flowing, marked by a roundness that is almost copybook in its style. In these years she often signs her name "Emilie." The unlinking of letters begins in the early 'sixties and is well along to completion ten years later. The letters become progressively more angular, and the pages show a sense of drive and forcefulness. The "ie" for "Emily" is permanently discarded after 1861. In the 'seventies the size of the letters reaches a maximum, the use of a pencil is more frequent, and in the later years of the decade supplants the pen altogether.

Particular changes are far more complicated and overlapping. Charts made of each individual capital letter for each successive year tell a story quite easy to follow, for each year some capital letters undergo striking changes not found in other letters. The same phenomena are observable in lower-case letters, with the further advantage that the alterations in the small letters can be subdivided according to their use initially, medially, and finally. For example, in 1859 her final "d" is formed by an upswept ascender curving right. In the years preceding and following it sweeps left. From '55 to '58 the small "h" used initially is hooked to the left. The list of these minute variations through the years is very extensive, and each serves as a reference to and a check upon the others. Given a sufficient number of words in any document, it is possible to assign a probable date within comparatively narrow limits.

Since I have never tried before to study handwriting with the purpose in mind of dating a manuscript by characteristic changes in it, I cannot say whether all handwriting is so subtly variable. The progressive unlinking of letters, in this case over an eighteen-year period, is enormously useful, and made possible by a physiological change that perhaps is comparatively rare. In her case I believe it theoretically possible, if enough manuscript existed, and if each manuscript used enough letters in sufficient combination, to track down dates of composition within the limits of a given week. But the quantity of manuscripts is wanting, and even if they existed it would take years to compute and equate the frequencies without the aid of an electric eye and a robot tabulator. Our laborsome method of charts must remain but a very rough estimate where handwriting alone is the clue. At best, it must allow a margin of error measured in several months. At worst, as in instances where the documents are so brief that tell-tale combinations of letters do not appear, the probable limits of error can extend through two to three years. It is at this point particularly that we turn to paper groups for aid.

Emily Dickinson was fastidious in her stationery selection. Whether it was wove or laid paper, it is almost invariably of an identifiable quality, and though over the years there is a great variety of it, when the types have been identified and grouped, a distinct paper pattern emerges. I suggest that for the moment we consider the rule, not the exception. It is true that she had several paper types at her desk at one time, and that she might on occasion use a sheet in 1875 left over from a batch presumably exhausted in the 'fifties. Such exceptions are easy to spot, and when they occur they rule out the aid which paper groups often can give.

The task of arranging paper into groups is tedious in the extreme, and has not yet been completed. It involves identifying whenever possible (and it is possible 95 per cent of the time) every paper type that she used, measuring it, matching the groups, and sub-dividing them according to their millimeter measurements. Since the identification of a document by its group is desirable as a check on the handwriting, this work must be pursued with no reference whatever to handwriting or other identifying quality.

Much of the laid paper she used was embossed with, say, a head of Minerva, or a capitol dome, or a basket of fruit, or the name of a stationer or manufacturer. The wove paper is generally water-marked and often dated. Let us suppose that all Weston's Linen 1868 paper has been identified and grouped, and that it totals 75 items. Millimeter measurements show that it falls into three sub-groups. That is to say, the sheets have all been folded once, to make four pages, with the spine vertical on the left, the way boxed stationery usually is sold. When we open it out for measurement, we find that the four outer corners for the entire quantity are identical in size. But the middle vertical measurements—the part that becomes the spine when folded—are in three distinct divisions: group A measures 180 mm; group B, 183 mm; group C, 177 mm. These groups, then, were trimmed folded, and represent three distinct batches. Let us say that the number of sheets in each group is roughly even, about 25 in each. Turn now to absolutely identifiable documents in each group. There are five in group A—all in the year 1872; ten in group B—covering 1874–75; eight in group C —all 1877–78. Turn back to group A. Of the remaining items in it, 20 had been dated about 1872–73 on the basis of handwriting; and three are unmistakably later. The remaining two are too brief to guess at closely from handwriting. They are clearly not later than 1876 nor earlier than '73. All that can be said of them is that they belong with group A, and fall within a pattern common to that batch.

Now group B, where the ten identifiable items fall within the years 1874–75. Let us suppose that 12 of the 15 items remaining have been assigned dates, on the basis of handwriting, ranging from 1874 to '78. The remaining three had been classified as doubtful, with a tentative range of dates between 1872–74. I think it reasonable at this point to assume 1872 is too early a date for any paper in group B. It seems more likely that group A was purchased from the stationer and used sometime before group B; that group B, the same *kind* of stationery but from a different batch, was purchased later; that therefore the evidence of the group as a whole points to a date not earlier than 1874 for the three doubtful items.

Similarly in group C, if but one item were conjectured to fall before 1877, I should think the burden of convincing us of the possibility would be more difficult, once the pattern of the group is shown to extend forward from that year, not back of it.

For purposes of clarity, the illustration has been simplified, but it is representative of the use to which paper groups may be put. Evidence from it can never be final, nor can it be used except in conjunction with other evidence. But where it exists, it must be considered.

I think it important to underline at this point that I am presenting problems, not reaching conclusions. To establish a text for Emily Dickinson, particularly of her poems, in terms of exact chronology will never be possible, for all the reasons that have been set forth. The evidence must derive solely from handwriting and from paper groups, and whether taken separately or together, they cannot do more than suggest areas of time. The most that can be done is to give the physical evidence in the greatest possible detail.

It remains finally to say something about the text of the poetry. There would obviously be no problem if every poem were left in a single and final version. But such is not the case. At a rough estimate, I should say that 80 per cent of the poems exist in finished versions, copied fair, with no alternate lines or variant readings suggested. Of the remaining 20 per cent—some 400 poems—she offers variant readings, for the most part with no indication which reading she might ultimately have selected in a final version. Any editorial choice therefore becomes impossible in a definitive edition, since it can represent only an editorial preference.

In one instance I thought she herself had provided a solution. One of the poems which she copied into a packet had several suggested readings for eight different words in the course of the five stanzas, but with no indication of her choice. (Sometimes, though infrequently, her choice is indicated by an underlining of the word she prefers, or by a deletion of the one she has rejected.) Then I found the same poem included in a letter to Higginson with choices made in every instance. Here, then, seemed proof that she had established her final version. But in another letter to another correspondent, written at substantially the same time, she has included the same poem—also evidently a final version—wherein she adopted six of the choices made in the Higginson letter, but selected two from among her variants in the remaining instances. If any conclusion is to be drawn from this citation, it would seem to be that there are no *final* versions of the poems for which she allowed alternate readings to stand in the packets.

Later when anthologists are compiling selections for lay readers, they may do what they wish about selecting the "appropriate" version. The text for my edition in preparation must simply record the lines as she wrote them, noting the alternates and the variant readings. It would be misleading to give the impression that many such exist. Even of the 300 or 400 poems that show them, by far the largest part offer alternates for but one or two words in any poem.

Some dozen or so work sheets exist: those scraps of paper which represent the first draft of a poem—often potentially a great one. They are the jottings which throw brilliant flashes upon the creative spirit in travail. Such is the poem "Two butterflies went out at noon," which has been reproduced in facsimile in *Bolts of Melody*. So far as I know, it never proceeded beyond the work-sheet stage. What shape she might finally have given it! But we sit, helpless to gain her insight, knowing only that such speculations "tease us past thought, as doth eternity."

Here then are the problems. Our tools are method only. As we crave solutions, daydreaming what we might learn from Dickinson herself if we could visit the Stygian world and hold parley with her Shade, I am reminded of a story told me some years ago of William Lyon Phelps. "Will Rhett Butler return to Scarlett O'Hara?" a student queried after finishing *Gone with the Wind*. "That is an interesting question," he answered. "I am dining with Margaret Mitchell tonight, and I will try to bring you back the answer." "And what did she say?" the student asked next day: "What was Rhett's choice?" "She said," replied the professor, "that she hadn't the slightest idea."

JOHN BUTT

Editing a Nineteenth-Century Novelist

(*Proposals for an Edition of Dickens*)

JOHN BUTT *points out that although manuscript and proof sheets exist for Dickens' novels, they had been ignored until recently by Dickens' critics. Butt does not propose to use this material in the way that Greg or Bowers might advocate. Butt's recommendation, for example, that the* "editor of David Copperfield *and of any subsequent novel issued in monthly parts must take the part-issue as his copytext and correct it in the light shed by the manuscript, the proofs, and [the Charles Dickens Edition],"* *does not accord with Greg's dicta regarding copy-text. There has been, perhaps, an international conspiracy to impose one standard of textual editing on the world, but it appears not to have been successful.*

T HE ENERGY EXPENDED during the last forty years in supplying reliable editions of our major writers has not yet been directed towards our great novelists. R. W. Chapman's Jane Austen is an outstanding exception; but Richardson, Scott, Dickens, George Eliot, and others we are forced to study in more or less misleading and inaccurate reprints. We may recall the misappre-

Reprinted from *English Studies Today*, Second Series (Bern, 1961), 187–95, with the permission of A. Francke.

hension of Dr. Leavis, who was led to make certain claims for Henry James's early manner on the assumption that the reprint he used of *Roderick Hudson* followed the text of 1874, though in fact it was derived from the much revised text of 1907. In the present state of editions, we are all of us liable to make mistakes. I recall some members of a class of students at work on *Great Expectations* maintaining that Magwitch had returned to see Pip before his dramatic arrival in Pip's chambers in London. They claimed that Magwitch was the man who arrived one evening at the Three Jolly Bargemen and took Joe's file out of his pocket, and they were therefore prepared for Magwitch turning up again. They had some justification, too; for where Pip remarked "I knew it to be Joe's file, and I knew that he *knew* my convict," the text some of them were using read (incorrectly) "I knew it to be Joe's file, and I knew that he *was* my convict" (my italics). Another instance will be found in Dr. Fielding's admirable book *Charles Dickens: A Critical Introduction.*[1] In writing about *The Old Curiosity Shop,* Dr. Fielding remarks:

> ... Dickens's first thought had been to make little more than a short story of it, and in that form it had already been introduced in the fourth number, when Master Humphrey had mused on a child he had met, who "seemed to exist in a kind of allegory" and thought ...

Dr. Fielding then quotes as follows from Master Humphrey's musings:

> It would be a curious speculation ... to imagine her in her future life, holding her solitary way among a crowd of wild grotesque companions; the only pure, fresh, youthful object in the throng ... I checked myself here, for the theme was carrying me along with it at a great pace.

Dr. Fielding very naturally assumed that this passage marked the dawning of a new idea; whereas in fact it was an afterthought inserted in the first revised edition.

What we need to avoid such errors and misapprehensions is a reliable and critical text. Most modern reprints of Dickens's novels are plain texts with no apparatus or commentary other than a critical introduction and a reprint of the latest preface written by the author. I have not conducted a searching enquiry into the text of these reprints, but I suspect that at best they follow the text of the last edition published in Dickens's life-time, the so-called Charles Dickens Edition, bound in red covers and bearing a facsimile of the author's signature in gold upon the front. Dickens made a few revisions in the text of this edition and added descriptive headlines on alternate pages.

Should a modern editor be content to follow the "Charles Dickens" text? We must see what choice is open to him. The manuscripts of all the novels from *The Old Curiosity Shop* onwards survive complete. These are corrected first drafts and are the copy which Dickens sent to press. Proofs also survive in abundance, sometimes to the extent of two or more copies of a proof of a single monthly number. It is clear that these proofs are copies of "first proof" or first revise; the final revises, where they existed, were presumably retained by the printer, who subsequently destroyed them. But even of "first proofs," though we do not know how many copies were issued, we have enough material to judge with what degree of accuracy the compositor followed his copy and the author corrected his proofs. The compositor was faced with a difficult task. He had before him in all the later novels from *Dombey and Son* onwards a manuscript written in a small and not too tidy hand, dense with erasures and interlineations, the caret-marks not prominent, a manuscript idiosyncratic in spelling, punctuation, and the use of capitals, peculiar in its proper names—not Tomlinson but Towlinson, not Cox but Tox—and lapsing from time to time into phonetic spelling to represent dialect speech. It is remarkable not that there are some errors of substance in proof, but that there are so few of them. In accidentals the compositor took some liberty with copy, and Dickens seems to have acquiesced. He punctuated lightly, but did not remove in proof the compositor's additional commas and semi-colons. Similarly he was sparing in his use of hyphens, but did not protest when they were added in such words as "half-a-crown" and "ninety-two." He was also prepared to give way to a less liberal use of initial capitals. But he seems to have required some idiosyncrasies of spelling to be respected, especially the suffix "-or" for "-our," in such a word as "humor," though even in this he is far from being consistent.

Though he was pretty careful in correcting errors of substance, he does not seem to have collated the proof with his manuscript, even assuming that it invariably accompanied the proof. Occasionally he lets a plausible error pass, and occasionally he invents a new reading to correct an error, instead of reverting to the manuscript reading. There is an instance of plausible error overlooked in the fifth chapter of *David Copperfield*, where David has been sent to school ahead of his fellows and has had a placard tied upon his back: "I could not read a boy's name," says David, "without inquiring in what tone and with what emphasis he would read, 'Take care of him. He bites'."—"Without inquiring" is the printer's error for "without imagining"; but though "without inquiring" is manifestly inferior, it has never been corrected.

There are many examples of what might be termed "incorrect revision by the author." I must limit myself to one. You will recall that in the first chapter of *David Copperfield*, Betsey Trotwood had plugged her ears with "jewellers' cotton," but was forced to remove the cotton when addressed by Mr. Chillip, the doctor. She removed it on three occasions, and in the manuscript three different verbs are used to describe her action:

> "What!" replied my aunt, pulling the cotton out of one ear like a cork . . .
> "Well?" said my aunt, jerking the cotton out of the ear nearest to him . . .
> "Well?" said my aunt, taking out the cotton on that side again.

"Jerking" proved too difficult for the printer; the best he could offer was "picking." Dickens understandably disliked it, but substituted "taking," although the verb was already used to describe the last of the three actions. I am inclined to think that the editor is justified in restoring the manuscript reading on this occasion, as well as on the last.

In this respect the last two chapters of *Edwin Drood* are of special interest, for Dickens did not live to correct the proofs. They are therefore the only two chapters in the whole of his published work where the manuscript is the sole authoritative text, and we may see what the printer made of it, unassisted by the author's correcting eye. The printer's errors are almost all of a type to escape the easily satisfied reader: "When a man rides an amiable hobby that shies at nothing and kicks nobody, it is only agreeable to find him riding it with a humorous sense of the droll side of the creature." Most of us will feel satisfied, but an R. W. Chapman would surely guess that Dickens wrote "it is always agreeable," and not "it is only agreeable"; and Chapman would have confidently substituted "enrobed" for "enrolled" when Mrs. Billickin "sent into her back parlor for her shawl . . . and having been enrolled by her attendant, led the way." He might also—correctly—have inserted a missing indefinite article before "emphasis" in the following sentence:

"My informiation," retorted the Billickin, throwing in an extra syllable for the sake of emphasis at once polite and powerful.

The Billickin's engaging idiosyncrasy of throwing in an extra syllable to which Dickens draws such clear attention, should have been enough to put any proof-reader on his guard. How was it possible to ensure that she was reported correctly without the most careful collation? It is true that not much has been lost, but a keener pair of eyes might have preserved for us the two oddities in the following passage:

"Mr. Grewgious," replied Mrs. Billickin, "pardon me, there is the stairs. Unless your mind is prepared for the stairs, it will lead to inevitable disapintmink. You cannot, Miss," said Mrs. Billickin, addressing Rosa, reproachfully, "place a first floor, and far less a second, on the level footing of a parlor. No, you cannot do it, Miss, it is beyond your power, and wherefore try?"

When full allowance has been made for the superiority of the manuscript in such instances as these, it remains true that proofs generally supercede the manuscript since on a great many occasions they record revisions where the compositor has followed the manuscript correctly. But it must be remembered that they are "first proofs" only. When MS and proof agree in reading "as if she had only been taking a look," and the first edition reads "as if she had only been taking a casual look," it becomes clear that Dickens made further revisions in the now lost "revise," and that therefore just as first proof supersedes the manuscript in textual authority, so the first edition supersedes the proofs. This is of course what we should expect, but it is satisfactory to have the means of demonstrating it.

Just as the manuscript reading will sometimes serve to correct the first edition, so the first proofs have their value; and a peculiar value it is. For the novels issued in monthly parts, Dickens was restricted to monthly numbers of thirty-two pages: no more, no less. Although he was accustomed to reckon that thirty sheets of his handwriting would produce roughly thirty-two pages of type, his erasures and interlineations often disturbed his calculations. When proofs reached him, he sometimes discovered that he had written too little, and sometimes too much. It was mechanically simple to supply an additional paragraph or two in proof when he fell short of the required amount, but it was more troublesome to deal with "over-matter." The printer could help him by adjusting spaces so as to save a line or two, and sometimes he would increase the customary number of lines on a page; but Dickens had usually to cut out something he had written, and it was then his custom to attack passages of dialogue, where the maximum saving could be made at a minimum expense. There can be little doubt that these excised passages were removed simply because there was no room for them, and not because they dissatisfied him. In evidence of this are proof-corrections in these very passages, made presumably before the decision to cut had been taken; it may also be observed that comparable deletions are not made in proofs which contain no over-matter. There is surely a case for restoring excised passages, even though Dickens never troubled to do so himself in subsequent editions. It would be inadvisable to replace them in the text; but they might occupy a prominent position at the foot of the page, in type larger than that to be used for recording variants.

I pass now to the extent of his revision in these later editions. When a novel first appeared in monthly parts, the opportunity for

revision was occasionally taken—in *Pickwick Papers*, for example
—even between the part-issue and the first complete edition, although the edition in volume form followed immediately upon
the publication of the last part. The first complete edition was, in
fact, printed from the same plates used in the part-issue, and revisions incorporated in the text at this stage are therefore rare. Errata
observed were listed on a separate page of the preliminary matter
included with the last part, and this page of errata was normally
included in the first complete edition without correction of the
errors in the text. This is true only of the novels issued in monthly
parts. Since the last three weekly novels were printed in double-
column in magazines, the type had necessarily to be reset for the
first complete edition. An opportunity for revision therefore occurred at this point, and the part-issues of at any rate *Hard Times*
and *Great Expectations* were revised for the first complete editions.

   The principal opportunities for revision of the later novels occurred in the three collected editions. These are the Cheap Edition, begun in 1847 (the year of *Dombey and Son*) and completed
in 17 volumes in 1868; the Library Edition, published in twenty-
two volumes in 1858 and 1859; and the Charles Dickens Edition,
which I have already mentioned, and which was begun in 1867.
New prefaces were written for the Cheap Edition, and corrections
were made in the text of some earlier novels, notably *Oliver Twist;*
but so far as the later novels are concerned, I have not yet found any
significant variants in it or in the Library Edition. Some revision
was made in the text of the Charles Dickens Edition, however, and
there is one piece of evidence which suggests that the copy sent to
the printer—at any rate for *David Copperfield*—was a corrected
copy of the Cheap Edition. In the first chapter Betsey Trotwood
wishes to summon Peggotty, and asks Mrs. Copperfield what she
calls her girl. Mrs. Copperfield, with her mind still running on the
unborn child, replies "I don't know that it will be a girl, yet,
ma'am"; at which Aunt Betsey exclaims, "Bless the Baby! I don't
mean that. I mean your servant-girl." *Servant-girl* is the reading of
the First Edition and the Library Edition. Cheap Edition and
Charles Dickens Edition read *Servant*, thus failing to preserve Aunt
Betsey's emphatic distinction. But in the Cheap Edition the word

occurs at the end of a line and carries a hyphen, thus showing that the following line, with the single word *girl* in it, has dropped out and has been overlooked in the proof-reading. The Charles Dickens Edition (which I shall call CD in future) carelessly follows the corrupt text.

This trifling example serves as a warning against a wholesale adoption of the CD text. There are other instances of CD sophistication which have been preserved in subsequent reprints, whose publishers have assumed that because CD was the last revised edition, it is therefore correct in all particulars. I quote an instance from the end of *Little Dorrit*, where Flora Finching bids farewell to Little Dorrit knowing that Arthur Clennam has ceased merely to be her protector and is about to become her husband. She puts the point as follows: "being aware that tenderer relations are in contemplation beg to state that I heartily wish well to both." So reads the first edition; but instead of *tenderer*, CD reads *tender*, an obvious corruption.

I think it may be assumed that after sending his corrected copy to press for this edition, Dickens read proofs only of those pages which he had corrected and therefore did not notice newly-created errors. The upshot is, I think, that the editor of *David Copperfield* and of any subsequent novel issued in monthly parts must take the part-issue as his copytext and correct it in the light shed by the manuscript, the proofs, and CD.

During the process of collation a great quantity of variant readings have sprung to light. How many should be recorded, and of what kinds? The larger the critical apparatus the more unusable it becomes. All variants of spelling, and where the sense is not affected of punctuation, should therefore be rejected, and all records of mere error perpetrated by CD or other editions subsequent to the first; but an exception should be made for readings of the first edition where in the text the reading of the manuscript is restored. Readings rejected in MS and in proof are so numerous that no publisher will provide space for all of them; moreover some of the original readings of the MS are so heavily erased as to be almost illegible. But the editor should be allowed to use his judgment in recording an occasional rejection. Thus I should like to see recorded in *David Copperfield*, ch. 29, that the song Rosa Dartle sang had at one time been "The Last Rose of Summer" before the title was removed, and that the sermon to which the love-sick David listened in ch. 26 had at one time begun "In the first chapter and first verse of the Book of Dora, you will find the following word Dora." The apparatus must also be used to show what passages were added in proof to complete a number which would otherwise have been under weight, and what passages were deleted in proof to bring the number down to its specified size.

One word more about textual policy before I turn to other matters. In *Dickens at Work*[2] Professor Kathleen Tillotson has already shown to what minute and careful revision *Sketches by Boz* was subjected, first for the collected edition in two series of 1836, secondly for the Monthly Parts version begun in 1837, thirdly for the one-volume edition of 1839, and lastly for the Cheap Edition of 1850. It is surely remarkable that Dickens should have had leisure for three of these four revisions at a time when he was furiously busy with *Pickwick Papers*, *Nicholas Nickleby*, and *Oliver Twist*. Four major revisions were also undertaken for *Oliver Twist*, striking testimony to the importance Dickens attached to that novel. So far as collation has yet proceeded, these two books stand apart from the others in the complexity of their textual history, and will require from an editor special consideration in the choice of copy-text.

Under the general heading of text must also be considered the author's prefaces, his descriptive headlines, and the division of the novels into serial parts. It was Dickens's custom to write a preface for inclusion with the preliminaries in the last monthly part. When he re-issued his novels in the Cheap Edition, he scrapped some of these prefaces and wrote fresh ones, others he revised, and to others he added a note or final paragraph. In modern reprints it is customary to print the last preface only; but in a reliable edition all prefaces should be included, or the variants of those that were merely corrected. This is a policy which has been adopted only by the "National" and the Macmillan editions.

Descriptive head-lines appear for the first time in the Charles Dickens Edition, and they refer only to the right hand page of each opening. Since it is highly improbable that a new edition will run page for page with CD, a different place must be found for them. Perhaps they will best be located in the apparatus criticus, where the passage of the text to which each refers can be most readily indicated; or perhaps they could be placed in the margins.

No modern edition indicates the division of a novel into its monthly or weekly parts, nor is the division immediately apparent in any of Dickens's collected editions. Yet the serial pattern had a great influence upon his work, and the divisions should be indicated. This can be done by inserting the name of the novel and the number of the serial part within square brackets at the head of the first chapter in each number. The running-headline might also indicate the number as well as the chapter.

I now pass from questions of text to the expository material which an editor should be expected to supply. Of first importance are Dickens's working notes for several of the novels. These are still preserved with the manuscripts. They take the form of draft-titles and of plans for individual numbers; there is also a scheme of plot for *The Old Curiosity Shop*—the only novel for which such a scheme exists—and there is a plan for bringing *Great Expectations* to a close. These notes have never been printed in extenso, and to print them at all offers problems; since the arrangement of the notes, the size of the handwriting, the very colour of the ink must often be taken into account in elucidating them. Ideally a photograph of each page should be accompanied by a transcript, but this might be ruled out on grounds of expense. We may have to be content with a transcript, located in an appendix to the novel, and illustrated by one specimen plate.

Only less important are the illustrations and the cover-design to the monthly parts. After the death of Seymour, who illustrated the first two numbers of *Pickwick Papers*, Dickens's illustrator was Hablòt Browne up to and including *A Tale of Two Cities*, but with the following exceptions: Cruikshank for *Oliver Twist*, and Cattermole in association with Browne for *The Old Curiosity Shop* and *Barnaby Rudge*, and Leech, Stanfield and others for the *Christmas Books*. For *Hard Times* and *Great Expectations* there were no illustrations, either in the weekly part-issues or in the first complete editions. For *Our Mutual Friend* Dickens chose Marcus Stone, the son of his old friend Frank Stone; and for *Edwin Drood* he chose Luke Fildes, but entrusted the cover-design to his son-in-law, Charles Collins, the brother of Wilkie. These cover-designs form the front page of the wrapper of the monthly part-issues, and they were normally designed by the illustrator. From *Dombey and Son* onwards they were used to foreshadow the drift of the novel as Dickens originally conceived it. But since the design was necessarily put in hand before more than four or five numbers were written, it sometimes provides evidence of a change in the completed novel from the original conception. The cover-design of *Edwin Drood* was drawn from the most precise directions and it has therefore been subjected to the closest scrutiny by those who wish to know how the novel was to end.

Clearly all these cover-designs should be reproduced, as they are in the National edition and Macmillan's; and the case for reproducing the original illustrations is no less clear, for they too were frequently ordered by Dickens and were sometimes revised before they satisfied him. Where Dickens's directions to his illustrator survive, these too should be incorporated in an appendix.

It might also be interesting to reproduce some illustrations to subsequent editions published in Dickens's lifetime, since they also may be presumed to bear his imprimatur. But they are not so close to his original conception, and not so necessary to a sympathetic understanding of the text. Their omission would be a legitimate saving in the cost of production; but I am not sure whether an exception might be made for *Hard Times* and *Great Expectations* which would otherwise be published without illustrations.

So much for expository material derived from the manuscripts and original editions. What else is required of an editor? Some notes perhaps; an introduction certainly. As to notes Dickens is a classic of another age, and his work presents a fair and ample field for annotation. But when one considers the changes of meaning in word and phrase since Victorian times, the obsolescence of proverbial sayings, the wide range of social and political allusion, and the already immense literature on the original of Dickens's characters and on Dickensian topography, one recognizes that no editor can satisfy the potential demand. I doubt if he should try. I doubt if he should anticipate the standard works which will sometime be written on Dickens's London, Dickens's treatment of his originals, and Dickens's English.

But something can be done in the introductions to group and deal summarily with the more important detail. These introductions should be primarily concerned with the history of the composition of the novel in question. The history of composition is perhaps of more importance when a novel is published serially than when published all at once. At any rate a serial novel is likely to have a longer history. Thanks to the survival of so many of Dickens's letters, it is possible to trace the history of each novel in considerable detail from the first dim stirrings to the publication of the final part-issue. Such an annotated time-table should be found in the introduction to the novel, perhaps in the form of a chart; and with it there should be a description of the manuscript and a bibliographical account of the life-time editions. I should also include a descriptive account of the social, political and autobiographical background of such novels as manifestly require it. That is all that is needed; and if I continue for one moment more, it is only to trail my coat and say that there should be no critical appreciation. There have been plenty of these already, and at their best they "date" more rapidly than the rest of an editor's work. If the novelist were Blackmore, there might be a case for seizing the opportunity of reappraisal. But for Dickens that opportunity is always open without trespassing upon editorial space.

N O T E S

1. London, 1958.
2. John Butt and Kathleen Tillotson, *Dickens at Work*, London, 1957.

DENNIS WELLAND

Samuel Clemens and His English

Publishers: Bibliographical and

Editorial Problems

DENNIS WELLAND *calls attention to the circumstances that may lead to variations between British and American editions and to the usefulness of publishers' records in understanding these circumstances and dealing with the variants. The "sea-change" that often occurs when a text crosses the Atlantic dictates Welland's advice to editors and bibliographers dealing with such books: "regard all texts as guilty until they are proved innocent."*

I

NINETEENTH-CENTURY PUBLISHERS on both sides of the Atlantic often found that they could serve their own financial interests and gratify the literary tastes of their readers at the same time by taking advantage of the absence of a law of international copyright. Pirated American works were as marketable and apparently as popular in Britain as pirated British books were in America, and no purpose would be served by debating which of the two countries was more to blame. Many an author whose works were pirated might condemn the commercial opportunism of the publisher and deplore the liberties taken with his text, either by accident or design, but he would not be wholly averse to the widening of reputation and popularity that resulted from piracy. Nor were all publishers rogues. As early as 1837 Henry Carey of Philadelphia sent the young Dickens £25, urging its acceptance "not as compensation, but as a memento of the fact that unsolicited a bookseller has sent an author, if not money, at least a fair representative of it."[1] American writers sought regular, paid publication in Britain and British publishers were not blind to the advantages of securing for themselves rights as exclusive as possible in the works of those Americans whose writings appealed to British taste. The desirability of a law of international copyright made, not unnaturally, a stronger appeal to authors than to publishers, some of whom seem actively to have opposed or at least delayed its introduction. Nevertheless, while the legal aspects of the matter were debated at length, many writers and publishers, sensing mutual advantage, worked quietly and empirically to secure copyright protection on the basis of such legislation as already existed.[2]

The implications of this copyright situation for the bibliographic study and editing of an American author may well be considerable, for it would be erroneous to suppose that when the English edition was not a piracy, it was only an authorized issue of the American edition with an English publisher's name and binding. What might seem the obvious expedient of shipping over sheets of the American edition for English distribution was, more often than not, impracticable if the English rights were to be secured. Discrepancies between the American and the English text can of course be established by collating the two, though it is sobering to discover how often this task has been neglected by bibliographers, sometimes with disastrous results. Yet collation is not everything: it may show what the differences are but, except in the more obvious areas such as typographical errors, it will not explain how these differences came about. To the textual critic this will often be the more important question, though its answer will be more frequently conjectural. It will usually depend on the survival of publishers' records or correspondence between American author and English publisher involving, perhaps, the American publisher as well; these materials, if they have survived at all, are frequently not accessible to the scholar.

This inaccessibility is not necessarily ascribable to hostility on the part of the publishers. Often the publisher's files have been thinned out or destroyed when a house goes out of business or changes hands. Ethical problems, as well as problems of copyright, may well be involved in allowing research workers unrestricted access to the files. Furthermore, publishers exist to publish books: they will rarely have the staff to aid research workers that a scholarly library can provide; much less have they the staff to undertake research work in response to detailed inquiries from bibliographers and others. Even when the records survive and the good will is there, problems of physical space may well make it quite impossible for the publisher to provide even the minimal facilities for the scholar to do his research on the premises. The collection of the data on which the present article draws has been made possible only by remarkable generosity on the part of the publishers concerned, which the writer gratefully acknowledges. But he has to emphasize that, in order not to impede day-to-day business, it has had to be undertaken at odd times over a period of years. To extend such facilities indiscriminately would mean a serious disruption of the publishers' normal and primary operations.

This somewhat forbidding and portentous introduction is intended to explain why this paper addresses itself to a general problem by discussing a particular case. The case is that of the American author who achieved the greatest popularity among his British— indeed, his European—contemporaries, Mark Twain. It happens to be a case which is singularly well documented, although many of the documents are dispersed through most of the major libraries in the United States and become fully explicable only in the light of the records of two English publishing houses. Hamlin Hill's *Mark Twain's Letters to His Publishers* and his earlier *Mark Twain and Elisha Bliss* have proven invaluable in recounting Clemens' dealings with his American publishers. Until now, however, his relations with publishers on the other side of the Atlantic have been obscure. From a very early stage in his writing career Mark Twain actively sought a British and a European audience; the ways in which he went about this and the effect it had on his work will be treated in a book on which the present writer is currently engaged. The object of this paper is less to report on work in progress than to point to certain general bibliographical problems (with clear editorial implications) which that work has turned up, and to discuss them in terms which may be of interest to bibliographers and editors of nineteenth-century literature. Reference to the English publication of a few of Mark Twain's books will exhibit an unexpected number of ways in which differences could occur in the English text and may suggest general issues not necessarily peculiar to his experience.

II

Clemens' initial encounter with an English pirate occurred when the notorious John Camden Hotten of Piccadilly spawned a *Jumping Frog and Other Tales* in 1867, euphemizing piracy by the bland statement on his title page—"from the Original Edition." Emboldened by success (the book sold well), Hotten then brought out an unauthorized *Innocents Abroad* in two parts, with an introduction by Edward P. Hingston, the friend of Artemus Ward; he followed this with *Mark Twain's (Burlesque) Autobiography and First Romance*, advertising it, with no apparent justification, as the "Author's edition, containing twice as much as any other." He also issued selections of the sketches under a series of catch-penny titles, often including apocryphal pieces among them. Clemens' dealings with Hotten have recently been summarized in an informative essay[3] which perhaps lets Hotten off a little lightly but makes it clear that Clemens, more sinned against than sinning, took retaliatory action that was not wholly scrupulous. The campaign he conducted against Hotten in tones of moral indignation in the correspondence columns of *The Spectator* was in some respects disingenuous and calculated to attract the maximum attention to the authorized editions which were by then being published in London by George Routledge & Sons. Nevertheless, the encounter with Hotten dramatized for Clemens the desirability of an international law of copyright, a cause for which he was to campaign vigorously and with devotion long after his English publishers had found an adequate means of safeguarding the English editions of Clemens' books.

George Routledge & Sons had since 1854 maintained a New York branch at 416 Broome Street, and it may have been their New York agent, Joseph L. Blamire, who first drew their attention to *The Jumping Frog*. They too published it in London in 1867; whether it was by previous arrangement or not remains obscure. Certainly Clemens had made Blamire's acquaintance by 1870, and Blamire made many of the arrangements for Clemens' visit to England in 1872 as well as negotiating the English rights for the books he had written. Routledge published *Roughing It* early in 1872 (the British Museum copy was accessioned on 15 February) and described it on the title page as a "Copyright Edition." Jacob Blanck thinks it probably appeared a few days before the American edition.[4] In a letter to Blamire Clemens had promised "to ship the revised Roughing It today,"[5] a statement which suggests some authorial changes in the English text, but which probably referred only to a set of revised proofs of the American edition. In England the book was published in two volumes, the first (chapters 1 to 45 inclusive) entitled *Roughing It*, the second *The Innocents at Home*. The three appendices to the American text were omitted by Routledge, but instead "Mark Twain's (Burlesque) Autobiography" was included at the end of the second volume. There are some printer's errors in the English text and some Anglicizations ("ploughed" for "plowed," for example), but no significant changes. Indeed, in Chapter 44 the reference to "the accompanying portrait" is retained, even though the edition was not illustrated.

In 1872 also the Routledges reissued their *Jumping Frog* volume, and Blanck notes that in one printing the title page carried the statement "Messrs. George Routledge & Sons are my only authorized London publishers. Mark Twain" (BAL 3338). This statement also appeared on the title page of *A Curious Dream and Other Sketches* published by Routledge in the same year. Meanwhile Routledge was also planning to bring out a collected edition of the sketches and an authorized edition of *The Innocents Abroad*. Clemens had asked Bliss to send Blamire a complimentary copy of the American edition as early as March 1870,[6] and there is no obvious reason for their delay in publishing this volume unless Hotten's prompt piracy had dissuaded them. The Routledge edition followed Hotten's pattern of a two-volume publication, the second volume being entitled (as with Hotten's) *The New Pilgrims' Progress*. Clemens was induced to provide a special preface for each volume and to introduce a number of revisions. As in *Roughing It* there are printer's errors and Anglicizations, but a number of new footnotes appear, some that explain allusions which the English reader might not know, others that are purely humorous. Sentences are added here and there in the text and there are also a number of omissions of a phrase or a sentence from the 1869 American text.[7] They may have been made in order to justify the entry "Author's English Edition" on the title page, and to constitute a legal claim of sorts to copyright in England of a book which had been published in America more than two years earlier, and already pirated in England. As far as one can tell the copyright in all these works did in fact hold: despite Mark Twain's increasing popularity they were not pirated.

Routledge's *Sketches Selected and Revised* is of bibliographical significance as the first collection of Mark Twain's sketches to be published in book form with the author's approval. It antedates the corresponding American volume by three years. Simultaneous publication in the United States would seem an obvious and desirable step, but Bliss was reluctant to consider it in 1872, arguing that it would be too close to the publication of *Roughing It*. Orion Clemens wrote to his brother explaining Bliss's view that "few people want to buy two books from the same author at the same time,"[8] yet in England Routledge was deliberately giving the public the chance of buying *four*, and the record of reprintings suggests that he was right in doing so. Was Bliss overcautious? Was Mark Twain more popular abroad than at home? Were the book-buying habits of the British different from those of the Americans, or does Clemens' preference for the subscription method of publication in the United States explain the difference? There is as yet no conclusive answer to any of these questions. The one thing which is clear is that the preface Mark Twain furnished for the English *Sketches* gives that text a particular authority:

> Messrs. George Routledge and Sons are the only English publishers who pay me any copyright on my books. That is something; but a

courtesy which I prize even more, is the opportunity which they have given me to edit and revise the matter for publication myself. This enables me to leave out a good deal of literature which has appeared in England over my name, but which I never wrote. And, as far as this particular volume is concerned, it also enables me to add a number of sketches which I *did* write, but which have not heretofore been published abroad. This book contains all of my sketches which I feel at all willing to father.

Hartford 1872   MARK TWAIN

The first English edition of *The Gilded Age*, published late in December 1873, is also textually unique by virtue of an "Author's Preface to the London Edition" in which Clemens moralized on the corruption prevalent in American politics, but asserted "a great strong faith in a noble future for my country" and blamed Britain for at least some of the corrupt figures on the American scene.

Thus, of the volumes of Twain's writing published by Hotten and Routledge none is identical with the American original: some have new introductory or prefatory matter; others have typographical variations; one at least contains minor revisions; while others represent the first publication in book form of fugitive pieces. In an autobiographical memoir Clemens wrote for Charles Dudley Warner about this time he commented: "In England the Routledges and Hotten have gathered together and published all my sketches; a great many have not appeared in book form here. There are four volumes of these sketches. . . ."[9] The absence here of any criticism of Hotten will be remarked, as will the general note of satisfaction with his English publishing arrangements; in fact those arrangements were beginning to enter a new and expansive phase.

III

In 1873 Hotten died suddenly. The business was bought by a junior member of the firm named Andrew Chatto, who took into partnership with him the minor poet, W. E. Windus. In November 1873, knowing Clemens to be in London on a lecture tour, Chatto wrote him a conciliatory letter and enclosed "a set of the sheets of a volume of your writings, in order that you may (as I understand you expressed a desire to do) correct certain portions of the contents."[10] The sheets were one of Hotten's last piracies which he had published earlier that year under the cumbersome title *The Choice Humorous Works of Mark Twain, Now first Collected with Extra Passages to the "Innocents Abroad," now first reprinted, and a life of the author. Illustrations by Mark Twain & other Artists: also portrait of the author.* The biographical sketch was a compilation of Hotten's based largely on *Roughing It* and on Hingston's introduction to *The Innocents Abroad;* it is initialled "J.C.H." and dated March 12 1873. Chatto evidently wished to reissue the book and did so in 1874, retitling it *The Choice Humorous Works of Mark Twain, Revised and corrected by the Author With a Life and also a Portrait of the Author, and numerous Illustrations.* He omitted seventeen pieces from the earlier edition and re-titled one other; the "Life" was shortened by about four pages but in such a way as to minimize the amount of re-setting necessary; the income Mark Twain was "stated on very good authority" to have received from *The Innocents Abroad* is raised from "seventeen thousand dollars" to "twenty-four thousand dollars," this time on "unimpeachable authority," and the statement "112,000 copies of the book were sold" is added. There is no written proof that these changes were made at the author's direction but Clemens not infrequently saved himself correspondence by a visit to a publisher and a conversation: these changes he may well have made in Chatto's office and not by letter at all. The eagerness with which Clemens was to offer Chatto his next book and the fact that he never challenged Chatto's title would suggest that he did personally authorize this selection.

The questions to which *The Choice Humorous Works* gives rise are not without bibliographical significance. Were the seventeen omitted pieces dropped because Mark Twain had not written them or merely because he no longer wished to own them? What is the status of the pieces—there are eleven of them—which appear here but are not included in the Routledge 1872 volume which was also authorized? Did Clemens' knowledge of the imminence of this volume explain his apparent softening toward Hotten in the autobiographical note for Warner, or was he there tacitly acknowledging the extent to which Hotten, pirate or no, had helped make his name a household word in Britain? If his authorization of this volume can be accepted, why did he allow Routledge, as late as the spring of 1876, to issue *Information Wanted, and other sketches by Mark Twain* with the customary statement that he was Mark Twain's only authorized London publisher? In any case, by the time that book appeared he was committed to Chatto & Windus for the publishing of *The Adventures of Tom Sawyer* which they were already setting in type.

The full reasons for this change of publisher need not be enumerated here. Hamlin Hill has summarized them (pp. 93–98, notes), and they are in any case predictable in broad outline. On a later and different occasion Clemens enunciated the principle that "there is neither wisdom nor fairness in changing publishers except for good and palpable business reasons,"[11] and in this case the good and palpable business reasons were the more advantageous terms Chatto was prepared to offer him for the new book. In negotiating those terms his friend Moncure Daniel Conway proved himself so able that Clemens was to appoint him his English agent on a regular 5% commission basis, an indication of the importance Mark Twain was coming to attach to the English market. Conway played Chatto off against Routledge in 1876 with evident shrewdness, but it is not easy to see why Routledge did not make a more determined effort to retain Mark Twain on his lists. The sales of his books were obviously satisfactory, and although a notebook entry suggests that Clemens liked the Routledges as people less than he was to come to like Chatto, there is no evidence of any actual disagreement with them. In 1881 they were to make an attempt to win him back for the publication of *The Prince and the Pauper*, but by then he was too well satisfied with Chatto & Windus to wish to change.

Why Chatto was so ready to offer generous, even munificent, terms is easier to understand. As a writer and as a lecturer Mark Twain was extremely popular in Britain and would be a commercial asset to the new publishing house. Moreover the willing transfer to that firm of a popular author who had dealt so scathingly and contemptuously in the press with its former head would dramatize vividly the changed character of the firm under its new directors. When Conway offered Chatto the rights to *The Adventures of Tom Sawyer* the publisher made a bid for it without even seeing the manuscript. He could not have foreseen the reputation the book was to acquire, and his previous experience of Conway's enthusiasms might justifiably have made him sceptical of this recommendation, but his business acumen led him to take it and pay handsomely for it.

There were two manuscripts of *Tom Sawyer*, an autograph original and an amanuensis copy.[12] The latter had been lent to W. D. Howells who, as is well known, had suggested certain modifications and emendations which he had pencilled none too legibly on it. It was this copy which Clemens entrusted to Conway at Hartford in January 1876, which Conway took across the Atlantic, and which he handed to Andrew Chatto as the text for the English edition. For a variety of reasons, as Hamlin Hill has shown (pp. 95ff.), Elisha Bliss was dilatory in preparing the American edition. Chatto, egged on by the ever-impetuous Conway, lost no time. On 29 March 1876 he acknowledged receipt of the manuscript which "is now in the printers hands to be set up." Some of the surviving galleys are dated; apparently Spottiswoode, the printer, had the first batch of galleys back to Conway on 11 April, the seventh two days later, and the seventy-ninth (down to Chapter XXIV) by 1 May. On 3 May Conway returned "the last revise of the last proof" and on 10 June the book was advertised in *The Athenaeum* as "New copyright work by Mark Twain. Now ready." It is an impressive rate of book production by any standards.

By 25 August Chatto had already decided that the market would stand an illustrated edition and he asked Conway to obtain proofs of the American illustrations, but they were still not available. Indeed, Conway's eagerness to promote the book was proving embarrassing: he had read extracts from it at a lecture in London in April, reviewed it anonymously on publication, and, unaware of the American publication delays, had published a review of it in the *Cincinnati Commercial* in June which other American papers had drawn on, reprinting especially all its extensive quotations from the text.[13] This amused Clemens more than it irritated him, but worse was to come. By the end of October the Canadian publishing house of Belford had brought out a cheap pirated edition and was, Clemens told Conway in November, "flooding America" with it: he estimated that Bliss could not "issue for 6 weeks yet, & by that time Belford will have sold 100,000 over the frontier & killed my book dead. This piracy will cost me $10,000" (Hill, p. 106).

The one thing that emerges with complete clarity from the subsequent flurry of correspondence between Chatto, Conway, and Clemens is that no one had any sure idea of how far English copyright protected a book published in England by an American author against piracy in Canada. Belford told Chatto truculently: "We know Americans are in the habit of taking out copyright in England, but we doubt if it would hold there: we are well advised that it gives no right in Canada" (Hill, p. 106). By the end of January 1877, after a visit to the United States and Canada, Chatto had established that English copyright on first publication extended to all the colonies, but that some, including Canada, had the right to import foreign reprints of English copyright books: he guessed that Belford might be observing the strict letter of the law by printing copies on American soil and then "importing" them into Canada. Whether the subsequent distribution of such copies in the United States was an offence against American copyright law he did not know; Clemens was the only person who could test this by legal action and Chatto was understandably reluctant to predict the outcome. Clemens meanwhile was persuaded by Bliss that Canadian law allowed copyright in Canada only to such English publications as were registered in Canada sixty days before publication. Conway, whom Clemens was inclined to accuse of negligence over this, was able to cite cases where this rule had certainly not obtained. Desperate but inconclusive discussions were held as to whether reassignment of the English copyright to either Conway or Chatto would affect the issue. Meanwhile Belford continued marketing *Tom Sawyer*.

In the absence of legislation, copyright lore flourished. The British Imperial Act of 1842 had guaranteed copyright to a book first published in the British dominions provided that the author, whatever his nationality, was at the date of publication resident in the dominions. In 1870 Clemens asked Blamire "if it would pay me to go over the Niagara river and get a British copyright"[14] for *The Innocents Abroad*, evidently imagining that copyright could be given retroactively. By the summer of 1873, he was sending Bliss explicit instructions from London to keep Routledge informed of the exact date of publication of *The Gilded Age*: "Routledge will publish on that day or the day before" (Hill, p. 77). He told another correspondent that "it is now a fact beyond question that I shall have to remain in London till Oct. 25 and thus be able to secure English copyright" (Hill, pp. 78–79). Determined to avoid confusion over *Tom Sawyer* in 1876, he had sought the advice of A. R. Spofford, Librarian of Congress, who told him that "the first publication in England is essential to Copyright there but previous entry here will secure you in the United States" (Hill, p. 98). The pattern established with Chatto thereafter was usually to issue in England one day before the date of American publication. Canada passed an act in 1875 requiring citizenship or bona fide residence as a condition for copyright, restricting this to books printed and published in Canada. A principle of reciprocity also obtained, but as the United States had no corresponding provision Clemens could not benefit from that. However, a trip to Canada, so as to be registered in a hotel there on publication day, was to become a ritual for Clemens in his unceasing campaign against Belford and his fellow pirates.

"There seems to be no convenient way to beat those Canadian re-publishers anyway," Clemens had wistfully told Bliss in 1871 (Hill, p. 67), but he never gave up trying. Yet when Routledge negotiated the English rights of *The Gilded Age* one clause stipulated that the Canadian market was to be supplied by a two shilling edition imported from England: "The Routledges would not yield up Canada to Bliss," Clemens wrote to his wife, adding that this was very much to the authors' advantage.[15] There does not seem to have been any Canadian piracy problem with that novel, but it had not the attractiveness of *Tom Sawyer* and was in any case on sale simultaneously in the United States. It was the lack of synchronization that gave Belford his opportunity with *Tom*

Sawyer, and Mark Twain tried very hard never to repeat that error.

Thus when Bliss eventually brought out *The Adventures of Tom Sawyer* in America it was the third publication of that book, but bibliographically the situation is even more complex than that suggests. Both authorized editions had been printed from a manuscript, but the first to appear, the English edition, was set from an amanuensis copy with corrections by Howells. The proofs had been read by Conway. Bliss, however, had worked from an autograph manuscript and Clemens had presumably read the proofs. Which, then, constitutes the more authoritative text? For, as Jacob Blanck notes (BAL 3367, note), there are textual differences. The example he cites is from Chapter 1. In one text Tom promises himself "But I bet you I'll lam Sid for that. If I don't, blame my cats." In the other he remarks circumspectly "But I bet you I'll lam Sid for that. I'll learn him!" Those critics who see Howells as perpetually emasculating Mark Twain's vernacular raciness in the interests of gentility would probably detect Howells' influence behind the second of these readings and attribute it to the Howells-corrected English manuscript. Unfortunately for this theory, the reverse is the case. Howells took no exception to "blame my cats" and the English text retains the phrase, though it is one unfamiliar to the English ear. "I'll learn him!" which the English reader would more readily have understood, appears in the American text. Presumably Mark Twain had second thoughts about it before the later edition was printed.

Yet in another instance the English edition appears to follow the author's second thoughts more closely than the American. In Chapter XX Becky comes upon the teacher's anatomy book with its frontispiece of "a human figure, stark naked": that, at least, is how the manuscript originally read. "I should be afraid of this picture incident" wrote Howells in the margin, and Mark Twain, among other modifications, cancelled "stark naked." The English edition observed this cancellation, the American edition retained the phrase. Textual problems of this nature will presumably be resolved as definitively as possible in the edition of Mark Twain currently in preparation at the University of Iowa. They are problems which arise directly out of the author's desire for English publication, the necessity to secure English copyright by prior publication, and the fact that this could most easily be ensured by providing the English publisher with a copy manuscript from which to work. Similar problems may well exist in other cases.

IV

In 1880, doubtless anxious to avoid a repetition of the *Tom Sawyer* confusion, Clemens decided that for *A Tramp Abroad* Bliss should "furnish advance sheets to Chatto as fast as possible" (Hill, p. 120) —sheets from which the English edition could be set, so that the two publishers might, as the phrase went, "simultane" with each other. Again he was doomed to disaster. This time the American edition came out first, thus effectively preventing Chatto from copyrighting the English edition.

Foreseeably, Mark Twain erupted, distributing blame in all directions. The facts are clear. As early as 11 November 1879 Chatto & Windus wrote to warn Clemens that although they had registered the title at Stationers Hall and obtained copyright on that, complete copyright could not be obtained without depositing a copy of the book itself, and without this precaution the Canadian printer could not be forestalled. On 11 March 1880 they reminded him that they needed to know the date of publication and were still awaiting proofs of the final part of the text as well as the illustrations. This crossed with a letter from Bliss written on the same day, informing them with incredible casualness, "Mr. Clemens wishes us to notify you that you can publish as early as you please. We shall not wait for its publication there."[16] Conway subsequently told Clemens "There was over a hundred pages of the book short here [in England] when the book was issued [in the United States]" (Hill, p. 124). However, Chatto was able to report on 16 April that a copy of their edition "was rushed through the press in three days in order to keep the ground if possible against pirates," but it was, of course, unillustrated. The speed of publication and the fact that the book was set from American advance sheets would argue against the likelihood of significant textual variants. "I hope there may not be too many heart-breaking misprints in it," Chatto had written, "—some of them no doubt will be owing to the uncorrected proofs we had to print from."

After fulminating against all concerned, Clemens belatedly realized that the fault was primarily his own for not having honored his undertaking to supervise the matter himself, and letters of apology duly went to Chatto and to Conway. In any event no great harm was done: there was, in May, the threat of a pirated one shilling version of the book appearing in England, "which," said Chatto, "we shall be powerless to oppose, but by keeping a bold front we hope to scare off intruders and so escape the danger." He appears to have succeeded, and Clemens was, in December, surprised and gratified by the royalties on his English sales. However, Chatto's fears for the Canadian market were justified: a pirated Canadian edition was on sale almost as soon as the American. "I think they hurt us to the extent of 20,000 copies, perhaps," was Clemens' estimate (Hill, p. 127). Oddly, the American edition of *A Tramp Abroad* printed the name of Chatto & Windus on the title page, below that of the American Publishing Company. This may have been conceived as a possible deterrent to Canadian pirates: if so, it was an unsuccessful bluff, and to add insult to injury the pirates were in this instance understood to have obtained their advance sheets from printers in Hartford presumably working for Bliss (Hill, p. 127). There is a comic, even farcical, aspect to the full correspondence about *A Tramp Abroad*, but it seems that once again Mark Twain was better served by his English than by his American publishers.

About this time also he became aware of yet another way in which his contractual relationship with Chatto & Windus was to prove convenient and lucrative to him. At Clemens' express request Chatto officially handled all European rights for him from 1881 onwards. Hitherto Tauchnitz had dealt directly with Clemens for the rights to *Tom Sawyer*, *The Innocents Abroad*, and *Roughing It*. The two men had met in Paris in 1879 and Clemens described him to Howells as "a mighty nice old gentleman" whose terms he was quite happy to accept without question: "one can't have the heart to dicker with a publisher who won't steal."[17] Clearly Clemens did not realize the security of his own position until Chatto explained to him in 1881 that "English copyright covers and protects us from continental reprints such as those of Tauchnitz."

If Clemens was not prepared to dicker with Tauchnitz over terms, Chatto certainly was; his more experienced knowledge of the European market enabled him to know just how much he could get for the European rights and how far he could bargain with Tauchnitz. That "mighty nice old gentleman" was also an experienced and shrewd publisher; his fairness is not in question, but there is ample evidence that Chatto was often able to obtain from him a price considerably higher than a less experienced negotiator could have commanded. He also adopted the practice of sending advance sheets of each new book to Tauchnitz so that the European edition could appear almost simultaneously with the English. Left to handle such matters himself, Clemens might well have been as casual and as forgetful as he was in some of his other correspondence with publishers, and his European reputation would have been slower in growing.

Special reference needs to be made here to Mark Twain's last travel book. Possibly because an international copyright law had become effective in 1891, bibliographers down to and including Jacob Blanck have always regarded *More Tramps Abroad* as the English title of *Following the Equator*, in the same way that the English title of *A Connecticut Yankee at King Arthur's Court* has always been *A Yankee at the Court of King Arthur*. However, as the present writer has demonstrated elsewhere,[18] the textual differences between *More Tramps Abroad* and *Following the Equator* are very considerable and are directly related to the circumstances of English publication. Clemens wrote the book entirely in London, exhausted after his world tour, emotionally drained by the death of his favorite daughter, and driving himself to complete the book as quickly as possible in order to ease his financial problems. The manuscript was hurried around to Chatto & Windus where Andrew Chatto, who generally acted as his own reader, went through it himself and persuaded the author to make a number of cuts and revisions. A typescript was made and sent to Frank Bliss in Hartford as the basis for the American text. Chatto's printers worked from the author's manuscript, a practice which, in the early days of typewriting, some printers seem actually to have preferred.

Both the manuscript and the typescript are now part of the Berg Collection in the New York Public Library, and a comparison of them shows how extensively and even ruthlessly Bliss had cut the text in order to adapt the book to his conception of the tastes of the subscription market. A more lavish piece of book production, *Following the Equator* seems to have relied on full-plate and inset illustrations in the text where *More Tramps Abroad* contained only three full-page illustrations and one in the text. To accommodate the illustrations and to enable each chapter to begin on a fresh page, Bliss was unscrupulous in his cutting; he also indulged his own taste by omitting a good deal of material (especially on the primitive races and on British policy in South Africa) which did not appeal to him. The differences between the two texts are still further complicated by Bliss's retention of some passages which Chatto omitted (in some cases they would probably have been actionable in Britain), by differences of chapter division, and by variations in the Pudd'nhead Wilson maxims used at the head of each chapter.

That Clemens himself never seems to have been aware of these discrepancies is less remarkable in light of his remark to Howells, "I wrote my last travel book in hell; but I let on, the best I could, that it was an excursion through heaven. Some day I will read it, and if its lying cheerfulness fools me, then I shall believe it fooled the reader" (*Mark Twain–Howells Letters*, II, 690). For a moment during the writing of it he had been "more than satisfied with it" and had told Bliss "I wouldn't trade it for any book I have ever written—and I am not an easy person to please"[19]. That may have been bravado; his more cautious later estimate will probably be closer to that of most readers, but whatever its quality the book deserves, as part of the Mark Twain canon, an established text. And for reasons enumerated in the article referred to, *More Tramps Abroad* should be seen as the more authoritative edition and *Following the Equator* as an abridged version of it.

Not every American writer was as popular in England as Mark

Twain or, perhaps, as well served by his English publishers. In other cases even greater discrepancies may exist between American and English editions, for international copyright carries no guarantee that texts will be identical, and many authors more recent than Mark Twain, English and American, have seen their works undergo various degrees of sea-change in crossing the Atlantic. It would seem that editors and bibliographers would be well advised to regard all texts as guilty until they are proved innocent.

NOTES

1. David Kaser, *Messrs. Carey & Lea of Philadelphia* (Philadelphia, 1957), pp. 112–13.

2. England had had an international copyright law since 1838 but it operated only reciprocally; the United States could not benefit from it since it had no international copyright law until 1891. The British Imperial Act of 1842 afforded some measure of protection to a book by an author of any nationality, provided that it was first published in Britain and that he was at that time resident there. In 1868 this was extended to allow residence anywhere in the British dominions at the time of first publication. See Edward H. Hudon, "Mark Twain and the Copyright Dilemma," *American Bar Association Journal*, LII (1966), 56–60.

3. Dewey Ganzel, "Samuel Clemens and John Camden Hotten," *The Library*, 5th ser., XX (1965), 230–42.

4. Jacob Blanck, *Bibliography of American Literature* (New Haven, 1957), II, entry no. 3337, note; hereafter cited as BAL.

5. S. L. Clemens to Joseph L. Blamire, "Hartford, 23^d," no month or year, Clifton Waller Barrett Library of the University of Virginia Library, to whom my thanks are due. © 1969 by the Mark Twain Company. For permission to use the unpublished material identified in this note and in notes 9, 11, 14, and 15, I am grateful to the trustees of the estate of Clara Clemens Samossoud.

6. S. L. Clemens to Elisha Bliss, 3 March 1870. Typescript copy in the Mark Twain Papers, University of California, Berkeley (hereafter cited as MTP).

7. These variants have been studied by Arthur L. Scott, "Mark Twain's Revisions of *The Innocents Abroad* for the British Edition of 1872," *American Literature*, XXV (1953), 43–61.

[184]

8. Hamlin Hill, *Mark Twain's Letters to His Publishers* (Los Angeles, 1967), p. 54; hereafter cited as Hill.

9. The Pierpont Morgan Library, New York, to whom my thanks are due. © 1969 by the Mark Twain Company.

10. Quotations from and references to letters from Andrew Chatto or from Chatto & Windus are made by kind permission of that house; they will not hereafter be separately acknowledged in the notes, but I am grateful to Mr. Ian Parsons for permission to make use of the firm's letter books in this way.

11. S. L. Clemens to Andrew Chatto, 11 November 1881. The Henry W. and Alberta A. Berg Collection of the New York Public Library, Astor, Lenox, and Tilden Foundations, to whom my thanks are due. © 1969 by the Mark Twain Company.

12. The former is now the property of George Washington University, Washington, D.C., the other is in the Mark Twain Birthplace Memorial Shrine at Florida, Missouri, and has been described by the curator, Mr. Ralph Gregory, in a privately printed pamphlet "William Dean Howells's Corrections, Suggestions and Questions on the English Manuscript of *Tom Sawyer.*"

13. For a fuller discussion of this see Dennis Welland, "A Note on Some Early Reviews of *Tom Sawyer,*" *Journal of American Studies,* I (1967), 99–103.

14. Quoted by Clemens in the letter to Bliss identified in note 6 above. © 1969 by the Mark Twain Company.

15. Letter in MTP. © 1969 by the Mark Twain Company.

16. Letter in the ownership of Messrs. Chatto & Windus.

17. *Mark Twain–Howells Letters,* ed. Henry Nash Smith and William M. Gibson (Cambridge, Mass., 1960), I, 262.

18. "Mark Twain's Last Travel Book, *Bulletin of the New York Public Library,* LXV (1965), 31–48.

19. S. L. Clemens to Elisha Bliss, 26 March 1897. The Yale Collection of American Literature, The Beinecke Rare Book and Manuscript Library, Yale University, to whom my thanks are due. © 1969 by the Mark Twain Company. I was not aware of this letter at the time of writing the article under discussion; it proposes *Imitating the Equator* as an alternative title for the book in addition to those mentioned on p. 38 of the article.

RUSSELL K. ALSPACH

Some Textual Problems in Yeats

RUSSELL K. ALSPACH *distills much that he and his collaborator,*
Peter Allt, learned preparing the variorum edition of Yeats's
poems, in particular the textual and critical implications of Yeats's
"inveterate" but inconsistently realized revisions. He calls atten-
tion especially to the dangers of depending unwarily on loosely
used distinctions between "early" and "late" in the canon. The
wisdom of his insistence on recording variants in accidentals
("who is to judge where the meaning or rhythm is affected?")
is clearly demonstrated, and of course has application beyond
Yeats. The problems Alspach examines witness how much textual
work needs to be done even on the giants of our literature.

THIS PAPER IS BASED on the variorum edition of Yeats's poems
that Peter Allt, late lecturer in Anglo-Irish literature at
the University of Groningen, and I have been preparing jointly
for some ten years. Because of Peter Allt's untimely death in an
accident in London two years ago the finishing of the work fell to
me. His death was a severe personal blow, and it was a great loss to
Yeats's scholarship.

Reprinted from *Studies in Bibliography*, IX (1957), 51-67, with the permission of the author and the Bibliographical Society of the University of
Virginia.

In our work, we confined ourselves to versions of Yeats's poems published by him in magazine or book. We included no manuscript versions—they are quite numerous and widely scattered, and comparatively few are available for study. (And no manuscript version has the final polishing of proofreading by Yeats.) Nor did we include versions of his poems quoted by other writers, e.g. Katharine Tynan[1] and Dorothy Wellesley.[2] At best these are secondhand. As our standard text we used the two-volume limited and signed edition of *The Poems of W. B. Yeats* published by Macmillan of London in 1949. The publisher's brochure that accompanied this edition reads in part:

> For some time before his death, W. B. Yeats was engaged in revising the text of this edition of his poems, of which he had corrected the proofs, and for which he had signed the special page to appear at the beginning of Volume I. The outbreak of the Second World War, however, came at a crucial stage in the production of the work, and Messrs. Macmillan & Co. Ltd. had to consider the effect of austere conditions on a publication which had been projected on a lavish scale and which, after the untimely death of this great writer, would have formed a worthy monument of him. It was finally decided that production should be discontinued until after the war, and it is only now, a decade later, that it has become possible to offer the work as it was originally planned.

With this definitive edition at hand it is possible to trace the evolution of a Yeats poem from its first published version through all its revisions to its final form and to see how in the process Yeats's concept of what he wanted the poem to say developed.

Under revisions I include all changes, even those in punctuation. Perhaps this is dangerous ground; much has been said about Yeats's carelessness in, and lack of knowledge of, punctuation. But the testimony varies. We know, for instance, that he wrote to Robert Bridges in 1915 that "I chiefly remember that you asked me about stops and commas. Do what you will. I do not understand stops. I write so completely for the ear that I feel helpless when I have to measure pauses by stops and commas."[3] But Mrs. Yeats told me in the summer of 1954 that she believed shifts in punctuation were very much a problem in any textual study of her husband's work, that W. B. was careful about "stops and commas," and that several times he had become quite irate with a publisher who had taken it upon himself to change the poet's punctuation. It took me a long time to convince my colleague on the variorum that punctuation must be noted. His point of view originally, and the point of view of others, was that it should be noted only where the meaning or rhythm is affected. But who is to judge where the meaning or rhythm is affected? Certainly not the textual critic or scholar who is working in the realm of facts and not of aesthetics. And in the case of Yeats the conflicting testimony about his knowledge of punctuation must be kept in mind. I believe further that a close study of the punctuational changes in his verse will convince others, as it has me, that these changes were in the main deliberate and not accidental.

That Yeats was an inveterate revisor soon became apparent to discriminating readers of his poetry during the years in which it was being published. He continued to revise until the end; he was never content. He comments often about his revisions. The best-known of these comments is the quatrain he wrote for the second volume of *The Collected Works* of 1908:

> The friends that have it I do wrong
> Whenever I remake a song,
> Must know what issue is at stake:
> It is myself that I remake.[4]

Not so wellknown, but pertinent to this study, is his statement in the preface written in 1927 for the thirteenth reprinting and revision of *Poems* (1895): "This volume contains what is, I hope, the final text of the poems of my youth; and yet it may not be, ... One is always cutting out the dead wood."[5] We can, I think, profitably examine the last words of this statement, "One is always cutting out the dead wood," and the implications that arise from it.

In any textual study of Yeats's poems no edition, printing, impression, or reissue can be ignored. For example, the volume *Later Poems* was published in London in 1922 and reprinted there the same year. These printings are identical. In February 1924 it was reprinted again; this time there are a number of changes. In April

1924 it was published in New York, and this printing differed from the London printings of 1922 and February 1924. In 1926 and 1931 there were further reprintings in London: these printings differ from all previous printings and from each other. (A New York reprint of 1928 is identical to the first New York printing, that of 1924.) A second example is the trade edition of *The Wild Swans at Coole,* published in London and New York in 1919. These are identical. But a London reprint of 1920 has several changes. It is here, for instance, that we have for the first time the final form of "An Irish Airman Foresees His Death." A third example is the *Selected Poems* of 1929, published only in London. (Parenthetically, this is usually ignored by Yeats's textual critics, but textually it is very important. Many of the changes ascribed to *Collected Poems* (1933)[6] actually appeared first here.) *Selected Poems* was reprinted in 1930, 1932, 1936, 1938, 1951, and 1952—the last two in the Golden Treasury series. The printings of 1929, 1930, and 1932 are identical; but there are changes for the 1936 printing. From then on the printings are the same.

Nor can it be assumed that simultaneous periodical publication in Britain and America meant identity of form. In her admirable study of Yeats's revisions of his later poems, Professor Witt[7] has discussed a case in point: that of "Among Schoolchildren" published first in both *The Dial* and *The London Mercury* for August 1927. Other examples are numerous. "The Two Kings" appeared in *Poetry* and *The British Review* in October 1913. In the 252 lines of these first printings there are over fifty changes, great and small, between the two. In "Upon a Dying Lady," in *The Little Review,* August 1917, and *The New Statesman,* 11 August 1917, there are some twenty changes in the seventy-three lines. And between the versions of "The Second Coming" in *The Dial,* November 1920, and the London *Nation,* 6 November 1920, there is a startling change. Line 19 reads in *The Dial,* "That thirty centuries of stony sleep," and in *The Nation,* "That twenty centuries of stony sleep." Even with Yeats's handwriting it's a little difficult to make "thirty" out of "twenty."

So far in these examples I have been pointing up the truth of Yeats's assertion about "always cutting out the dead wood," an assertion that would have lead one to believe that if he had the latest-dated Yeats volume he had the latest versions of its contents. But there are curious exceptions, exceptions where "dead wood" persisted beside "live wood." One of these is *The Wind Among the Reeds*, published in London and New York in 1899, and reprinted in both places a number of times. The last printing was London, 1911, called the "sixth edition."[8] All printings are identical. But in the meantime *The Wind Among the Reeds* was revised for the first volume of the 1906 *Poetical Works* published only in America,[9] and again revised for the first volume of the 1908 *Collected Works* published only in England. In 1908, therefore, we have in print three versions of the poems in *The Wind Among the Reeds*: the original version, the version in *The Poetical Works* I (1906), and the version in *The Collected Works* I (1908). To add to the mixup, *The Poetical Works* I (1906) was reprinted nine times, with no changes, to 1922. The same anomaly happens with the 1931 printing of *Later Poems* that, while it has revisions, does not have all the revisions made for the 1929 *Selected Poems*. And the 1936 revised printing of *Selected Poems* does not have all the revisions of the 1933 *Collected Poems*. An accurate study of the development of a Yeats poem demands, it seems to me, the ability to work one's way through this maze in order to recognize the "dead wood" and the "live wood."

Closely allied to the "dead wood" and "live wood" textual problem is the problem of the "early" Yeats and the "later" Yeats. Any one even faintly familiar with Yeats is aware of this much-discussed division of his work. The difficulty is the wide variance of opinion about where "early" stops and "later" begins. One critic dates the "early" Yeats from 1889 to 1901, another from 1889 to 1910, and another from 1889 to 1914. Perhaps we cannot do better than take the poet's own dates in definition of "early" and "later."

He first uses the words "Early Poems" in 1906 as a subheading in *The Poetical Works* I. Under "Early Poems" he includes the long narrative poem "The Wanderings of Oisin" and certain of the ballads and lyrics from his first two published volumes: *The Wanderings of Oisin and Other Poems* (London, 1889) and *The*

Countess Kathleen and Various Legends and Lyrics (London; Boston and London, 1892). He uses the same subheading with almost the same inclusions in 1908 in *The Collected Works* I. In 1913 in the Tauchnitz edition of *A Selection from the Poetry of W. B. Yeats* (Leipzig) he modifies the subheading to "Early Poems (1885–1892)" and includes under it thirteen lyrics from the 1889 and 1892 volumes; later in the same year in *A Selection from the Love Poetry of William Butler Yeats* (The Cuala Press, Dundrum, Ireland) the subheading is again modified, this time to "Early Poems 1890–1892": the contents are four lyrics from the 1892 volume. In 1921 in *Selected Poems* (New York) the heading and the number of poems are the same as in the Tauchnitz edition but with some variation in the selection. In 1925, in the title of the volume *Early Poems and Stories* (London; New York), he uses the words for the last time; there is a slight shift in the inclusions but they are practically the same as in *The Poetical Works* I (1906). From here to the definitive edition of 1949 these early poems with the exception of "The Wanderings of Oisin" are called "Crossways" and "The Rose," descriptive titles Yeats had originally used when he took the shorter poems from the volumes of 1889 and 1892 and published them in *Poems* (1895). Apparently, then, Yeats thought of his early poetry as that written up to 1892. For he could, in 1906, have included *The Wind Among the Reeds* (1899) and *In the Seven Woods* (The Dun Emer Press, Dundrum, Ireland, 1903) among his "early" poems. And although by 1925 critical opinion was already dividing his work at this date or that date, Yeats stuck to his own division.

The term "later poems" he uses, and by using defines, just once: as the title of the 1922 *Later Poems,* that includes verse from the following volumes: *The Wind Among the Reeds* (1899), *In the Seven Woods* (1903), *Poems 1899–1905* (London and Dublin, 1906), *The Green Helmet and Other Poems* (New York and London, 1912), *Responsibilities* (London; New York, 1916), *The Wild Swans at Coole* (London; New York, 1919), and *Michael Robartes and the Dancer* (Cuala Press, Dundrum, 1921). The line of demarcation seems clear.

But having decided the dates of "early," the textual critic must next determine just what an early Yeats poem is: i.e., is it an early poem through all its revisions, or is it an early poem through only some of its revisions, or is it an early poem in only its first printing? Of the forty early poems, including "The Wanderings of Oisin," in the definitive edition there is not one that was not revised in greater or less degree. Eleven got their final polishing for the definitive edition of 1949, seventeen for *Collected Poems* (1933), four for *Selected Poems* (1929), three for the 1927 revision of *Poems* (1895), two for *Early Poems and Stories* (1925), one for the 1912 revision of *Poems* (1895), and two for the first edition of *Poems* (1895). Thirty-two of the forty were revised finally, then, from 1929 to 1939: the last ten years of Yeats's life. And, as a rule, the later the final polishing the heavier the revisions throughout. The problem becomes more complicated when we study an early poem like "The Ballad of the Foxhunter," published first in the magazine *East and West* for November 1889, then in *United Ireland* for 28 May 1892, then in *The Countess Kathleen*, etc. (September, 1892), then in *Poems* (1895), and so on. In discussing this poem, one critic speaks blithely of "the early version" and then proceeds to quote the first four stanzas of the version in *Poems* (1895). But this is the fourth version. He ignores the three earlier versions. Here are lines 5–8 as they appear in each of the versions up to 1895.

In the first, that in *East and West* (November 1889) they read:

> And of my servants some one go,
> Bring my brown hunter near,
> And lead him slowly to and fro,
> My Lollard old and dear.

In the second version (*United Ireland*, 28 May 1892) these become

> And some one from the stable bring
> My Dermot dear and brown,
> And lead him gently in a ring,
> And slowly up and down.

The third version (*The Countess Kathleen*, etc., September 1892)
is identical with the second; the fourth (*Poems*, 1895) changes
from the third:

> And some one from the stables bring
> My Dermot dear and brown,
> And lead him gently in a ring
> And gently up and down.

It will be noted that in line 5 "stable" has become "stables" and in
line 8 "slowly" has become "gently." One wonders by what magic
this last version, differing so markedly from the first version and
in degree from the second and third versions, becomes "the early
version."

The same difficulty is present in "The Madness of King Goll"
that likewise has several early versions: the first in *The Leisure
Hour* for September 1887, the second in *Poems and Ballads of
Young Ireland* (Dublin, 1888), the third in *The Wanderings of
Oisin*, etc. (1889), and the fourth, and except for minor changes
the final version, in *Poems* (1895). Each of the first three is extensively revised, yet we have a critic saying that "The Madness
of King Goll" was revised so thoroughly that the 1895 version is
practically a new poem, the implication of the context being that
there was but one earlier version. Another critic of Yeats's revisions,
in commenting on the line "And every mumbling old man said"
from the second version of the poem, remarks that the metre
exacts "an unnatural emphasis [on the word "old"]" and that
Yeats improved the metre for *Poems* (1895) by changing the line
to "And every ancient Ollave said." But in the first version this
line has a metre similar to the final metre: "And every whispering
Druid said."

There are other examples at hand, but these illustrate sufficiently
something of the problem inherent in the term "early poem" and
likewise the possible errors inherent in a study of "the early version" of a poem. To come back to my question, "What is an 'early
Yeats poem'?", I should answer it by saying that it is a poem written
originally before 1892. And immediately I should add that in any

discussion of such a poem the details of its early publication must be given and the exact printing date of any quotation.

Revisions of the early poems continued, as I said, right up to the end. It is not until the definitive edition, for example, that we can clear up the vexing question of whether line 39 in "The Song of the Happy Shepherd" should be "Rewarding in melodious guile" or "Rewording in melodious guile." The textual history of the line is curious and provocative. In the first printing, in *The Dublin University Review* for October 1885, and in successive printings up to the 1901 revision of *Poems* (1895), it was "Rewording." In the 1904 revision of *Poems* (1895) it became "Rewarding." In *The Poetical Works* I (1906) and *The Collected Works* I (1908) it is "Rewording." But in the 1908 revision of *Poems* (1895) and in all subsequent printings through *Collected Poems* (1933) it is "Rewarding." In the definitive edition it becomes "Rewording"— a reversion to the original word and concept. (I am aware that what sometimes seem to be reversions in an author's work are nothing more in fact than the careless use of an earlier edition as copy for a later edition, but the reversions discussed in this paper were, I believe, purposely made by Yeats and represent a rejection of his own revisions.) Another revision in the same edition is a punctuational change—again a reversion—in line 7 of "Ephemera," "When the poor tired child, Passion, falls asleep." In the first printing, *The Wanderings of Oisin*, etc. (1889), the terminal punctuation was a period; but in the next printing, *Poems* (1895), the period was replaced by a colon that remained through *Collected Poems* (1933). The colon shifts the implication of the next two lines: "How far away the stars seem, and how far / Is our first kiss, and ah, how old my heart!" In the definitive edition the period reappears.

He even revised, in the definitive edition, his spelling of certain Gaelic names. In "The Wanderings of Oisin," for instance, "Aed" becomes "Aedh," and "Blanid" becomes "Blanaid" (although the trade editions of 1950 and 1951 do not have the latter change[10]). He makes several slight punctuational revisions in the same poem; an example is the deletion of the terminal commas of lines 405 and 406, Book I. Here are lines 404–407 as they appear in all printings from *Poems* (1895) through *Collected Poems* (1950–51) except the definitive edition:

> He hears the storm in the chimney above,
> And bends to the fire and shakes with the cold,
> While his heart still dreams of battle and love,
> And the cry of the hounds on the hills of old.

And here they are in the definitive edition:

> He hears the storm in the chimney above,
> And bends to the fire and shakes with the cold
> While his heart still dreams of battle and love
> And the cry of the hounds on the hills of old.

Apparently Yeats felt that the elision of the commas after "cold" and "love" make the last three lines more clearly modify, rather than be in apposition with, the first line.

Collected Poems (1933), given frequently by textual critics as the source of numerous revisions, has actually not very many and they are not very extensive. Among them are the insertion of a comma after "last" in line 33 of "The Rose of Battle": "And when at last, defeated in His wars"; the hyphenation of "bean-rows" and "honey-bee" in line 3 of "The Lake Isle of Innisfree"; the final changing of "will" to "with" in "When You Are Old": "And loved your beauty with love false or true" [the printings oscillate between "with" and "will," the first "will,"[11] that displaces the original "with," being perhaps due to a misprint]; the substitution of "fear" for "fears" in line 6 of "Who Goes with Fergus?": "And brood on hopes and fear no more"—it had been "fears" from the first printing in 1892; and a change in the punctuation in line 13 of "The Two Trees": "There the Loves a circle go." This line, that Yeats first used in *Selected Poems* (1929), he originally punctuated "There the Loves—a circle—go." In 1933 he eliminated the dashes. In line 18, Book I, of "The Wanderings of Oisin," "Where passionate Maeve is stony-still;", that makes dubious sense without a hyphen between "stony" and "still," he hyphenates the phrase—another reversion, for it had been hyphenated in the first printing; and, also in "The Wanderings of Oisin," he changes the spellings of some of the Gaelic names. One of those changed is "Conhor" that becomes "Conchubar" and necessitates a rewording of line 80, book III, from "And the names of the demons whose hammers made armour for Conhor of old" to "And the name of the demon whose hammer made Conchubar's sword-blade of old."

Selected Poems (1929) includes thirteen of the shorter early poems and "The Wanderings of Oisin." Of the thirteen shorter poems, six are revised slightly. Two have major revisions, "The Man Who Dreamed of Faeryland" and "The Two Trees," revisions often credited to *Collected Poems* (1933). One critic strides in thus: "Yet in rewriting the poem ["The Man Who Dreamed of Faeryland"] for the 1933 *Collected Poems*. . . ." Our critic buttresses this surprising statement by boldly assigning the following versions of lines 41 and 42 to the 1901 revision of *Poems* (1895):

> Were not the worms that spired about his bones
> Proclaiming with a low and reedy cry . . .

and then says they were revised in 1933 to

> Did not the worms that spired about his bones
> Proclaim with that unwearied, reedy cry . . . .

He is almost right about line 41, but quite mixed up about line 42. In the original printing in *The National Observer* for 7 February 1891 the lines read:

> Were not the worms that spired about his bones
> A-telling with their low and reedy cry.

Line 41 stayed unchanged until *Selected Poems* (1929) when it was revised to "Did not the worms that spired about his bones": its final form. Line 42, however, went through several changes. The first was for its second printing, *The Book of the Rhymer's Club* (London, 1892), where it had a terminal comma added. It kept this form until *Early Poems and Stories* (1925) where it became "Proclaiming with a low and reedy cry," that was changed finally in *Selected Poems* to "Proclaim with that unwearied, reedy cry." The remaining revisions in the poem are likewise incorrectly assigned to 1933. We have lost four years in a poet's development.

(Incidentally, no comment is made on one of the most striking 1929 revisions: "That if a dancer stayed his hungry foot / It seemed the sun and moon were in the fruit" that replace "A Danaan fruitage makes a shower of moons, / And as it falls awakens leafy tunes.")

The extensive revisions in "The Two Trees" for *Selected Poems* are exemplified by the changes in lines 13–20. The original version of these lines that except for two unimportant punctuational changes lasted from its first printing in *The Countess Kathleen*, etc. (1892) through the final reprinting in 1929 of *Poems* (1895), reads,

> There, through bewildered branches, go
> Winged Loves borne on in gentle strife,
> Tossing and tossing to and fro
> The flaming circle of our life.
> When looking on their shaken hair,
> And dreaming how they dance and dart,
> Thine eyes grow full of tender care:
> Beloved, gaze in thine own heart.

Here is the revision for *Selected Poems*:

> There the Loves—a circle—go,
> The flaming circle of our days,
> Gyring, spiring to and fro
> In those great ignorant leafy ways;
> Remembering all that shaken hair
> And how the wingèd sandals dart,
> Thine eyes grow full of tender care:
> Beloved, gaze in thine own heart.

becoming, I think, a clearer statement of the desirability-of-innocence theme so superbly expressed ten years earlier in "A Prayer for My Daughter."

For "The Wanderings of Oisin" there are fifty-two changes, forty-two of which are punctuational with seven of the forty-two changes being reversions. The remaining ten changes are word and phrase revisions, with five "maidens" becoming "ladies." One wonders whether to ascribe this to the years or better diction.

Revisions for *Early Poems and Stories* (1925) and for the 1927 edition of *Poems* (1895) are considerable, among others being "Fergus and the Druid," "A Cradle Song," "The Sorrow of Love," "The Lamentation of the Old Pensioner," and "To Ireland in the Coming Times" for the 1925 volume; "The Ballad of the Fox-hunter" and "The Countess Cathleen in Paradise," for the 1927 volume. "The Dedication to a Book of Stories selected from the Irish Novelists" was revised originally for its publication in *The Irish Statesman* for 8 November 1924; it was printed in *Early Poems and Stories* in its revised form. "Cuchulain's Fight with the Sea" has numerous revisions for both volumes; we might glance at these revisions, in particular the revised ending and some criticisms of it.

For *Early Poems and Stories* Yeats changed the title from "The Death of Cuchulain," deleted seven lines, and redid forty-two of the remaining eighty-six lines. For the 1927 *Poems* he deleted one line and redid twenty-two—ten of which he had just finished revising in 1925. Probably the most striking of the changes is the new ending of the poem, done for *Early Poems and Stories*. Here is the ending[12] Yeats revised:

> In three days' time, Cuchulain with a moan
> Stood up, and came to the long sands alone:
> For four days warred he with the bitter tide;
> And the waves flowed above him, and he died.

and here the revision:

> Cuchulain stirred,
> Stared on the horses of the sea, and heard
> The cars of battle and his own name cried;
> And fought with the invulnerable tide.

Criticism of the old vs. the new ending varies widely. We have this from one critic: "The second [ending] is fine too, but has not the same sense of water flowing on and on that is heard in the other. 'And the waves flowed above him and he died' hold the invulnerability of the sea, and the majesty . . . of death." But another writes that the new ending "transformed a mediocre poem into a work of quite extraordinary power." A third apparently thought both endings were the same: "The changes [in the revision of the entire poem] do not, however, concern the contents—apart from one small detail: the name Finmole has disappeared, . . ." A little textual reading, not studying, would have helped number three. Incidentally, I agree with the second critic—that the poem is transformed into a work of extraordinary power.

"The Lamentation of the Old Pensioner" was made over for the 1925 volume into an entirely new poem. This rewriting has been discussed again and again; so far as I know, however, no one has commented on the brilliantly bitter and savage satire in the mere use of the word "transfigure."[13]

Numerous other revisions of the early poems occur in the following volumes[14]—going back chronologically from 1925: the 1912 reprinting of *Poems* (1895), *The Collected Works* I (1908), the 1901 reprinting of *Poems* (1895), the 1899 reprinting of the same volume, the 1895 *Poems* itself, *The Countess Kathleen*, etc. (1892), and *The Wanderings of Oisin*, etc. (1889). The last two are listed because of the many changes Yeats made between initial periodical publication and publication in these first two volumes of his verse. There is, as I have implied, a tendency either to ignore the earliest changes or to be unaware of them and to assign the first revisions to *Poems* (1895).

I have emphasized by mention or discussion a number of the volumes for which the early poems were revised. A ranking of these volumes based on the number of revisions would show, in my opinion, *Poems* (1895) as easily the first, followed by *The Countess Kathleen*, etc. (1892), *The Wanderings of Oisin*, etc. (1889), the 1912 reprinting of *Poems* (1895), *Early Poems and Stories* (1925), the 1899 reprinting of *Poems* (1895), *The Collected Works* I (1908), the 1901 and the 1927 reprintings of *Poems* (1895) in that order, *Collected Poems* (1933), and *The Poems of W. B. Yeats* I (1949). A ranking based on the significance of the revisions would show *Poems* (1895) as again first, followed by the 1925, 1912, 1908, 1892, 1899, 1901, 1927, 1889, 1933, and 1949 volumes. *Selected Poems* (1929), despite its importance, is not listed because it includes less than half the early poems. I think my ranking of the order of significance would be authenticated by a detailed study, a study that I believe would likewise show that reversions in later printings of the early poems most often go back to the 1889 and 1908 volumes.

Before leaving the early poems I'd like to call attention to some of the lines that should have been revised. One example is lines 15 and 16 or "The Sad Shepherd": "But naught they heard, for they are always listening, / The dewdrops, for the sound of their own dropping."—almost unchanged in all printings; another is lines 5–8 in "The Falling of the Leaves," with its tongue-twisting line 6:

> The hour of the waning of love has beset us,
> And weary and worn are our sad souls now;
> Let us part, ere the season of passion forget us,
> With a kiss and a tear on thy drooping brow.

the third is lines 32 and 33 in Book 1 of the "Wanderings of Oisin," " 'Why do you wind no horn?' she said, / And every hero droop his head?"—a hackneyed rhythm "reminiscent," as Peter Allt once remarked to me, of " 'Shoot if you must this old grey head / But spare your country's flag,' she said."; and, as a last example, line 51 in the same book of the same poem, "Through bitter tide on foam-wet feet?" Yeats had a deal of trouble with this line. Finn is asking Niamh why she is paying a visit to his country. In *The Wanderings of Oisin*, etc. (1889) part of line 50 and line 51 read:

> Young maiden, what may bring
> Thy wandering steps across the sea?

In *Poems* (1895) this becomes

> What may bring
> To this dim shore those gentle feet?

In the 1899 revision of *Poems* (1895) 50 and 51 are

> What dream came with you that you came
> To this dim shore on foam wet feet?

Fifty remained the same, but fifty-one received its final form in *Early Poems and Stories* (1925):

> Through bitter tide on foam-wet feet?

Part of Niamh's answer—lines 57–59, in the final form they got in the 1912 revision of *Poems* (1895)—is perhaps even worse,

> . . ., these four feet [of her horse]
> Ran through the foam and ran to this
> That I might have your son to kiss.

The later poems, using Yeats's own division, include everything from *The Wind Among the Reeds* (1899) to *Last Poems and Plays* (London; New York, 1940), a total of 346 poems. The observations made and the conclusions reached about any textual study of the early poems are likewise applicable to the later poems. This is borne out by the incidental references I have made so far to the texts of a few of the later poems.

Beginning in 1903 a new textual source, the Dun Emer press, after 1907 called the Cuala press, comes into the picture. The Dun Emer press was started by Yeats's sister Elizabeth. Yeats himself took an active part in its work and for some years chose and edited the books it issued as well as having most of his own poems, beginning with *In the Seven Woods* (1903), printed by it. As a matter of statistics, there are 308 poems in the definitive edition that date from 1903 to January 1939; of these 264 are in Dun Emer-Cuala books and of that number 94 are first printings.

Because of Yeats's close supervision of the Cuala press books, one might be led to believe that here is a textual source more important than others, and that here if anywhere would be a finality not found in other printings. But not so; the Cuala press printing of a poem is not on that account likely to show more permanence than any other printing of a poem.

But apparently the magic of the words "Cuala Press" indicated to at least one critic that if a Yeats poem was printed in a Cuala press edition the poem would never again be changed. So in discussing "Broken Dreams" and "The Second Coming" from "the 1918 and the 1920 volumes, . . . *The Wild Swans at Coole* and *Michael Robartes and the Dancer*," he gives these two Cuala press volumes as the sources for his quotations from the two poems. But in both cases he quotes 1933 versions. This is not too serious for "Broken Dreams" where the changes are minor, but it is rather disastrous for "The Second Coming." The version of that poem in *Michael Robartes and the Dancer* has, as lines 13 and 17,

> Troubles my sight: a waste of desert sand; . . .
> Wind shadows of the indignant desert birds.

Whereas we are told they read

> Troubles my sight: somewhere in sands of the desert . . .
> Reel shadows of the indignant desert birds.

Hence by an assumption of the inviolability of a Cuala press printing the chance of commenting on two of Yeats's most brilliant changes is lost: of pointing out, for instance, how "somewhere in sands of the desert" brings into the poem a sense of the vastness and desolation of "the lone and level sands" stretching "far away"; and how "Reel" for "Wind" expresses far more effectively the bewildered terror of the desert birds. These revisions in "The Second Coming" were actually made for *Later Poems* (1922) and were retained to the end, but because when he quotes the poem our critic italicizes "Spiritus Mundi" in line 12 it is evident that he used the 1933 version where the italicization first appears. (Incidentally, there was no "1918" *Wild Swans at Coole;* the Cuala edition was 1917 and the trade edition 1919. The colophon in the Cuala edition of *Michael Robartes and the Dancer* says it was finished on All Soul's Day, 1920, the title page reads 1921.)

I have indicated that just as we are in trouble with the careless use of the phrase "early poem," so with the phrase "later poem." Here, for example, we have one of Yeats's biographers talking about the poems in *In the Seven Woods* (1903) and saying that "The first, and perhaps the finest poem in the new 'middle-aged' group, was 'The Folly of Being Comforted'," and he then cites lines 7–14 of, presumably, the 1903 version of that poem, but actually of the 1933 version that except for one minor change made for the definitive edition is the final version. Now textually, he could hardly have picked a more difficult poem than "The Folly of Being Comforted." From its publication in *The Speaker* for 11 January 1902, down through the definitive edition, there are 36 changes in the publicized versions and a complete shift of meaning in lines 8–11,—

a shift that appears first in the Tauchnitz *A Selection from the Poetry of W. B. Yeats* (1913) and is completed in *Collected Poems* (1933). Lines 8–11, in the 1903 Dun Emer and trade editions of *In the Seven Woods*, were

> Time can but make her beauty over again
> Because of that great nobleness of hers;
> The fire that stirs about her, when she stirs
> Burns but more clearly;

The terminal semi-colon at line 9 makes that line modify line 8; the comma after "her" in line 10 makes the remainder of that line and line 11 modify the first part of line 10. In 1913, after some intermediate and relatively unimportant changes, the punctuation was changed significantly:

> Time can but make her beauty over again;
> Because of that great nobleness of hers
> The fire that stirs about her, when she stirs
> Burns but more clearly.

Now line 8 stands by itself, line 9 modifies lines 10 and 11, and there is a specific meaning in lines 10 and 11. The next significant change was for *Later Poems* (1922) where a colon replaces the semi-colon in line 8; the last was for the 1933 printing where a terminal comma after "stirs," in line 10, finally gave Yeats, it would seem, the meaning or meanings he wanted. It is this 1933 version that we are presented with as the 1903 version: proof that when a "later" as well as an "early" Yeats poem is discussed and quoted the exact printing date of the quotation must be given and pertinent facts from the poem's printing history.

   The more important revision volumes for the later poems are *The Wind Among the Reeds* (1899)—on the basis of the many revisions from initial magazine printings; *Poems 1899–1905* (1906); *The Green Helmet and Other Poems* (1912); *Responsibilities* (1916); *Later Poems* (1922); *The Tower* (London; New York, 1928); *The Winding Stair and Other Poems* (London; New York, 1933); *Collected Poems* (1933); and *A Full Moon in March* (London, 1935). It would be misleading to list these volumes in an order based either on number or significance of revisions, for in only two of them, *Later Poems* and *Collected Poems,* are more than a handful of the later poems printed or reprinted. As a matter of fact, the later poems in their entirety appear only in the definitive edition of 1949 and the trade editions of 1950 and 1951.

These, then, are some of the textual facts and problems the student of Yeats must deal with. There are others: for instance, the existence of one version of a poem in the prose works and another version in the poetry volumes, examples being "The Moods," "Into the Twilight," and "The Happy Townland";[15] or the scores of title changes Yeats made;[16] or the changes made for, apparently, the sake of the rhythm only: "They'd mauled and bitten the night through" to "They mauled and bit the whole night through";[17] or "They'll cough in the ink to the world's end," to "All shuffle there; all cough in ink."[18]

Finally, two amusing revisions, the second probably a misprint.

In the first printing of the poem "Lullaby" in *The New Keepsake* (London, 1931) lines 3–6 read

> What are all the world's alarms?
> What were they when Paris found
> Sleep upon a golden bed
> That first dawn in Helen's arms?

As revised for its next printing in *Words for Music Perhaps and Other Poems* (Cuala Press, Dublin, 1932) they become

> What were all the world's alarms
> To mighty Paris when he found
> Sleep upon a golden bed
> That first night in Helen's arms?

In the succeeding printing, *The Winding Stair and Other Poems* (1933), line six reverts to

> That first dawn in Helen's arms?

and remains so.

The second, the probable misprint, concerns line 36 of "Adam's Curse": "To love you in the old high way of love." In three of the printings, *The Gael* (February, 1903),[19] *The Poetical Works* I (1906), and *Selected Poems* (1921) the words "high" and "way" have been joined, and the line reads "To love you in the old highway of love."

I give these two revisions to the Freudians "for free."

N O T E S

1. *Twenty-five Years: Reminiscences* (1913), and *The Middle Years* (1916).

2. *Letters on Poetry from W. B. Yeats to Dorothy Wellesley* (1940).

3. Allan Wade, *The Letters of W. B. Yeats* (1954), p. 598.

4. *The Collected Works in Verse and Prose of William Butler Yeats* (8 vols., Stratford-on-Avon, 1908), II. [viii].

5. (London).

6. *The Collected Poems of W. B. Yeats* (London; New York: 1933).

7. Marion Witt, "A Competition for Eternity: Yeats's Revision of His Later Poems," *PMLA*, LXIV (1949), 40–58.

8. A correspondent has informed me that he has seen a sixth edition with an American imprint on the verso of the title page. I have seen only the London edition.

9. *The Poetical Works of William B. Yeats* (2 vols., New York, 1906). Vol. I, Lyrical Poems; vol. II, Dramatical Poems.

10. *The Collected Poems of W. B. Yeats* (London, 1950), p. 437; (New York, 1951), p. 374.

11. In the 1912 revision of *Poems* (1895). The "will" remains in the 1913, 1919, 1920, 1922 (2), 1923, and 1924 reprintings of *Poems* (1895); in *Early Poems and Stories* (1925); in the first two printings of *The Augustan Books of English Poetry/W. B. Yeats* (London, 1927, 1928); and in the first three printings of *Selected Poems* (London, 1929, 1930, 1932). But in *A Selection from the Love Poetry*, etc. (1913) and in *Selected Poems* (1921) it is "with."

12. Except for minor altering these lines had not been changed from their original form in *United Ireland*, 11 June 1892, until the major revision discussed here.

13. I refer, of course, to the last line of the three stanzas in the rewritten version: "Ere Time transfigured me" at the end of the first stanza, and "That has transfigured me" at the end of the second and third stanzas.

14. There were revisions for all the volumes in which the early

poems were printed; those volumes I mention were the more extensively revised.

15. "The Moods." Originally in *The Bookman* (August 1893). With minor changes, and no title, reprinted in *The Celtic Twilight* (London, December 1893; New York, 1894), in the revised *The Celtic Twilight* (London; New York: 1902; rptd. London and Stratford-upon-Avon, 1911), and in *The Collected Works* V (1908). But for *The Wind Among the Reeds* (1899) the title was restored, marked changes were made in several lines, and in this form it was printed in *The Poetical Works* I (1906), *The Collected Works* I (1908), and so on through the definitive edition. "Into the Twilight." Originally in *The National Observer* (29 July 1893) entitled "The Celtic Twilight." With a new title "Into the Twilight" and minor changes reprinted in *The Celtic Twilight* (1893,1894), in the revised *The Celtic Twilight* (1902, rptd 1911), in *The Collected Works* V (1908), and in *Early Poems and Stories* (1925). In the course of these printings a few additional changes were made. But for *The Wind Among the Reeds* (1899) marked changes were made . . . . [The remainder of this note is the same as that for "The Moods."]

"The Happy Townland." Originally in *The Weekly Critical Review*, June 1903; then with a new title "The Rider from the North" in *In the Seven Woods* (1903); with the original title restored, in *Poems, 1899–1905* (1906), and so on through the definitive edition. But for *The Collected Works* V (1908), *Stories of Red Hanrahan* (London and Stratford-upon-Avon; New York: 1913), *Early Poems and Stories* (1925), and *Stories of Red Hanrahan* (London, 1927) lines 1–12, much changed, are in the story "The Twisting of the Rope," and lines 1–32 and 41–60, with the same changes in lines 1–12 but the other lines unchanged, are in the story "Hanrahan's Vision."

16. See Witt, *op. cit.*, for a brief discussion of title changes in the later poems.

17. From "The Three Beggars." The earlier version of the line is in the first three printings: *Harper's Weekly* (15 November 1913), *Responsibilities* (Cuala Press, 1914), and *Responsibilities* (London; New York: 1916); the later and final version begins with the fourth printing: *Later Poems* (1922).

18. From "The Scholars." The original version of lines 7–10 that lasted from their first printing in the *Catholic Anthology* (1914–1915) (London, 1915) through the 1926 revision of *Later Poems* (1922) are

> They'll cough in the ink to the world's end;
> Wear out the carpet with their shoes
> Earning respect; have no strange friend;
> If they have sinned nobody knows:

The revised version, first in *Selected Poems* (1929), is

> All shuffle there; all cough in ink;
> All wear the carpet with their shoes;
> All think what other people think;
> All know the man their neighbour knows.

19. A magazine published in New York 1881–1904 and October 1923–May 1924.

HARRY M. GEDULD

Back to Methuselah:

Textual Problems in Shaw

HARRY M. GEDULD *emphasizes how modern drama has been neglected by textual critics. He reveals the bibliographical complexities of* Back to Methuselah—*compounded by Shaw's position as his own publisher—and suggests several fascinating problems that await the serious editor of Shaw. His evidence leads one to share his doubt that "there exists a reliable 'standard edition' of any of Shaw's works" and his distrust of the "textual reliability of the editions of all other extensively-published modern dramatists."*

IGNORANCE OF or indifference to the problems of machine-printed books has sharply declined in recent years. So far, poetry and the novel have been the main beneficiaries of this new focus of scholarship, exemplified in the variorum Yeats and the volumes of the Center for Editions of American Authors. However, drama remains neglected for the most part. Such indifference to the textual problems of modern drama is as unwarrantable as was the earlier and more general indifference to the textual problems of machine-printed books. For the range of variants, the complexities of textual transmission, and the resulting corruption are no less extensive in the play than in the poem and the novel, and thus knowledge of the bibliographical problems involved is no less fundamental to critical interpretation of the play.

In 1960, in preparation for a variorum edition of Shaw's "Meta-biological Pentateuch," I completed a study of all available texts of *Back to Methuselah*. My conclusion, based on the collation of twenty-three editions and a study of much secondary evidence, is that there is no reliable "standard edition" of this work, and I shall provide here, in summary, evidence to support my conclusion. This evidence should in turn lead us not only to doubt whether there exists a reliable "standard edition" of any of Shaw's works, but also to suspect the textual reliability of the editions of all other extensively-published modern dramatists. Hopefully, therefore, the problems encountered in the study of *Back to Methuselah* will highlight the need for careful study of other machine-printed plays. But in advance of that study it is fair to guess that virtually all the most commonly used play texts are in need of re-editing. It should be emphasized that my evidence here is basically biblio-graphical and must therefore be considered preparatory to the editorial work that should be undertaken.

The need for a variorum edition of Shaw was discussed at the Second MLA Conference on Shaw in 1960.[1] Several scholars main-tained that it would probably be best to defer a variorum edition as premature. But it is surely pertinent to question when—if ever—the time will be ripe for critically edited texts. Shakespeare's text had to wait three hundred years. Are we to set aside the text of Shaw for scholars of the twenty-third century? Now it seems to me that before our critics can proceed reliably, we should expect them to know exactly what Shaw wrote, or what he intended to write, or both, and the extent and nature of his revisions. Whole libraries of conjecture (and doubtless many graduate seminars) would have been avoided if one of Shakespeare's contemporaries had attempted a critical edition of *Hamlet*, indicating the extent to which the first quarto is dependent on the *Ur-Hamlet*. Unfor-tunately, there were no Elizabethan textual scholars concerned with the works of William Shakespeare.

Shaw scholars may find food for thought in the fact that there is no library which possesses all the editions of Shaw's work published during his lifetime. Many librarians think it superfluous for a library to possess more than one edition (often the latest) of a "modern work." It took me more than three years to buy, borrow, or obtain access to the many texts of *Back to Methuselah* that I collated for my variorum. Some of these editions and impressions were not obtainable in any library (for a variety of reasons, including the fact that they were "paper-bound reprints" or "foreign editions"), but they were almost all of significance in tracing the transmission of the text. Presumably the accessibility of texts will not become easier with the passing of years. Indeed, I believe that only the most diligent scholar could now obtain all the editions of *Pygmalion* and *Saint Joan* published in Shaw's lifetime.

The first public announcement of *Back to Methuselah* appeared in *The Times* of London for 28 May 1920; it was evident from this report that Shaw had completed his manuscript of the play on the 27th:

> Mr. Bernard Shaw, speaking at Croydon last night, said that that day he had finished a new play, "or rather," he added, "it is really a series of five separate plays. I have been struggling with them for a very long time past, and it has been a great relief to me to write the final words."[2]

In accordance with his usual custom, Shaw began work on the Preface after completing the play. This part of the work was finished in Ireland, and the entire manuscript was typed and sent to the printers, R. & R. Clark of Edinburgh, by 15 September 1920.[3]

Shaw was his own publisher, but during the twentieth century most of his books were issued by Constable and Company, Ltd., in London. Instructions for printing were sent by Shaw directly to his printers—not through Constable's office. He dealt "personally with printer and binder . . . paying direct for the paper, setting up of type, machining and binding work. . . . The wide range of Shaw's knowledge included a very fair acquaintance with the different sorts of type."[4] During his lifetime, Shaw himself always retained complete control of the British printing and publishing arrangements involving his work.[5]

For the first British edition of *Back to Methuselah* he adhered to the book design he had selected for himself in 1897. R. & R. Clark were instructed to print the work as a "Green Cloth" edition, in typefounder's Caslon, long primer solid with even roman small caps, lower case italics with square brackets, and occasional lower case roman words letter-spaced. Shaw liked the use of very black printing ink, and he aimed at blocks of letterpress without the obvious intrusion of rivulets of white page into the text.[6] The book was to have a Green Cloth binding in conformity with the other volumes of Shaw's plays that had been issued by Constable.

First proofs were ready by November 1920,[7] but unfortunately the proofs corrected by Shaw are no longer extant.[8] However, J. Shand noticed that "Shaw's first proof corrections are often heavy, sometimes involving considerable re-setting and re-make-up."[9] After the first proofs had been corrected, a second set was prepared —by late December 1920 in the case of *Back to Methuselah*. "In a second proof . . . he could not have been more considerate, calculating the exact number of words, or even letters, to balance further cuts" (Patch, pp. 49–50). When Shaw had revised the second proofs they were passed for the press. All revisions before the final proofs had been passed were the concern only of Shaw, his secretary, and his printers, for as he explained to Lawrence Langner of the Theatre Guild, "if you once let an imperfect text loose, you can never overtake it and I always have to destroy my unused proofs with the greatest care . . ." (Langner, p. 34).

Back to Methuselah was first published on 23 June 1921. There is now no evidence that a rehearsal copy of *Back to Methuselah* was ever printed,[10] and all the proofs in the possession of Shaw's printers were reportedly destroyed by enemy action in World War II. Our consideration of the textual transmission of *Back to Methuselah* must therefore begin with the first impression of the Brentano edition, printed May 1921 in the United States, and with the first impression of the Constable Green Cloth edition (1921). Despite minor corruptions in the Brentano text, it is evident from a full collation that it was set from the same proofs as were used for the first impression of the Constable Green Cloth edition. The corruptions in the American edition, which were entirely due to the carelessness of the printer, are carefully listed by Shaw himself in a pencilled note preserved in the Hanley Collection at the University of Texas. Several of the corruptions are spelling errors (e.g., "parisitic" at xiii.31); others appear to be the result of misreading the final proofs (e.g., "pretty" at xxxvii.7).[11] But in other respects the texts are identical.[12]

After the first impression had been published, Shaw began revising the text of the Green Cloth edition. Thus commenced a process of revision that was to continue until Shaw's death in 1950.

The various changes introduced in the second and third impressions of the Green Cloth edition (1922 and 1926) are retained in all later texts. These involve minor changes of five different kinds:

1. Simple corrections (e.g., correction of Darwin's age: see xxx.21)
2. Stylistic improvements (cf. first and second impressions at lxxxiii.12–15)
3. Changes aiming at greater precision in fact or detail (cf. first and second impressions at xliv.26–27)
4. Abridgement (cf. first and second impressions at xxix.20)
5. Softening or eliminating material—perhaps in response to adverse criticism which Shaw considered justified (cf. first and second impressions at xxix.8–16).

Subsequent impressions of the Green Cloth edition in 1927, 1928, and 1929 went unrevised, and this Green Cloth text of 1926 was the basis of the Globe edition (1926) and all impressions of the Constable Pocket Edition (1926).

In the late 1920's William Maxwell, Clark's master-printer, informed Shaw that the plates for the Green Cloth edition were wearing out. He suggested the printing of a new Standard Edition in large crown octavo. About this time Shaw was also considering the printing of a Limited Collected Edition of his works in medium octavo—a larger page than the new Standard Edition. Shaw, influenced by the work of William Morris, at first insisted on hand-setting for the Limited Collected Edition; but when Maxwell showed him two specimen pages, one hand-set and one in Monotype Caslon, Shaw instantly preferred the typographical quality of the machine-set page.[13] The Limited Collected Edition was printed in Monotype Caslon pica solid and was published by Constable on 22 September 1930; *Back to Methuselah* was volume sixteen. In the new Standard Edition the typefounder's Caslon of the Green Cloth edition was abandoned in favor of small pica Fournier 1½-points leaded. And because Shaw had been disappointed by the fading of the old Green Cloth bindings, fadeless red Sundour binding was used for the Standard Edition. *Back to Methuselah* in the Standard Edition was first published by Constable on 5 November 1931.

Final proofs of the Limited Collected Edition are preserved in the study at Shaw's Corner, Ayot Saint Lawrence. A set of these proofs was despatched to the Wm. H. Wise Company in the United States to be used for setting the Ayot Saint Lawrence edition,[14] in which *Back to Methuselah* was volume sixteen. The differences between the texts of the Limited Collected Edition and the Ayot Saint Lawrence edition amount to six or seven minutiae of punctuation and two or three corrections of spelling. Again we have a repetition of circumstances that accounted for the differences between the American and British editions in 1921. The Dodd, Mead edition of 1949 is the only text that derives from the Ayot Saint Lawrence edition. But the Limited Collected Edition provided the basic text for the Standard Edition (1931), the *Complete Plays* (1934), the *Prefaces* (1934), the Limited Editions Club edition (1939), and the Penguin editions of 1939–40 and 1954. It is also the text that was revised for the World's Classics edition (1945) and the Galaxy (American) edition of 1947.

In the Limited Collected Edition of 1930, Shaw incorporated the dialogue for Part V of the play (209.9–34) which he had originally written for the Birmingham Repertory production of 1923. These lines substituted for about ten lines of stage direction that appear in every edition of the play before 1930. Much later, in 1949, Shaw further corrected the text of the Standard Edition which was then issued in two states: with the Postscript and without it.

Shaw introduced only minor revisions into the text of the Limited Collected Edition of 1930 when he prepared the Limited Editions Club edition in 1939 (e.g., compare lxxv.7–15 in the two texts). However, this last is the only illustrated edition of *Back to Methuselah*, and its wood engravings were done by John Farleigh working under the direction of Shaw.[15] The edition was designed by Edward Alonzo Miller and printed at the Marchbanks Press in New York. The fifteen hundred signed and numbered copies of the edition were for sale only to members of the Limited Editions Club.[16]

In the Limited Collected Edition of 1930, Shaw incorporated Press to select one of his works for publication as number 500 in the World's Classics series. Shaw's choice was *Back to Methuselah*, for as he tells us at the end of the Postscript, "Back to Methuselah is a world classic or it is nothing." Apart from providing the World's Classics edition with a Postscript, Shaw undertook a substantial revision of the entire text. Most of the changes were made in the Preface, reducing it from approximately 28,500 words to about 22,500. The revisions involve additions and substitutions as well as excisions on practically every page of the text of the Preface. They affect the text as follows:

1. Minor punctuation variants
2. Minor grammatical corrections (e.g., "or" becomes "nor" at xxiii.21)
3. Replacing foreign words with English equivalents (e.g., "*de rigueur*" becomes "held obligatory" at lxxxiii.34)
4. Omission of additional examples and of remarks about them (e.g., compare the revised text with lxxvii.15–16)
5. Abridgement by removing an entire section (e.g., lv.11–lvi.24)
6. Abridgement by partially removing and adapting the remainder of a passage (e.g., x.34–xi.13; xlv.13)
7. Abridgement by omitting a sentence, a phrase, part of a sentence, or a single word (e.g., compare the revised text with lviii.13)
8. Abridgement by using a briefer alternative word or expression (e.g., "evaporated" for "vanished almost unnoticed" at lxvi.7–8; also compare the revised text with xli.12)
9. Elaboration of the text by additions (e.g., compare the revised text with xiv.19, lviii.22, and lxxv.5)

10. Addition of new examples or references (e.g., compare the revised text with xviii.1–xix.19)

11. Additions to clarify allusions that may have become obscured by the passage of time (e.g., compare the revised text with xxxvii.1–2)

12. Changes introduced to improve the style (e.g., compare the revised text with lix.33–lx.9)

13. Changes to secure greater fairness (e.g., "Ulster man" becomes "The Belfast Orangeman" at lxxv.24–25)

14. Clarification or intensification of matter related to ideas that were uppermost in Shaw's mind during 1944, when the text was revised (e.g., compare the revised text with lxxii.8–9, and see further Shaw's *Everybody's Political What's What?* [1944], p. 352)

15. Softening severe criticism of specified individuals (e.g., compare the revised text with xvi.26)

16. Shifting attacks from people to institutions (compare the revised text with xii.6) or from the philosopher to his philosophy (lxix.30–31).

17. Generalized criticism becoming specified (e.g., "blockheads" become "laboratory workers" at xxix.20–21)

18. Modernization because of "material progress" since 1921 (e.g., lxix.30–31), because of the changed rank of individuals (e.g., Bernard Partridge becomes Sir Bernard Partridge at xxv.27), or because of the death of a person (e.g., xxv.33).

Because of Shaw's many revisions and because he himself permitted the re-issue of the so-called Standard Edition in 1949 after the publication of his revised World's Classics text, there is no authorized, definitive text of *Back to Methuselah* (nor, one suspects, of most of his other works). To create such a text for *Back to Methuselah* the editor will have to resolve questions of the kind posed by the World's Classics and Standard Edition texts at 51.10–11 and 177.27–35.

At 51.10–11 Burge speaks of "doing something or other to keep the Irish quiet." The World's Classics text amplifies this to "doing whatever is necessary to keep Ireland and India quiet." The second reading undoubtedly updates the text, but it gives to Burge in the

1920's an implausible (and out-of-character) foresight in imperialist politics that is Shaw's hindsight in 1944. Would it therefore be advisable to reject the World's Classics reading here? At 177.27–35 appears a prophecy which anticipates the survival of the military and the destruction of seven capital cities in Europe by intensive bombing and poison gas. The World's Classics text alters the prophecy to the "capital cities of the world were wiped out of existence. . . ." Shaw's hindsight has not produced a text that is historically more accurate. Poison gas did not destroy civilian populations in World War II nor were all the capital cities of the world wiped out. On the other hand, Shaw's anticipations about warfare, and especially the role of the airplane and poison gas, are lost. Of a different order of relevance is the likelihood that this abridgement was intended to accommodate *Back to Methuselah* to the inflexible World's Classics format. The editor will have to decide here between different kinds of authorial intentions.

For critics of Shaw the "moral" of the textual history of *Back to Methuselah* is that you cannot trust Shaw to provide a standard edition—even when he tells you that he is providing one. Whatever he changed, he changed silently (as in the texts of *Back to Methuselah*), and as he was his own publisher the opportunities for revision were unlimited. Thus, in the absence of a critically edited Shaw, every text must be suspect, and hence one cannot offer critical commentary on a Shavian work with absolute conviction that the text quoted represents exactly what Shaw finally intended to be read.

There is, it seems to me, a discernible Shavian "philosophy" of textual revision, and this philosophy actually runs counter to what Shaw himself asserted in his Preface to *The Sanity of Art* (London, 1895): "The writer who aims at producing the platitudes which are 'not for an age, but for all time' has his reward in being unreadable in all ages. . . . I also am a journalist, proud of it, deliberately cutting out of my works all that is not journalism, convinced that nothing that is not journalism will live long as literature, or be of any use whilst it does live." In fact, the World's Classics edition of *Back to Methuselah* amply demonstrates that Shaw revised his work with the intention of establishing a text that would outlive his own age: hence his itch to alter material that seemed to have "dated" factually or in emphasis or to have become obscure with the passing of time. Hence also Shaw's growing respect for the feelings and reputations of individuals and his corresponding insensitivity towards institutions and categories of people. For when he softened or eliminated criticism of specific persons, he was in effect de-emphasizing topicality—especially those details that in fifty or a hundred years might require footnotes to be intelligible. And, undoubtedly, he considered "continuing intelligibility" a prime requisite for *Back to Methuselah*, his "gospel of the coming century."

NOTES

1. See "Bernard Shaw—Ten Years After (1950–1960)," *The Shaw Review*, IV, no. 2 (1961), 29–32.

2. P. 10; see also *The Croydon Times*, 29 May 1920, p. 5.

3. See Shaw's letter of this date to Siegfried Trebitsch, in the Berg Collection, New York Public Library.

4. Blanche Patch, *Thirty Years with G.B.S.* (London, 1951), pp. 48–49.

5. Information supplied to the author of this article by Messrs. R. & R. Clark and Messrs. Constable and Company, Ltd.

6. Shaw's ideal letterpress is to be seen in the Constable Standard Edition of *The Intelligent Woman's Guide* (London, 1928).

7. See Shaw's letter to Graham Wallas, 15 Nov. 1920, in the London School of Economics Library.

8. One uncorrected set survives. This is the set despatched by Shaw to Lawrence Langner of the Theatre Guild of New York. Shaw requested Langner to destroy or return these proofs after the Theatre Guild had considered the play for possible production. Langner did neither; see his *The Magic Curtain* (New York, 1952), p. 34. This set of proofs is now in the Theatre Guild Collection at Yale and is dated by the printer 24 Feb. 1921. The set is marked on the fly-title "In the Beginning," "Private and Confidential to Mr. Lawrence Langner."

9. See *Alphabet and Image*, VIII (1948), 22–23.

10. F. E. Loewenstein, Shaw's authorized bibliographer, did not in-

clude the work in his *The Rehearsal Copies of Bernard Shaw's Plays: A Bibliographical Study* (London, 1950).

11. Page and line references are to the second state of the third impression of the Constable Standard Edition (1949), the last complete text (i.e., with the Postscript) published in Shaw's lifetime.

12. The Tauchnitz edition of 1922 is based on the first impression of the Green Cloth edition.

13. See also *Alphabet and Image*, VIII (1948), 17–18.

14. 1,025 sets of the Limited Collected Edition and 1,790 sets of the Ayot Saint Lawrence edition were printed.

15. John Farleigh also illustrated Shaw's *The Adventures of the Black Girl in her Search for God* (1932). See further the Shaw-Farleigh correspondence in *The London Mercury*, March 1937, and Farleigh's *The Graven Image* (London, 1940), pp. 381–82.

16. All copies were signed by Farleigh. Later, Shaw signed a small number of these copies for friends.

JAMES B. MERIWETHER

Notes on the Textual History of

The Sound and the Fury

JAMES B. MERIWETHER *has published a number of more exclusively editorial studies, but none which more fully demonstrates the ways in which the history of composition and publication and other biographical data inform textual problems. Here is compelling evidence that contexts of fact condition interpretations of fiction.*

T HE PUBLISHING HISTORY of William Faulkner's novel *The Sound and the Fury* is not complex. The text of the original edition, published in 1929, was a careful and accurate one in most respects, and neither authorial revision nor an unusual amount of textual corruption appear to have occurred in any of the later editions and impressions in English.[1] Yet for several reasons *The Sound and the Fury* provides an opportunity for particularly useful textual study. The relationship between the novel and a commentary upon it which Faulkner wrote in 1945 has been often misunderstood, and the text of the most widely used edition is less reliable than it should be, and is commonly assumed to be—a matter of

Reprinted from *Papers of the Bibliographical Society of America*, LVI (1962), 285–316, with the permission of the author and the Bibliographical Society of America.

some importance, it would seem, though the corruption involved is minor, for a book which demands so close a reading as does *The Sound and the Fury*. Probably no twentieth-century American novel has elicited more intense critical analysis, and it is obvious that we need to know as much as possible about the text of a work where every italic, every capital, every point of punctuation may carry an important burden of meaning. Careful study of the broken time-sequence of the interior monologues in the first two of the book's four sections,[2] or of its much-disputed symbolism,[3] or of the complex, elliptical, densely textured style[4] must rest upon as firm a textual foundation as can be established. The purpose of this article is to assist the critical study of *The Sound and the Fury* by bringing together here certain information about its text, including details of its writing, of its publishing history, and of Faulkner's comments upon it.

Faulkner often referred to *The Sound and the Fury* as his own favorite among his books, the one which represented his most ambitious, uncompromising attempt at perfection in the novel, and the one which had moved him most in the writing.[5] (In the writing rather than in the reading. Faulkner was extremely reluctant to reread his books when they were finished, and it is possible that he never read *The Sound and the Fury* again after its original publication.[6]) The fourth of his novels, it was published 7 Oct. 1929[7] by Jonathan Cape and Harrison Smith in New York, approximately a year after Faulkner had finished it, perhaps a year and a half after it had been begun.

Since there has been conflicting testimony concerning the date when Faulkner wrote it[8] and what happened to the manuscript before it was accepted by Cape and Smith,[9] it is worthwhile to determine what we can about the prepublication history of *The Sound and the Fury*. Despite some confusion about the length of time involved in writing it, there is good reason to accept the statement that Faulkner at least twice made, that it took him six months. In answer to the question "How long does it take you to write a book?" he told a class at the University of Mississippi in 1947, according to a student who made careful notes, that the time varied—he wrote *As I Lay Dying* in six weeks, *The Sound and the Fury* in six months, and *Absalom, Absalom!* in three years.[10] Ten years later at the University of Virginia he said that the novel had been written in the six months between the spring and fall of 1928, and that it had been "finished in all the hooraw of Smith and Hoover in November."[11]

The time when the book was written was one when personal problems had placed him under severe strain, Faulkner told Maurice Edgar Coindreau in 1937,[12] and earlier he had noted that it was conceived at a period of crisis in his career as a writer too. His third novel, *Sartoris*, had been finished in the early fall of 1927,[13] but had been rejected by Boni and Liveright, publishers of his first two novels, with whom he had a three-book contract.[14] "I believed . . . that I would never be published again. I had stopped thinking of myself in publishing terms," Faulkner wrote in 1932 of his discouragement at the continued rejection of *Sartoris* by various publishers.[15] Under these circumstances he had written *The Sound and the Fury*—"written my guts" into it, he said, "though I was not aware until the book was published that I had done so, because I had done it for pleasure." About 1933 Faulkner recalled that "When I began it I had no plan at all. I wasn't even writing a book. I was thinking of books, publication, only in reverse, in saying to myself, I won't have to worry about publishers liking or not liking this at all." One day, he said, after *Sartoris* had been turned down again and again, "I seemed to shut a door between me and all publishers' addresses and book lists. I said to myself, Now I can write."[16]

Years later, Faulkner's old friend Phil Stone, the Oxford lawyer who was so close to him, and who did so much for him, during the first part of his career, recalled that Faulkner had told him nothing about *The Sound and the Fury* until it was finished. Although he had kept in close touch with Stone during the writing of *Sartoris*, Stone had not even known he was writing anything until the completion of *The Sound and the Fury*.[17] But afterward came the experience, still cherished by Stone, of sitting "night after night in Bill's little room in the little tower of the old Delta Psi chapter house" at the University of Mississippi while Faulkner read aloud *The Sound and the Fury* to him page by page.[18]

Presumably it was the original manuscript, not his later typescript, that Faulkner read to Stone in Mississippi, for it was in New York, in his friend (and literary agent) Ben Wasson's room on Macdougal Street, opposite the Provincetown Playhouse, that Faulkner completed typing the novel. According to Wasson, Faulkner brought the manuscript to New York and there typed the final version himself.[19] On the last page of the carbon which he bound and retained for his files, Faulkner added by hand, at the end of the typed text, the place and the date: "New York, N.Y. | October 1928."[20] Wasson recalls that when he finished it, Faulkner offered him the whole typescript with the words "Read this, Bud. It's a real sonofabitch."[21]

In addition to a carbon of his final typescript, Faulkner preserved among his papers a manuscript, lacking only one page of being complete.[22] As was his custom, he used thin sheets of legal-size paper, leaving a wide left-hand margin for corrections.[23] A page-by-page comparison, with spot collation, of manuscript, carbon typescript, and published book reveals that each version follows the previous one closely, though with a great deal of verbal polishing and minor revision from manuscript to typescript, and a certain amount of further polishing from typescript to published book. The manuscript itself gives evidence of very extensive rewriting, with many passages added, some canceled, and with its pagination revealing that many of the pages Faulkner preserved represent revisions and expansions of previous ones. Apparently the manuscript represents finished work, Faulkner not troubling to preserve anything prior to it. In typing it out in New York, Faulkner inevitably gave it a certain amount of revising, and at some point after this typing revised it yet further, producing the differences between the carbon typescript and the finished book either by later changes in the ribbon copy (which presumably went to the publisher and eventually became printer's setting copy) or by changes in the proofs.

One or more complete drafts, or none; extensive working notes, or none, may have preceded the extant manuscript but not have been preserved. For this particular novel, we might well suppose such measures a necessity; for this particular novelist, we may well assume that they were not.[24] In the case of another work in which there are complex dislocations of time, *A Fable*, we know that Faulkner used such notes, putting on the wall of his study a day-by-day chronology of the action of the novel.[25] But when in Japan in 1955 he was twice asked if he had worked from notes in writing the first section of *The Sound and the Fury*, he once ignored the question, once replied with a curt "No." We might be tempted to agree with the unbelief of the questioner who on that occasion stated, "I made a thorough study of the first section and I felt that it was humanly impossible to write it down from the very beginning without notes," and Faulkner did admit to his Japanese audience that he occasionally used such notes, throwing them away when he was through with them.[26] But lacking proof to the contrary it seems unwise to assume that Faulkner could not have constructed the novel in his head and set it down without working notes, even if he did not do so in the case of *A Fable*.[27]

If Faulkner "had no plan at all" when he sat down to write at this time, save the ambition to create for himself something moving and imperishable, he did have in mind when he began writing a basic image which was to dominate the work. This was "the picture of the little girl's [Caddy's] muddy drawers," as she climbed the pear tree to look in the window while her brothers waited below.[28] But Faulkner conceived it as a short story before it became a novel. As he said in Japan in 1955, it

began as a short story, it was a story without plot, of some children being sent away from the house during the grandmother's funeral . . . and then the idea struck me to see how much more I could have got out of the idea of the blind, self-centeredness of innocence, typified by children, if one of those children had been truly innocent, that is, an idiot. So the idiot was born and then I became interested in the relationship of the idiot to the world that he was in but would never be able to cope with and just where would he get the tenderness, the help, to shield him in his innocence. . . . And so the character of his sister began to emerge, then the brother, who . . . represented

complete evil . . . appeared. Then it needs the protagonist, someone
to tell the story, so Quentin appeared. By that time I found out I
couldn't possibly tell that in a short story. . . .

So the novel grew, Faukner said, with the three brothers each permitted to tell their version of the story, "and then I had to write
another section from the outside . . . to tell what had happened
on that particular day."[29]

When Faulkner showed the completed typescript of the novel to
Ben Wasson in the fall of 1928 he remarked that he did not expect
it to be published,[30] and it was in fact rejected by Harcourt, Brace.
But Harrison Smith, who as an editor at Harcourt, Brace had
been influential in the firm's decision to accept *Sartoris* earlier that
fall,[31] had in the meantime set up in the publishing business himself, and he decided to gamble upon the book, and its author,[32]
though he warned Faulkner when he accepted it that *The Sound
and the Fury* would not sell.[33]

The new firm of Cape and Smith published its first book, Evelyn Scott's Civil War novel *The Wave*, on 1 July 1929.[34] At about
that time Faulkner wrote from Pascagoula, Mississippi, a letter
about the proofs—presumably the galley proofs—of *The Sound
and the Fury*, which he had just corrected. His letter was in reply
to one from Wasson, who had joined the Cape and Smith staff as
an assistant editor,[35] and who seems to have made certain editorial
changes in the first section of the book which Faulkner, in correcting the proofs, had restored to his original readings.

Wasson had apparently copy edited the interior monologue of
Benjy, the idiot, which opens the book, in order to indicate the
breaks in time sequence by means of wider spacing between lines
in the text, instead of adhering to Faulkner's original system (which
appears in both the manuscript and the typescript he preserved) of
indicating these shifts by means of a change from roman to italic
type, or back from italic to roman. Wasson in his letter must have
argued that this was unsatisfactory because there were at least four
different times referred to in Benjy's section, for Faulkner replies
that his roman-to-italic-and-back system, far from being intended
to represent only two different dates, was simply meant to indicate to the reader that some sort of shift in time was occurring. He

PREFACE

« Ce roman, à l'origine, ne devait être qu'une nouvelle, me dit, un jour, William Faulkner. J'avais songé qu'il serait intéressant d'imaginer les pensées d'un groupe d'enfants, le jour de l'enterrement de leur grand'mère dont on leur a caché la mort, leur curiosité devant l'agitation de la maison, leurs efforts pour percer le mystère, les suppositions qui leur viennent à l'esprit. Ensuite, pour corser cette étude, j'ai conçu l'idée d'un être qui serait plus qu'un enfant, un être qui, pour résoudre le problème, n'aurait même pas à son service un cerveau normalement constitué, autrement dit un idiot. C'est ainsi que Benjy est né. Puis, il m'est arrivé ce qui arrive à bien des romanciers, je me suis épris d'un de mes personnages, Caddy. Je l'ai tant aimée que je n'ai pu me décider à ne la faire vivre que l'espace d'un conte. Elle meritait plus que cela. Et mon roman s'est achevé, je ne dirais pas malgré moi, mais presque. Il n'avait pas de titre jusqu'au jour où, de mon subconscient, surgirent les mots connus *The Sound and the Fury*. Et je les adoptai, sans réfléchir alors que le reste de la citation shakespearienne s'appliquait aussi bien, sinon mieux, à ma sombre histoire de folie et de haine. »

On lit en effet dans *Macbeth*, à la scène V de l'acte V, cette définition de la vie : « *It is a tale told by an idiot, full of sound and fury, signifying nothing* », « C'est une histoire, contée par un idiot, pleine de bruit et de fureur, qui ne signifie rien ». La première partie du roman de William Faulkner est, elle aussi, contée par un idiot le livre entier vibre de bruit et de

FIRST PAGE of Coindreau's preface to *Le bruit et la fureur*. [Reproduced by courtesy of M. Coindreau and of Gallimard.]

said that he could recall without difficulty far more than the four dates Wasson had noted, and added that a more important reason for rejecting the device of breaks in the text is that the breaks changed the pace too abruptly, whereas the surface of the narration should have continuity. Faulkner felt that the italics did a better job of indicating to the reader the superficially unbroken confusion of Benjy's mind; to establish this when breaks were used to indicate time changes, Faulkner said, he would have to write a separate beginning for each change.

Faulkner went on to say that he wished it were possible to print the section in different colors of ink to indicate time levels or time shifts, an argument he recalled making to Wasson and Smith on a former occasion. But at any rate, he said, he had to reject Wasson's device of the breaks, which was aesthetically displeasing because of its dullness and disjointedness. If a change had to be made in his original device, he felt it would be better to rewrite the first section in the third person, like the final section.

He warned Wasson not to add anything else to the text, noting that he had struck out the few examples present in the proofs. And in conclusion he returned to his justification for the device of italics in the first section, emphasizing again that he had not intended to indicate thereby any specific time, but simply a shift in time, letting the material of each scene imply its own date.[36]

It is obvious from this letter that Faulkner. a proud and in some ways supremely confident craftsman, was thoroughly aware of the difficulties in design and printing caused by his book, and it is interesting to see that he could entertain the idea of several radically different solutions to these problems in Benjy's section. His decisive rejection of the possibility of indicating the time shifts by breaks in the text is revealing. A writer who would admit the possibility of rewriting the whole section in the third person, or of writing a new induction or beginning to each new time sequence, can hardly be called inflexible in his thinking about the book, and his two reasons for rejecting the breaks in the text have important implications. His concern with book design appears both in his argument that the breaks in the type page were displeasing to the eye, and in his explanation that such a break would distort the impression he was trying to give of the real confusion of time in the idiot's mind, a confusion that Faulkner wanted to emphasize by the seeming continuity of his interior monologue. Such a concern is not surprising in an author who had several times during the past decade made up little booklets of his verse, fiction, or drama, doing all the illustrating, lettering, and binding himself.[37] One of them, "Mayday," has drawings in color by Faulkner, and though he early discovered that he wrote better than he drew,[38] and though he apparently never attempted to illustrate his serious mature work, he had a natural interest in the Blakean combination of picture and word, which helps explain his anxiety that the design in type of the Benjy section should match as closely as possible his conception of the idiot's associative thought processes. We can imagine that Faulkner deeply regretted the impossibility of achieving this by printing in colors, and since he proposed such differing alternative methods of handling the problem, we can imagine too his satisfaction when *The Sound and the Fury* eventually attained a certain degree of popular as well as critical success and so confirmed the validity of the method he had insisted upon in 1929. In 1955 he was asked his present opinion of his original idea of using ink of various colors, and he replied that his "original fear that the reader might need such a device seems not to have been valid," and that he now had "no desire to see the novel so printed."[39]

It would be extremely interesting to see a set of the galley proofs of the book, if a set were ever to turn up. Early in the letter to Wasson Faulkner states that he has made additions to the italics in the first section of the novel where the original seemed unclear upon rereading, and there are cryptic references later on in the letter to the necessity for repunctuating in the italic passages, and to inconsistencies in Wasson's changes. It seems possible that certain puzzling or inconsistent places in the published novel may be due to editorial changes which Faulkner overlooked, or corrected inconsistently, in the proofs.

What the first few proof sheets of the book looked like before Faulkner corrected them may be inferred from an examination of a printer's sample octavo gathering (title-page, copyright page, and first fourteen pages of text) for *The Sound and the Fury* now

"Wait a minute." Luster said. "You snagged on that nail again. Cant you never crawl through here without snagging on that nail."

Caddy uncaught me and we crawled through. Uncle Maury said to not let anybody see us, so we better stoop over, Caddy said. Stoop over, Benjy. Like this, see. We stooped over and crossed the garden, where the flowers rasped and rattled against us. The ground was hard. We climbed the fence, where the pigs were grunting and snuffing. I expect they're sorry because one of them got killed today, Caddy said. The ground was hard, churned and knotted.

Keep your hands in your pockets, Caddy said. Or they'll get froze. You dont want your hands froze on Christmas, do you.

"It's too cold out there." Versh said. "You dont want to go out doors."

" What is it now." Mother said.

" He want to go out doors." Versh said.

" Let him go." Uncle Maury said.

" It's too cold." Mother said. " He'd better stay in. Benjamin. Stop that, now."

" It wont hurt him." Uncle Maury said.

" You, Benjamin." Mother said. " If you dont be good, you'll have to go to the kitchen."

3

PAGE 3 of the sample gathering (1929) of *The Sound and the Fury*. [Reproduced by courtesy of Random House, Inc., and of the University of Texas.]

"Wait a minute." Luster said. "You snagged on that nail again. Cant you never crawl through here without snagging on that nail."

Caddy uncaught me and we crawled through. Uncle Maury said to not let anybody see us, so we better stoop over, Caddy said. Stoop over, Benjy. Like this, see. We stooped over and crossed the garden, where the flowers rasped and rattled against us. The ground was hard. We climbed the fence, where the pigs were grunting and snuffing. I expect they're sorry because one of them got killed today, Caddy said. The ground was hard, churned and knotted.

Keep your hands in your pockets, Caddy said. Or they'll get froze. You don't want your hands froze on Christmas, do you.

"It's too cold out there." Versh said. "You dont want to go out doors."

"What is it now." Mother said.

"He want to go out doors." Versh said.

"Let him go." Uncle Maury said.

"It's too cold." Mother said. "He'd better stay in. Benjamin. Stop that, now."

"It wont hurt him." Uncle Maury said.

"You, Benjamin." Mother said. "If you dont be good, you'll have to go to the kitchen."

"Mammy say keep him out the kitchen today." Versh said. "She say she got all that cooking to get done."

in the Faulkner Collection of the Humanities Research Center of the University of Texas. In the published book the first italic passage occurs on p. 3.[40] On p. 3 of the sample gathering the passage appears in roman type, leaded out to form a gap of between one and two lines' width at the beginning and ending of the passage. With one exception, the remaining italic passages in the first fourteen pages of the published book (including the two fragments on lines 6 and 8 of p. 8) all appear in roman, with the breaks, in the sample gathering. The exception—one wonders why—is the second of the italic passages in the book, that on p. 5. As Faulkner told Wasson, the leading out creates an ugly type page and a disruption of the reader's experience of Benjy's interior monologue.

To assist in publicizing the novel, Cape and Smith sent a set of the galleys (Wasson recalls that she returned them) to Evelyn Scott for comment, since *The Wave* had become something of a critical and popular success. She responded so enthusiastically in a letter that Wasson asked her to revise and expand her remarks, particularly on the Benjy section. She did this, and her commentary was issued in a little pamphlet, its cover carrying out the black-and-white design of the covers of the novel, which was distributed along with the book.[41] Paperbound prepublication copies were also circulated. All in all, Cape and Smith were to be congratulated on the way they brought out a novel which represented a considerable gamble for a new firm. It was published 7 Oct. 1929, an autumn for greater optimism concerning America's literary than financial condition, and received very good reviews, upon the whole; but it did not sell. The first printing, only 1,789 copies, sufficed until the publication of *Sanctuary* in February 1931. In that month a small second printing of 518 copies was made, and the following November a third printing, of 1,000 copies, was made from a copy of the second impression by offset lithography.[42]

This final printing of 1,000 copies appears to have lasted several successive publishers for more than a decade. By the late fall of 1931 Cape and Smith were out of business, to be succeeded, as Faulkner's publishers, first by Smith and Haas, then by Random House. The volumes of the *Publishers' Trade List Annual* record the continued availability, at $2.50, of *The Sound and the Fury* from Smith and Haas through 1935, and from Random House from 1936 through 1943.

Granted the exceptional difficulty of the text, the complications caused by a number of individual or idiosyncratic features of Faulkner's spelling and punctuation, the distance of author from publisher, and the inconsistencies of copy editing noted by Faulkner in his letter to Wasson, it would have been a small miracle had the text of the first edition of *The Sound and the Fury* been less imperfect than it actually was. Despite a certain number of demonstrable minor printer's errors and inconsistencies, and a larger number of possible or debatable ones, it is on the whole a very good text, and much better than any of the four later, and unfortunately much more widely available, editions.

Listed below in Table A are the obvious or demonstrable errors in the 1929 Cape and Smith edition. It is noteworthy how few misspellings due to printer's errors there are; for a careful collation to turn up only three (those on pp. 93, 120, and 216) in a novel of 400 pages is an indication of careful printing and proofreading. Since Faulkner varied his usage, from section to section and even within the section, depending upon the state of mind of the subject of the interior monologue, it is not at all surprising that there are real inconsistencies, as well as apparent ones, in matters of punctuation, the handling of direct quotations, and the use of apostrophes. For example, it would seem that Faulkner intended to indicate something about the quality of Benjy's perception of the world about him by uniformly omitting the question marks in the questions that are asked in the dialogue of his section of the novel. Akin to this device, but not employed with complete consistency, is the separation of dialogue from its adjunctive "he said" or "she said" by periods, instead of commas. That is, Benjy's mind appears to be recording the finality of a statement, in dialogue, by putting a period at the end of the statement; its connection to the following "he said" appears only in the lower case letter of the "he." But where there is inconsistency in the practice, is Faulkner attempting to indicate some subtle difference in the situation, or Benjy's perception of it, or did copy editor or printer make a change? Again, it seems obvious that nothing but errors of commission by printers, omission by proofreaders, are involved in the occasional appearance in one-syllable contractions like *wont* of the apostrophes which Faulkner, it is clear from his manuscripts and typescripts, prefers to omit. But it is less clear what is involved in the occasional omission of apostrophes in two-syllable contractions like *wouldn't;* some of them appear to be meaningless omissions, others might just possibly be related to the changes of punctuation that appear in the italicized passages of Benjy's and Quentin's sections.

Other problems in the text of this novel, as in other books by Faulkner, occur from his preference for omitting the periods after the contractions *Mr., Mrs.,* and *Dr.;* his preference for occasional *-our* forms (*humour, labouring*) and the *-ise* ending for certain verbs (do these reflect the author's taste for earlier American forms, or more recent English practice?); his liking for *awhile* and *anymore* instead of *a while* and *any more;* and so on. There is even one apparently deliberate Gallicism: *quai* for *quay*.

In a work where symbolism, imagery, and literary allusions are so densely, and often so inconspicuously, woven into the texture of the prose, a high degree of editorial conservatism would be called for if a new edition of the novel were to be brought out now. Consistency might mistakenly urge the smoothing out of spelling, punctuation, and other features of the style which could significantly enrich the reader's understanding of a particular passage, but it is also obvious that certain inconsistencies are almost sure to be the fault of the printer and copy editor. Wherever the context, or comparison with prevailing practice elsewhere in the book, argue very strongly that the inconsistency is not substantive, it is listed in the table of errors below. Other cases are ignored, for though it is to be hoped that Table A here will shed light upon the textual problems of this novel, a more thorough investigation of the whole text ought to involve collation of the published version with the extant manuscript and typescript texts. Only such a collation would reveal whether the occasionally disturbing inconsistencies, not listed here, in the use of apostrophes in contractions, in the punctuation, and in the use of italics are the fault of the author, or are due to slipshod copy editing and proofreading.

TABLE A

Errors in the 1929 Edition of *The Sound and the Fury*

page and line	error	suggested correction	page and line	error	suggested correction
3.15	*don't*	*dont*	168.1	You	"You
4.18	dining-room	dining room	179.15	weetha.	weetha."
9.3	don't	dont	185.16	Geralds	Gerald's
9.24	baby," she	baby." she	188.9	I've	Ive
10.1	Don't	Dont	190.11	I'll	Ill
10.25	Don't	Dont	196.3	we'll	well
11.1	didnt	didn't	197.7	I'll	Ill
11.8	Can't	Cant	200.28	he'll	hell
30.20	said,	said.	202.12	I'm	Im
33.20	barn.	barn."	216.16	*Nom sum*	*Non sum*
38.13	don't	dont	233.16	She	she
38.14	*can't*	*cant*	240.29	enevelope	envelope
38.19	go,"	go."	246.18	eve'y	ev'y
43.23	said,	said.	252.20	don't	dont
45.7	father	Father	260.12	can't	cant
48.10	up"	up."	263.4	start.	start,
56.28	Benjy,"	Benjy."	270.13	o'clock	oclock
60.5	looney	loony	273.4	childrens'	children's
66.18	looneys	loonies	286.22	can't	cant
68.2	fire-	fire	292.22	don't	dont
74.22	*Benjy.*	*Benjy,*	295.18	can't	cant
75.5	Mr.	Mr	322.11	o'clock	oclock
84.5	fast,	fast.	324.2	He	"He
86.11	up,	up.	328.7	don't	dont
93.6	excrutiating-ly	excruciating-ly	335.25	stove	stove-
105.7	jeweler	jeweller	343.10	He	he
114.15	diningroom	dining-room	346.16	Cahline	Miss Cahline
122.12	didnt	didn't	347.14	you alls'	you all's
125.12	hear?	hear?"	355.9	beatin'	beatin
125.17	o'clock	oclock	357.14	here?"	here."
130.22	girls	girl's	357.17	here?	here?"
139.14	flat irons	flat-irons	369.13	!	!"
144.8	flat irons	flat-irons	393.21	somethin'	somethin
144.26	May flies	Mayflies	394.10	said.	said,
156.25	again,	again.			

In April, 1931 the first English edition of *The Sound and the Fury* was brought out in London by Chatto and Windus, in a printing of 2,000 copies.[43] Faulkner's second book to be published in England (it followed *Soldier's Pay* by less than a year), it had an

[233]

introduction by Richard Hughes, who praised highly the novel's technique and structure. These produce, he said, an effect "impossible to describe . . . because it is unparalleled," and he noted particularly the "exquisite care" that had been used in fitting together the pattern of Benjy's section, the parts of which had been written with such "consummate contrapuntal skill."

English readers might have had more confidence in Faulkner's skill if they had been given a better text by which to judge it. When Chatto and Windus brought out *Sanctuary* the following fall, they censored the novel by omitting 325 words, but in other respects did a more careful job of printing it than had been done in America, where it had been somewhat sloppily copy edited and proofread.[44] However, the English edition of *The Sound and the Fury* was indifferently copy edited, little consistency being exhibited in the many departures made from the original text in spelling and punctuation, and although only a few printer's errors can be identified as such, some of the many changes in the original punctuation probably should be attributed to this source rather than to the copy editing.

House styling and other changes of the sort that almost invariably occur when an American book is set up in Britain (or a British book in America) account for many, perhaps the majority, of the differences between the first English and first American editions of the novel. There are the usual Anglicizations of spelling: *parlour, ploughed, draught, tyre.* Though *gasoline* does not become *petrol,* and *curb* remains *curb, motor* is substituted for *auto.* Such changes can hardly be criticized, however, because of the inconsistencies in the American text caused by Faulkner's occasional use of English forms. More serious is the fact that a number of Faulkner's dialectal or colloquial words and expressions are modified (some perhaps by printer rather than editor): for *hit, bein, nothin, shamed, begun, belong at* are substituted *it, being, nothing, ashamed, began, belong to.* Apostrophes are inserted (with less than perfect consistency) in Faulkner's *cant, wont, dont,* and after *Mr* and *Mrs* periods are usually supplied. Hyphens are added to many compounds: thus *drug store* becomes *drug-store, woodlot* becomes *wood-lot.* Trivial in themselves, these changes are all away from Faulkner's practice of eliminating punctuation that breaks up or slows down the movement of the eye across the type page unless demanded by the meaning (rather than the form) of the words. And though again it is not carried through with any degree of consistency, a further modification of Faulkner's practice in this respect is the addition of apostrophes to indicate omission of unpronounced letters in spoken words: *'tis, makin', S'pose*. The *-ise* verb ending so often preferred by Faulkner is changed to *-ize: civilized, criticize, fertilizing, realize, recognize*.

The greatest number of changes in the English edition are in punctuation. As we have seen, inconsistencies in the American edition afford some justification for this, and if the changes by Chatto and Windus had eliminated some of the American inconsistencies there would be little ground for complaint. Unfortunately the changes produced less consistency, not more, and despite many dozens of alterations, the result is a less respectable text. Commas are inserted, commas are omitted; periods are exchanged for commas, and vice versa.

Although the great majority of the changes made in the English edition of the novel do not affect the basic meaning of the passages in which they occur, in sum they unquestionably mar the text of the work, particularly since most of them were made inconsistently. The English reader misses a good many of the finer shades of pronunciation and rhythm in the dialogue through changes made in spelling and punctuation. He loses the chance of the closer acquaintance with Faulkner's mind which familiarity with some of the little idiosyncrasies of usage in the American text afford. And perhaps worst of all, the inconsistencies caused by careless copy editing and proofreading are apt to shake the reader's confidence in his text, and to discourage the kind of close attention the writing deserves.

There are also a few ordinary typographical errors. These are listed in Table B on page 236 more for the light they shed on the printing and proofreading of the book than because of their importance, though in one or two instances there is significant change in the meaning of the sentence in which the error occurs. Page and line references are to the first English and first American editions.

TABLE B

ERRORS IN THE FIRST ENGLISH EDITION OF *The Sound and the Fury*

English		American •	
14.26	They they	18.13	Then they
19.26	fell	24.28	I fell
26.30	Gid	34.1	Git
48.2	I have just to	60.25	I just have to
71.12	unbottoned	89.29	unbuttoned
93.33	Will	117.27	Was. Will
107.28	necessarily	134.26	unnecessarily
127.9	Dog	159.13	Doc
131.22	shiny	164.28	shiny tight
135.2	go	169.8	go back
171.6	*girl*	213.25	*girl Girl*
175.23	and it	219.19	and i it
191.14	in	238.23	on
207.17	'is,	258.13	is,"
212.4	shes ays	264.4	she says
216.25	your own	269.24	your
227.25	arrangement	283.17	agreement
260.32	next	325.10	about next
291.9	cycamores	363.5	sycamores
313.15	you.	391.7	you."

(A number of possible errors in the dialogue are not listed because conceivably they could represent editorial modification of dialect.)

One of the most interesting chapters in the publishing history of *The Sound and the Fury* concerns the special edition of the novel which Random House proposed to bring out in 1933. Beginning with his ninth novel, *Absalom, Absalom!*, in 1936, Random House became Faulkner's publishers for all his books, but his connection with the firm dates from several years earlier. In 1931 they had brought out one of his short stories, *Idyll in the Desert*, in a little limited edition signed by the author, and early in 1932 they issued *Sanctuary*, with a special introduction by Faulkner, in their low-priced Modern Library series. It may have been the success of these two projects which encouraged Random House to contemplate bringing out *The Sound and the Fury* in a new, limited edition with an introduction by the author.

In this edition the first section was to be printed in ink of various colors to help clarify the chronology, as Faulkner had proposed when the novel was first published, and for it he underlined his copy of the book in crayon of different colors and sent it, with the introduction, to Random House.[45] The 1933 *Publishers' Trade List Annual* carried a Random House "tentative advance announcement for the fall of 1933" which listed "A new limited Edition" of *The Sound and the Fury*, "With a new introduction by William Faulkner. Typography by the Grabhorn Press. 500 copies, signed by William Faulkner. Ready in November. $7.50."

Random House deserves great credit for even contemplating such a project during depression times, for it would have entailed a heavy printing bill indeed. But though the edition was announced again in the 1934 *Trade List Annual* for fall, 1934, publication, it was abandoned before completion. No trace of either Faulkner's introduction or the copy of the book with the crayon underlining can now be found at Random House.[46]

Reference has already been made to the incomplete, four-page typescript among Faulkner's papers which appears to be a draft of his introduction for this edition, and it is worth further comment here. The first page is lacking. The second begins in mid-sentence with a reference to the reading he had done a decade and more before he wrote *Sanctuary* but from which he was still learning. In writing *Sanctuary*, and later *As I Lay Dying*, he noted, he found something missing from the experience that writing *The Sound and the Fury* had been. This—a feeling hard to define but including an actual physical emotion, faith and joy and ecstasy and an eager looking forward to what the process of creation would release from the paper before him—this, he felt, might have been missing with *As I Lay Dying* because he had known so much about that book before writing it. He waited nearly two years before beginning his next novel, and then tried to recreate for *Light in August* the conditions of writing *The Sound and the Fury*, by sitting down to face the first blank sheet with only a single image in mind instead of the whole book, in this case the image of a pregnant girl making her way along an unfamiliar road.

But the new novel failed to bring him the feeling he had had with *The Sound and the Fury*, though it progressed satisfactorily. Realizing that he had now become a far more conscious, deliberate craftsman, more aware of the standards and achievements of his great predecessors among novelists in French and English, he wondered if he were not now in the situation of knowing too much about the techniques of fiction, and if he had not already made use of the only image, that of Caddy in her muddy drawers trying to see the funeral from the pear tree while her brothers waited below, which had the power to move him as he wanted the act of writing to do.

Faulkner concluded the piece with the description already quoted of the writing of *The Sound and the Fury*, describing his reaction to the continued rejection of *Sartoris* which eventually determined him to forget about being published and to create then a work of art which would be for himself to cherish. And so, lacking either sister or daughter, he had set himself to create the tragic, lovely figure of Caddy.

Though we cannot be absolutely certain that this was designed for the introduction to the 1933 limited edition of *The Sound and the Fury*, it fits in date and in scope, as far as we can tell from the internal (and incomplete) evidence of the typescript itself, and it is difficult to imagine anything else that it would fit. It is altogether a remarkably self-revelatory piece, for Faulkner; it is equally far in tone and attitude from the protective mask of tough, hard-boiled cynicism he had worn in introducing a lesser work, *Sanctuary*, a short time before, and from the pose of being an untutored rustic, or ignorant natural genius, which he was already finding useful.

Even with the lack of the first page, this is an important document for the understanding of Faulkner, and it is to be hoped that his estate will permit its publication. The picture it gives of Faulkner the widely read, ambitious, consecrated artist makes it tempting to speculate what might have been the effect of the publication of such an introduction with a beautifully prepared and printed Random House-Grabhorn Press edition of *The Sound and the Fury* in the 1930's. It seems reasonable to suppose that it might have changed radically, perhaps effaced, the picture which so many of his American readers derived from an unperceptive reading of *Sanctuary* and its Modern Library introduction. The whole course of the reception of his books in this country might have been swayed, not so much perhaps in the direction of winning for him a larger audience, but at any rate of producing a better one. Instead, misapprehension about Faulkner the man went far toward confirming a certain fashionable condescension toward his work which prevailed for long in the literary circles of America, and which encouraged too many readers and too many critics in a superficial approach to his fiction.(As a French admirer of Faulkner put it in 1937, comparing the relative popularity of *Sanctuary* and *The Sound and the Fury* in America, "Certains esprits aiment les plaisirs faciles."[47]) It is mortifying to Americans to compare the reputation of Faulkner in his own country with that to be found in France at this period. Knowing very little about the man, the French judged him by his work, and accordingly placed him at or very near the top among writers in English in the twentieth century, almost from the beginning.[48]

That Faulkner's reputation in France was so high, so early, was due to the work of Maurice Edgar Coindreau more than to any other single person. Beginning in 1931 a series of superb translations and critical articles by Coindreau led the way in introducing Faulkner to his audience in France. Important among these were his translation of *The Sound and the Fury*, which no study of the text of this work can afford to overlook, and his preface to this translation, which it has been the misfortune of American critics of the novel largely to ignore.

To Coindreau, Faulkner wrote early in 1937 that "After reading 'As I Lay Dying,'[49] in your translation, I am happy that you are considering undertaking S&F." To his most recent novel, *Absalom, Absalom!*, Faulkner had appended a short "Chronology" of dates and "Genealogy" of main characters, and he may have had something of the sort in mind when he offered to give Coindreau "any information you wish and I can about the book," adding "I wi[s]h you luck with it and I will be glad to draw up a chronology and genealogy and explanation, etc. if you need it. . . ."[50]

Coindreau did not take up Faulkner on the offer of a chronology and genealogy, but for the explanation he journeyed to California —Faulkner at the time was serving one of his stretches in Hollywood, writing for the movies—in June 1937 and stayed a few days with him at his Beverly Hills duplex, 129 Ledoux Boulevard, while working on the translation. Although Faulkner would not reread the book, he cooperated wholeheartedly in the task of translation, freely discussing passages with Coindreau, who was delighted, and somewhat astonished, at Faulkner's grasp of the details of the novel. Nearly eight years after its publication, the author's memory of the book was almost perfect. On only two occasions, according to Coindreau, did Faulkner's memory fail to produce the solution to the ambiguities in the novel which so often posed a problem for the translator.[51]

"Ambiguity is one aspect of Faulknerian obscurity," Coindreau has noted. As translator of Faulkner, one of his major problems was that "It is more difficult to be obscure in French than in English"; therefore, since the "English language lends itself readily to multiple interpretations," but the French language does not, it required constant care on his part to minimize the clarifying effect of the French tongue in passages of deliberate original ambiguity.[52] In accomplishing this, according to Coindreau, Faulkner's explanations of the ambiguities were of the greatest assistance.

The French translation of *The Sound and the Fury*, then, is—or should be—of concern to any careful critic of the novel for several reasons. The preface is of enduring interest. The French text, like any really good translation, is itself a kind of commentary upon the original English, one which in this case is particularly valuable because of Faulkner's association with the process of translating it. Significant too is Faulkner's ready offer to provide Coindreau with the same sort of chronological-genealogical guide to the novel which had appeared in *Absalom, Absalom!*, and which he was a few years later to supply at some length for the readers of the Viking *Portable Faulkner*. But how many American critics have examined the text, or even read the preface, of *Le bruit et la fureur*? (This is to my knowledge the only occasion when Faulkner assisted in the translations of one of his works, but a number of the translations are undeservedly neglected by American critics, for they contain valuable and otherwise unavailable introductions.)

Just as Faulkner's interest in the Random House limited edition

in the early 1930's revealed his continued interest in the typographical problems of the most effective way of handling Benjy's interior monologue, his reaction in 1945 to Malcolm Cowley's
proposal to include an excerpt from *The Sound and the Fury* in a
Faulkner anthology he was editing showed that he had not forgotten the idea he had broached to Coindreau in 1937 of providing
for the novel some sort of reader's guide to its cast of characters.
Cowley wanted to use part of the fourth section, and Faulkner
sent him in October 1945 a kind of summary-commentary upon
the main characters which in addition traced back the Compson
family line through a number of generations not mentioned in the
original book. In the Viking *Portable Faulkner*, where it is printed
at the end of the volume at some remove from the excerpt from
The Sound and the Fury, it makes a very pleasant addition to the
anthology's collection of high spots from Faulkner's fiction.

In the letter to Cowley (now in the Yale University Library)
which accompanied the piece, Faulkner apologized for any discrepancies with the novel it might contain, saying that he had no
copy of *The Sound and the Fury* but that if the errors were too
extreme Cowley might correct them himself, or send it back to
him for whatever revision Cowley wanted. He mentioned the
chronology, including the ages of the characters, and the total sum
of the money Miss Quentin steals from Jason, as possible points
of error. Obviously Faulkner was pleased by the piece; he told
Cowley he liked it and remarked that he ought to have done something of the sort to tie it together when he first wrote the novel.

Cowley, noting many discrepancies between novel and Appendix, wrote Faulkner on 10 Nov. suggesting various changes,
including the restoration to Miss Quentin of the pear tree down
which she climbed in the novel (in the Appendix Faulkner had
made it a rainpipe). But Faulkner excused the discrepancies by saying that he had written the Appendix from the standpoint of a
dispassionate genealogist, recording *Compson* before moving on to
the next family tree.

Faulkner gave an additional excuse for the differences between
the two Compson accounts several months later, when he wrote
to Cowley that rather than reread *The Sound and the Fury* in order

to catch the discrepancies with the Appendix, which was now supposed to be printed in the new Modern Library edition of the novel, he would prefer to let them stand, with some sort of statement to the effect that the inconsistencies were proof that the book was still alive and growing, and that since he was more familiar with the characters now, after fifteen years, than he was when he wrote the novel, it was the novel rather than the appendix that was inconsistent.[53]

Though Faulkner's correspondence with Cowley about the *Portable Faulkner* is of great interest, it will not do to accept all his statements at face value. It is difficult to be certain exactly what reservations he may have had about Cowley's introduction to the *Portable Faulkner* and his design in editing it, and we must allow for the possibility of a certain amount of caginess in his remarks to Cowley about the Compson Appendix. On the whole it seems safe to say that Faulkner was intrigued at the notion of writing something that would serve to introduce a fragment of *The Sound and the Fury* to readers of the anthology; that in the writing it became more an afterword upon the Compson family than an introduction to the excerpt; that he was quite aware that his vision of the book had changed in the years since he had written it; and that he expected anyone who read the Appendix in conjunction with the novel to be aware of the differences between them, especially the important differences in point of view. His willingness to permit the Appendix to be printed as a kind of introduction to a new edition of the novel is another matter.

After a hiatus of three years, *The Sound and the Fury* was brought back into print late in 1946 by Random House in their Modern Library series, in a double volume with *As I Lay Dying*. Faulkner wrote Malcolm Cowley in January 1946 that he had been offered $250 to write a new introduction for *The Sound and the Fury* by Random House, which also wanted to include the Compson Appendix from the Viking *Portable Faulkner*. Faulkner turned down the offer to do a new introduction, and in a letter to Cowley in March he voiced the hope that his earlier introduction, the one designed for the limited edition planned in the 1930's, had been lost. He suggested that Cowley do the introduction. At about the same time Cowley wrote to Robert Linscott at Random House, suggesting either Conrad Aiken or Jean Paul Sartre for the introduction, and informing him that he was sending a copy of the Compson Appendix.[54]

Cowley warned Linscott about the discrepancies between the Appendix and the text of the novel, but Random House wisely decided to print the original unedited version of the Appendix, rainpipe and all, which has caused a certain amount of critical unrest. But the decision by the publisher to print the Appendix at the beginning of the novel seems considerably less judicious. In effect the Appendix was made to serve the function that had been envisaged for the introduction Faulkner refused to supply; the title-page of the volume claims for it "A NEW APPENDIX AS A FOREWORD BY THE AUTHOR."

The text of the Modern Library edition of *The Sound and the Fury* is thus off to a very poor start, spoiling the effect of the original beginning of the novel with Benjy's interior monologue, and failing to make clear to the reader that this "Foreword by the Author" had been written originally to clear up the questions raised by printing in an anthology a part of one of the book's four sections. In defence of the Appendix as an introduction to the novel is the fact that in every way it is different from the novel itself— in tone, in form, in style, as well as content. It bears much the same relationship to the novel that the historical prologues do to the dramatic sections of *Requiem for a Nun*. But although the sophisticated reader, aware of its origin, can enjoy the Appendix as the forty-seven-year-old author's commentary upon the thirty-one-year-old author's book, it is of dubious service to less wary readers and to students to present them with what appears to be a five-part novel, the first part of which relieves them of the burdens which the second part was designed to impose upon them in the way of careful and creative reading.

The Modern Library text suffers from more than just the presence of this Appendix-as-Foreword. Collation with the 1929 edition reveals the presence of no authorial revision or correction, and though a few minor corrections of errors and inconsistencies in the original were made,[55] a great many new printer's errors were committed. As Table C reveals, most of them are in themselves un-important, but a few affect substantively the meaning of the pas-sages in which they occur, and when added to the lesser errors of the original edition, the total effect is demonstrably unfortunate. *The Sound and the Fury* is one of the most exactingly written and precisely demanding novels in English, but it can fail to achieve its effect if the reader, conscious of a large number of inconsisten-cies and errors, is discouraged from the search for meaning in com-plex and difficult passages.[56]

Not listed in the table are a number of minor editorial changes, like *a while* for *awhile* and *any more* for *anymore*, which are made inconsistently, and where the first edition was likewise inconsistent. Also not listed are the numerous places where the Modern Library edition omitted the spaces which in the original, in Quentin's sec-tion, served as a kind of punctuation. Again, there is sufficient in-consistency in the way the matter is handled in the original to make it appear not worthwhile to note the variations in the Mod-ern Library edition.

The Modern Library text of *The Sound and the Fury* has been a number of times reprinted, and has also been reissued in the cheaper format of the Vintage and Modern Library Paperback imprints. There have also been two new American editions,[57] both of them negligible, textually speaking, being based on the Modern Library text without any particular effort at the correction of errors or elimination of inconsistencies. Of the two, the best text is that in the 1954 *Faulkner Reader,* which has the added advantage of printing the Appendix at the end of the book instead of the beginning. The Appendix appears at the beginning of the 1959 Signet edition; it is omitted entirely from the English Four Square paperback of the same year, which is based upon, but adds many new errors to, the text of the original English edition.

The Sound and the Fury was a critical success when it was first published and its author was almost unknown, and since that time its reputation has grown, with its author's, until perhaps no Amer-ican novel of this century is esteemed more highly throughout the world. But despite the large amount of criticism that has appeared,

TABLE C
Errors in the Modern Library *The Sound and the Fury*

Modern Library	Cape and Smith	Modern Library	Cape and Smith
23.19 went	went back	154.2 *oh*	*Oh*
25.18 wonder.	wonder	155.26 *and mud*	*the mud*
38.16 up on	up	158.30 *got a*	*a*
41.30 It was	I was	161.1 curb	curb,
46.28 ain't	aint	175.33 window	windows
47.2 back	black	193.25 *I wouldnt have*	I wouldnt have
47.4 Mr.	Mr	194.29 right.	right
52.24 *Frony,*	*Frony*	199.7 her	her.
57.4 *nobody*	*ain't nobody*	202.5 her;	her,
59.24 Cad	Caddy	227.29 trying	tr-trying
59.27 *said Benjy*	*said, Benjy*	228.15 Rogers."	Rogers'."
63.19 door	door.	229.12 can	cant
63.34 whispered	whispered.	270.21 fom	fum
66.25 whispered	whispered.	272.24 from	fum
68.34 ain't	aint	273.26 ask	act
69.18 lost	lost."	281.1 CHILL.	CHILL,
71.31 Don't	Dont	285.2 less	less,
74.22 can't	cant	285.29 H'h	Hah
74.34 firedoor	fire door	286.11 bread-board	bread board
82.6 Hush.'	Hush."	289.2 what	whar
99.15 flatiron	flat-iron	289.4 last	Last
109.9 that it would	that would	291.6 'lawd	Lawd
123.33 to	too	292.16 you	yo
124.18 *that breathed*	*that breathed*	294.24 yo	you
125.26 that	than	297.18 have	yet have
127.33 hit off	hit it off	298.18 other	the other
130.24 Massachusetts	in Massachusetts	300.15 ready—	read—
134.34 razor,	razor	300.26 and	on and
144.30 stage	stage,	317.29 don't	dont
145.8 standing	just standing	321.30 nor	nor of
145.33 took	took up	327.4 your eye	your
146.12 dirty-dress	dirty dress	327.5 an eye	a human eye
147.15 horse	white horse	331.31 dont	done
147.25 Feetsoles	Feet soles	336.6 They	Then
149.14 facade	façade		

it is obvious that we have as yet hardly seen a beginning to the intensive investigation of the book: of its sources, its imagery, perhaps even of such basic matters as its structure, and the function of its three interior monologues. There is every reason to expect *The Sound and the Fury* to be accorded increasingly close reading, increasingly careful critical study; and surely such a work deserves a better text than is now available to the public. We must mourn the opportunity that was lost during the depression of bringing it out under the author's supervision in an edition commensurate with its significance. But fortunately the manuscript and typescript versions were preserved, and these, with a meticulous examination of the first published text, would make it possible to bring out *The Sound and the Fury* in an edition worthy of the feeling which its author had for it. Perhaps it might appear as the first volume in a carefully prepared collected edition, which we need so badly in this country. (There are substantially complete collected editions in England, France, and Italy, but not here.) In such an edition of *The Sound and the Fury* the Appendix could be removed from the novel, an operation which would benefit the patient enormously, though of course it should be preserved for inspection elsewhere, to be considered in the same light as those other related writings, like "That Evening Sun" and *Absalom, Absalom!*, which tell us other things about the characters of the novel. Perhaps no more fitting memorial to Faulkner might be made than an edition of *The Sound and the Fury* which came as close as possible to realising in type the intent that its author reveals in the manuscript, typescript, and the first printed version of the text of this book, which he so often referred to as the one closest to his heart of all he wrote.

NOTES

1. There have been four separate editions in America, two in England. In order of publication these are: (1) New York: Jonathan Cape and Harrison Smith, 1929; (2) London: Chatto and Windus, 1931; (3) New York: Modern Library, 1946; (4) *The Faulkner Reader* [including *The Sound and the Fury*], New York: Random House, 1954; (5)

New York: New American Library (a Signet paperback), 1959; (6) London: Landsborough Publications (a Four Square paperback), 1959.

2. George R. Stewart and Joseph M. Backus have attempted this for the first section alone, in " 'Each in Its Ordered Place': Structure and Narrative in 'Benjy's Section' of *The Sound and the Fury*," *American Literature* XXIX (Jan. 1958), [440]–56. But several of the authors' time-level identifications are open to dispute, and as Carvel Collins has pointed out, it is dangerous to ignore the evidence of the other sections of the novel in concentrating upon the study of one of them. "Miss Quentin's Paternity Again," *Texas Studies in Literature and Language* II (Autumn 1960), [253]–60.

3. Most of the recent studies of this novel have dealt at least in part with the symbolism. For two of the most penetrating, see Carvel Collins, "The Interior Monologues of *The Sound and the Fury*," *English Institute Essays, 1952*, New York: Columbia University Press, 1954, pp. [29]–56; and "The Pairing of *The Sound and the Fury* and *As I Lay Dying*," *Princeton University Library Chronicle* XVIII (Spring 1957), 114–23.

4. No detailed study of the style of *The Sound and the Fury* has yet been made. But such a study must be based on as good a text as possible. An example of the danger of relying upon a faulty text occurs in *The Modern Novel in America*, by Frederick J. Hoffman, Chicago: Regnery (a Gateway paperback), 1956, pp. 178–79, where the complexity and versatility of Faulkner's style are praised, and the beginning of the fourth section of *The Sound and the Fury* is quoted as "a brilliant example of Faulkner's skill" with language. The passage is quoted from the Modern Library edition (p. 281), where it appears as two sentences plus a long, dangling fragment. But in the original Cape and Smith edition (p. 330) the passage appears as two long sentences; the dangling fragment is not a feature of Faulkner's style, but was created by a printer's error in the Modern Library edition, which substituted a period for a comma in the first sentence of the section.

5. It is well to be cautious before accepting at face value some of Faulkner's remarks about his own and other people's work. He delighted in smoothly sidestepping questions he did not want to answer. For example, when asked in Japan which of his works did he "like the least," he replied "The one that gave me no trouble . . . was *As I Lay Dying*." (*Faulkner at Nagano*, ed. Robert A. Jelliffe, Tokyo: Kenkyusha, 1956, p. 162.) But there is abundant evidence that *The Sound and the Fury* meant something special to him. He described it to an audience at Virginia as his "best failure. It was the one that I anguished the most over, that I worked the hardest at, that even when I knew I couldn't bring it off, I still worked at it." (*Faulkner in the University*,

edd. F. L. Gwynn and J. L. Blotner, University of Virginia Press, 1959, p. 61.) In so often speaking of the book as a failure, Faulkner may be calling attention to his standards, not his achievements.

6. Faulkner's last two editors, Albert Erskine and the late Saxe Commins, have both described to me on several occasions Faulkner's reluctance to reread his earlier works, even when, as in the Snopes trilogy, there was some professional and artistic reason to do so.

7. Publication dates of American editions of Faulkner in this article are taken from *Publishers' Weekly;* of English editions, from the *English Catalogue of Books.*

8. In one interview Faulkner was quoted as saying that it took him "five years of re-working and re-writing." (Cynthia Grenier, "An Interview with William Faulkner—September, 1955," *Accent* xvi [Summer 1956], p. 172.) On another occasion he said, "I struggled and anguished with it for a year." (*Faulkner in the University,* p. 207.) Interviews are not the most reliable source of information, and different critics have followed different sources in assigning a period of time to the writing of the book.

9. Lenore Marshall, in "The Power of Words," *Saturday Review,* 28 July 1962, p. 16, gives an account of receiving *The Sound and the Fury* at Cape and Smith in 1929 after *thirteen* rejections and calling it to the attention of Smith, who is said to have asked, "What's it about?" (See n. 32.)

10. The student was R. M. Allen, who shortly afterward prepared a careful draft of his notes with the assistance of another member of the class, D. P. Butler. Other students made copies of these notes, not always accurately, according to Allen, and in the Summer 1951 issue of *Western Review* (Vol. xv, 300–4) one of the students who had been in the class, Lavon Rascoe, published "An Interview with William Faulkner," which Allen felt was derived from his notes. This interview became well known and widely quoted, and therefore in 1954 Allen mimeographed thirty copies of his notes and distributed some of them in order to make available a more accurate text of Faulkner's remarks. Faulkner's statement cited here is from p. 2 of these 1954 notes; in the corresponding passage in the Rascoe version (p. 301) Faulkner is quoted as saying that *As I Lay Dying* took six weeks, *The Sound and the Fury* three years, with *Absalom, Absalom!* not mentioned. There is a photocopy of set 10 of Allen's notes in the Faulkner Collection at the Princeton University Library.

11. See F. L. Gwynn, "Faulkner's Raskolnikov," *Modern Fiction Studies* iv (Summer 1958), 169*n.* There are errors in the table on p. 170 which gives dates of composition for Faulkner's first six novels, but although Faulkner's memory for specific dates or years was often un-

reliable, it seems reasonable to take seriously his statement about the span of time required by the writing; to confirm the recollection of the Hoover-Smith election, fall 1928, as the date the writing was finished, we have the corroborative evidence of the carbon typescript.

12. Interview with M. Coindreau, May 1962. Coindreau had referred to this situation in the preface to his 1938 French translation of *The Sound and the Fury*, which he described there as "Ecrit alors que l'auteur se débattait dans des difficultés d'ordre intime" (*Le bruit et la fureur*, Paris: Gallimard, p. 14).

13. James B. Meriwether, *The Literary Career of William Faulkner*, Princeton University Library, 1961, p. 65.

14. Letter, Phil Stone to C. P. Rollins, 27 Jan. 1927. A carbon of this letter is in the Faulkner Collection of the Humanities Research Center, University of Texas. Stone states in the letter that Faulkner's three-book contract with Liveright called for a $200 advance on the first book, with $400 in advance on the next two.

15. Faulkner, introduction to the Modern Library issue of *Sanctuary* (New York, 1932).

16. Meriwether, *Literary Career*, p. 16. The quotation is taken from what appears to be a version of the introduction Faulkner wrote for an unpublished, limited edition of *The Sound and the Fury*. Preserved among the papers Faulkner loaned to the 1957 Princeton University Library Faulkner exhibition, it is now on deposit at the University of Virginia Library.

17. Interview with Mr. Stone, July 1956.

18. Letter, Phil Stone to James B. Meriwether, 7 July 1960.

19. Interview with Mr. Wasson, Sept. 1959.

20. Meriwether, *Literary Career*, p. 65.

21. Interview with Mr. Wasson, Sept. 1959.

22. Meriwether, *Literary Career*, p. 65. The missing page is no. 5.

23. Pages of this manuscript (pp. 34, 70, 148) have been reproduced in Meriwether, *Literary Career*, Figs. 10 and 11; and in the *Princeton University Library Chronicle* XVIII (Spring 1957), Plate III.

24. Faulkner often stated that *As I Lay Dying* had been a *tour de force* in conception and execution—"I knew when I put down the first word what the last word . . . would be," he said at Virginia in 1957 (*Faulkner in the University*, p. 207). Though *As I Lay Dying* is a much shorter and simpler novel than *The Sound and the Fury*, it will not do to underestimate the capacities of the mind that so completely conceived it before the writing began. In the introduction to the Modern Library *Sanctuary* he made the statement that *As I Lay Dying* had been written "in six weeks, without changing a word." As George Garrett has shown ("Some Revisions in *As I Lay Dying*," *Modern*

Language Notes 73 [June 1958], 414–17), the novel actually underwent a good deal of minor polishing and revision at every stage, from manuscript to typescript to printed book. It will not do, then, to take too literally the words of the *Sanctuary* introduction (which Faulkner often repeated elsewhere). One logical way of taking the statement would be to assume that Faulkner expected sensible readers to understand that the book could not possibly have been written literally "without changing a word," and was using this way—a by no means uncharacteristic blend of honesty, modesty, and ambiguity—to call attention to his quite extraordinary feat of concentration and control in the planning and writing.

25. *Life* xxxvii (9 Aug. 1954), [77]–78.

26. *Faulkner at Nagano*, pp. 102, 103, 105.

27. One reason that Faulkner might well have followed a different rule in writing *A Fable* is that for various reasons it took him much longer to write than did *The Sound and the Fury*. At the end (p. 437) of *A Fable* (New York: Random House, 1954) Faulkner gives Dec. 1944, as the date it was begun, Nov. 1953, as the date it was finished.

28. *Faulkner in the University*, p. [1].

29. *Faulkner at Nagano*, pp. 103–5. In 1937 Faulkner gave M. E. Coindreau the same account of the book's inception as a short story. (*Le bruit et la fureur*, p. [7]. See Plate I.)

30. Interview with Mr. Wasson, Sept. 1959.

31. Interview with Mr. Wasson, Aug. 1957.

32. According to Wasson, Smith knew about *The Sound and the Fury* when still at Harcourt, Brace. Some time after he had left to set up his own business, knowing that *The Sound and the Fury* had been submitted to them, he sent Wasson to Harcourt, Brace to ask what had happened. Wasson was told that the book had been rejected, and he brought the typescript back to Smith himself (telephone conversation with Mr. Wasson, July 1962).

33. Faulkner, introduction to Modern Library *Sanctuary*, p. vi. The contract with Cape and Smith was signed 18 Feb. 1929 (information supplied from records at Random House, Mar. 1957, by Saxe Commins).

34. *Publishers' Weekly*, 13 July 1929, p. 207.

35. *Publishers' Weekly*, 23 Feb. 1929, p. 880.

36. This letter is now in the Massey collection of Faulkner at the University of Virginia Library. It was lent to the Princeton University Library in 1957 for their Faulkner exhibition, and is briefly described in Meriwether, *Literary Career*, p. 17.

37. He made several copies of one of these, the play, "The Marionettes," about 1920. A page from one is reproduced in Meriwether,

Literary Career, Fig. 1. "Mayday," a later work, is described briefly by Carvel Collins in the introduction to his edition of Faulkner's *New Orleans Sketches*, Rutgers University Press, 1958, pp. 21, 29.

38. In 1925 he praised, not without envy, the skill of his artist friend William Spratling, "whose hand has been shaped to a brush as mine has (alas!) not. . . ." (*New Orleans Sketches*, p. 102.) The best of Faulkner's drawings are far from contemptible in design and execution, however, and as one would expect, even the poorer ones have individuality, even those so reminiscent of Beardsley and Held.

39. Quoted by John Cook Wyllie in the *Richmond News Letter*, 31 Jan. 1955, p. 11.

40. See Plates II and III. For permission to reproduce the material in these plates, thanks are due to Random House, Faulkner's publisher in this country, and to the Humanities Research Center of the University of Texas. For permission to reproduce Plate I, thanks are due to Gallimard, publisher of the French translation, and to Maurice Edgar Coindreau.

41. Evelyn Scott, *On William Faulkner's "The Sound and the Fury."* *Publishers' Weekly*, 21 Sept. 1929, p. 1138, carried a statement by Cape and Smith in their announcement of fall books that "After reading the galleys of this remarkable book, EVELYN SCOTT wrote us enthusiastically, 'His idiot is better than Dostoyevsky's!' " Other information from interview with Mr. Wasson, Sept. 1959.

42. Dates of printing appear on the copyright pages of the second and third impressions. For the number of copies in all three printings, I am indebted to Mrs. Evelyn Harter Glick, formerly of Cape and Smith, and of Smith and Haas, who collected the information with the intention of publishing a Faulkner bibliography in collaboration with Kenneth Godfrey. (The project, begun with great thoroughness, was unfortunately abandoned sometime in 1932.) Mrs. Glick also provided, from the Cape and Smith records, the information that no textual changes were made in the second and third impressions, a fact confirmed by both oral and machine collation, though in the third printing commas were inserted between the date of the month and the year in the headings of the second, third, and fourth sections. For their assistance with the task of collating these impressions, and also the texts of the Modern Library, Chatto and Windus, and *Faulkner Reader* editions, I wish to thank Mrs. Mary C. Bozeman, Mr. James B. Davis, Miss Margaret Meriwether, and Mrs. Nancy C. Meriwether.

43. Meriwether, *Literary Career*, p. 102. This edition appears not to have been reprinted until the 1954 "Uniform Edition" text was reproduced by photo-offset from the original impression.

44. James B. Meriwether, "Some Notes on the Text of Faulkner's *Sanctuary,*" *Papers of the Bibliographical Society of America* 55 (Third Quarter, 1961), 203–5.

45. In a letter from Faulkner to Malcolm Cowley, undated save for the day of the week (Saturday) but probably written late in 1945, Faulkner refers to the Random House limited edition and the copy he underlined in crayon for it. This letter is now in the Yale University Library, and I am grateful to the Library, and to Mr. Cowley, for permission to use it and the other Faulkner-Cowley correspondence cited in this article. Though the letter does not state that it is the first section which was so underlined, I assume that this is the case, since elsewhere Faulkner indicated that it was only this section which he conceived would benefit from printing in color. (See *Faulkner at Nagano,* p. 105.)

46. Information supplied by Albert Erskine, since 1958 Faulkner's editor at Random House, in interview, Nov. 1961.

47. M. E. Coindreau, preface to *Le bruit et la fureur,* p. 15.

48. For the French reception of Faulkner, see S. D. Woodworth's fine study, *William Faulkner en France (1931–1952),* Paris: Minard, 1959.

49. *Tandis que j'agonise,* Paris: Gallimard, 1934. With a preface by Valery Larbaud. Coindreau was working on this translation when he first met Faulkner, who inscribed for him his copy of the first edition (first state) of the novel: "William Faulkner | New York, N.Y. | 9 Nov 1931 | With gratitude to Dr Coindreau, the translator". (I am indebted to M. Coindreau for permitting me to use this inscription, seen May 1962.)

50. This letter, dated 26 Feb. 1937, is reproduced in Plate 11, *Princeton University Library Chronicle* xviii (Spring 1957).

51. Interviews with M. Coindreau, June 1957 and May 1962.

52. M. E. Coindreau, "On Translating Faulkner," *Princeton University Library Chronicle* xviii (Spring 1957), 110. M. Coindreau makes the same point in the preface to his translation (p. 15): "Ayant eu le privilège d'entendre M. Faulkner me commenter lui-même les points les plus obscurs de son roman, je ne me suis dérobé devant aucun obstacle." Here too M. Coindreau apologizes for the fact that "la précision de la langue française m'a amené, malgré moi, à éclaircir le texte."

53. Faulkner made the same point exactly, in almost the same words, some years later when he supplied a short prefatory note to *The Mansion,* the third volume of his Snopes trilogy (New York: Random House, 1959), which explained any inconsistencies with the other volumes as inevitable if his work was to have life, since "the author has learned . . . more about the human heart and its dilemma than he knew"

before. Faulkner's attitude about the inconsistencies within the trilogy, which help define the separate identities of its individual novels, sheds additional light upon his willingness to consider the Appendix as related to *The Sound and the Fury* but not part of it.

54. Faulkner-Cowley correspondence, Yale University Library. Cowley's letters reveal that he had the original typescript of the Appendix from Faulkner retyped, and it was one of the retyped copies that he appears to have sent to Random House for use in the Modern Library edition. Therefore, though the many differences between the Modern Library and *Portable Faulkner* texts of the Appendix reveal, in connection with the correspondence on the subject, that the Modern Library version is essentially unedited, it is still possible that some changes were made in it from Faulkner's original version.

55. The following errors listed in Table A were corrected in the Modern Library edition: 33.20, 75.5, 84.5, 105.7, 125.12, 144.26, 168.1, 216.14, 233.16, 240.29, 273.4, 324.2, 357.14, and 369.13.

56. For example, Stewart and Backus, in their study of the chronology of Benjy's section (see fn. 2), conclude that Faulkner's device of using the change from roman to italic type to indicate a time change to the reader is "worthless" because their study of the section revealed "that a change in type does not always indicate a break" in chronology. ("Each in Its Ordered Place,' " p. 446.) But it is clear from Faulkner's letter to Wasson that this is just what he intends the change in type to mean, and it is clear from the published book that this is almost always just what it does mean. Though there are obviously some minor inconsistencies in the use of the device, and further study is needed to settle this matter, to dismiss the validity of the device and ignore it as an indication of time change is to adopt an artistically and bibliographically unsophisticated view of the text of the novel.

57. See fn. 1.

VINTON A. DEARING

Computer Aids to Editing

the Text of Dryden

VINTON A. DEARING *is a pioneer in the application of mechanical aids to editorial problems. The present essay recounts how he learned to apply computer languages and quantitative methods to textual criticism. Dearing explains in detail how computers have been employed in collating and proofreading, preparing word lists, and for making textual family trees. In addition he provides practical advice and the algorithms for five programs, and illustrates how the data generated by these programs can inform the whole editorial process.*

THE CALIFORNIA EDITION of the *Works of John Dryden*, of which I am the textual editor, is an old-spelling critical edition. The text, it is hoped, comes as close as possible to Dryden's manuscripts while including all the changes that he introduced into their printings and reprintings. In the United States this ideal for scholarly editions of literary texts is principally associated with the name of Fredson Bowers, and the California *Dryden* is only one of many such undertakings to have benefited from his example and advice.

Attainment of the ideal is far from easy. It entails minute comparison of all manuscripts and printings that may be of interest in the history of the texts, including a number of copies of each printing in case small variations may turn up there. For the California *Dryden*, at least, it entails as well a careful examination of the major collected editions of modern times for useful emendations. Our aim was perfect accuracy and completeness in the recording of all significant differences between the texts examined, and our first volume set a very high standard in this respect.

The fruits of textual editing turn to ashes if the work proves not to be well done or if it is too laborious. With our second volume I began to sense that I was in danger of losing my harvest for the second reason, and turned then to the computer to lighten my labors without loss of accuracy—in fact, I gained an increase in accuracy.[1] A computer operates at the speed of light and never makes a mistake. The hyperbole here is so slight that it can be ignored: I have sometimes thought I had found a "machine error," but it has always turned out to be a human error.

The computers used in literary research do two things, and essentially two things only: they add and they transfer. The mathematical processes are all forms of addition: negative addition (subtraction) is a method of comparison, because subtraction yields zero only when the minuend and subtrahend are the same, a positive value only when the minuend is larger, a negative value only when the subtrahend is larger. In making its additions the computer normally follows its instructions (its program) serially, but it can be programmed to transfer ahead or back in the series of instructions and in particular to do so according to the results of its additions. For example, the computer can be programmed to subtract x from y to obtain z and to transfer to the zth instruction ahead, or to subtract 1 from x, and if the difference is not zero or negative to transfer back to a given instruction (but not farther back than the instruction establishing the initial value of x). This common device for causing the computer to repeat an operation the number of times given by the initial value of x is called looping.

By the processes of adding and transferring it is possible to perform all the operations of mathematics and logic on numbers. The letters of the alphabet, the marks of punctuation, and the space or blank are coded as numbers by the computer. Because various sequences of these numbers are the codings for words and sequences of words, which are in turn codings for pronunciation and meaning, the computer may have a place in any branch of literary and linguistic scholarship. The more adept and experienced a scholar is at determining his reasoning and emotional processes step-by-step and in detail, and at seeing when to ask and how to answer *why? when? where? how? how often?* and *how much?*, the more uses he will find for the computer. And the more adept and experienced he is at transferring methods used in one discipline to another, the easier he will find it to use the computer. All literary and linguistic research is at root a comparison of codings, whether the end in view is the determination of likeness and difference only, the setting up of some kind of order or hierarchy, or the determination of cause, meaning, or value. It is with these considerations in mind that I offer the following rather detailed account of the five computer programs we are using in preparing the text of the California *Dryden,* one each for collating, proofreading, and making word lists, and two for making textual family trees.

When I first investigated computers, the programs for the machine on my campus had to be written as series of numbers, and the series were long even for the simplest operations. Computer programming in those days required more time than I could afford, and it did not occur to me that someone might be willing to do the programming for me. In a year or two, however, machines became available that would accept programs written in the "language" of Fortran, and I was able to learn it from just a few lectures.

The computers used in literary study are essentially the same in their operations, so that learning one computer language provides a key to all the rest. Each make and sometimes each model of computer has its own "machine language," but there are a number of "compiler languages" that are easier to learn and that will be translated into the machine language of the computer by a compiler program supplied by the manufacturer or the computer center. Fortran is one of the easiest of the compiler languages to learn and there are Fortran compilers for many different machines, but it is not necessarily the best language to learn first, or to use at all. Cobol might be better in the abstract, for instance. The best language for a beginner is the one most familiar to the staff of the computer center where his work will be done. It is very likely to be the only language taught regularly and at no charge. It is easier to learn a computer language from an experienced instructor, and it is easier to get advice about specific programs and problems if one is writing in a language thoroughly familiar to the computer center personnel. Subsequently one can learn other languages from manuals and perhaps decide that another is more suitable, given the computer it is to be used with and the types of work it facilitates. (A program can be written in several sections, or subprograms, each in a different language if desired, if the necessary compilers exist for the computer in question.) Fortran and Cobol are the best established languages in this country, an important consideration if one wishes to make one's programs generally available, and when one realizes that a researcher may change his institution, or his institution may change its computers from time to time. Other things being equal I should today choose Cobol, but my guess is that Fortran is still more widely used in academic computing centers.

Before I learned Fortran a student introduced me to a professional programmer in the aircraft industry, Ronald Bland, who wrote the first version of the California *Dryden's* collation program. With it we have processed about one hundred thousand lines of Dryden's verse. Mr. Bland chose the machine language of the IBM 7090, then the major computer on my campus, as most suitable for the work, in spite of the fact that he had to learn it for the purpose. He did the programming in his spare time over a couple of months and charged it to experience. Since I knew exactly what I wished the program to do, for the most part Mr. Bland had to work out and write up the routines only once; if he and I had also had to experiment with various kinds of output, the work would have taken much longer.

As I look back, our method of procedure was interesting. It is not as difficult to compare texts by computer as it is to record the results of the comparison in a way that will be easy and unambiguous to read. My desires as to the print-out determined how Mr. Bland chose to do the comparison.

For example, let us assume five texts of *Absalom and Achitophel* that begin as follows: (1) "In pious times," (2) "In times," (3) "In old pious times," (4) "In times pious," and (5) "In olden times." Let us call the first variant word in each text the base word and define the word following the base word as the next word. Then, in following the decision procedure or algorithm below, the computer will, when text 2 is the other text, go from statement 1 to 2, 6, and 7; when text 3 is the other, from statement 1 to 2, 3, 4; when 4 is the other, from 1 to 2, 3, 4, 5; and when 5 is the other, from 1 to 2, 6, 7, 8, 9. Algorithms are normally written without full specifications as to the alternatives to "if" statements when serial progress through the statements may be inferred; thus in the example below statement 2 implies "If they do not differ go to 3."

1. Compare the base word in the base text with the next word in the other text.
2. If they differ go to 6.
3. Compare the next word in the base text with the base word in the other text.
4. If they differ go to routine for word added in other text.
5. Go to routine for transposed words.
6. Compare the next word in the base text with the base word in the other text.
7. If they are the same go to routine for word omitted from other text.
8. Compare the next word in both texts.
9. If they are the same go to routine for substituted word in other text.
10. Define "next word" as "next word after the word previously defined as 'next word.'"
11. If the limit of search has not been reached go to 1.
12. Go to routine for substituted word in other text.

Statement 12 would be reached when the texts did not agree again before the end or the end of some natural or artificial subdivision, such as a line of verse or prose.

From this algorithm it would be possible to construct a table of the variants as follows:

1	IN	PIOUS	TIMES
2		***	

```
3     OLD
4             TIMES PIOUS
5             OLDEN
```

The principal difficulty in construction lies in spacing out the texts so that the variations will be in columns. I agreed to Mr. Bland's suggestion that we simplify matters by accepting a modified columnar arrangement as follows:

```
1  IN  PIOUS TIMES
2      TIMES (
3      OLD  PIOUS (
4      TIMES  PIOUS
5      OLDEN
```

The left paren marks a word that is the same as, but cannot by the simpler construction routine be placed directly under, a corresponding word in the base text. This makes possible as well a much simpler comparison routine: read in from the left of the line in the base and the other text and if a variant is found in the latter then read in from the right until a variant is found (it may be the same variant as before). The construction routine is to print the variant word or words, if any, and anything between just as they stand in the other text, with an additional invariant word, if any, when the line in the other text is longer or shorter than the base line. (So that the variants will always line up on the left side, the computer checks and, if necessary, adjusts the spacing between the words in all texts to a single space; it must also divide prose texts into comparable lines before this simplified comparison is feasible—of which more below.) If there are two or more variants in the other text and words between that are the same as the base, as in

```
1  IN  PIOUS TIMES
6  IF  PIOUS DATES
```

it will be up to the reader of the table to cross out the invariant words. It takes much less of the reader's time, proportionally, to cross out such words than of the computer's time to insure that they do not occur.

Such an adjustment of means and ends—a "trade-off" as it is called—is normal in computer work of all kinds. Essentially, time, which usually means cost, is in question. Both programming time and computing time were reduced by our simplification; the time required for human analysis of the results was increased.

It is not possible to generalize satisfactorily about absolute rather than relative costs, as these vary from time to time; they depend on the installation, computer, programmer, language, and user. A program always takes longer to develop or adapt than one expects, but the added time may be offset by the tendency of programmers to do more than they are paid for, or for computer centers to supply certain services and materials free. Once a program is in operation, its costs can be calculated fairly easily on the basis of past experience, but associated costs may vary. For example, the assistants who prepare our texts for the computer receive raises as their experience increases; when they leave and are replaced by others, the salaries vary. This year for the first time we have had to pay for computer time. However, even with these charges, the associated costs, and my summer salary from the budget of the California *Dryden*, using the computer is still an economy. It increases my productivity on this and other projects, and I find that computer programming or directing other programmers sharpens my mind.

Mr. Bland delivered our collating program without any documentation, that is, without any explanation of how it did its work. This procedure is usual with computer programmers, but documentation is absolutely necessary if anyone else is to make changes. In this instance, I decided to supply the documentation myself, as I also wished to make some small changes. It took a year, for I also had to learn the machine language. In working in my changes I wiped out one or two neatly contrived operations of Mr. Bland's that I did not understand at the time and could not reconstruct after I had realized their usefulness.

Recently IBM System/360 machines have replaced the 7090–7094's as the principal computers on my campus, so that our collating program has been translated into a new computer language. This time the program was written in Fortran by Richard Bandat, who supplied full documentation. Mr. Bandat also worked in his spare time. Even though he knew both the old and the new languages well, and had a direct teletype connection from his home to computers owned and leased by his company, it took him almost as long as it took Mr. Bland. We paid him a lump sum on delivery, but it did not fully compensate him for his time. I personally gained in an unexpected way: I would have made the translation by a process of metaphrase, to use Dryden's terms, whereas Mr. Bandat was inclined to paraphrase, and I learned some useful technics by examining the results.

The output from our program looks like the following (this is a real example, slightly doctored to indicate more fully the program's capabilities):

ABSALOM AND ACHITOPHEL LINES 100–199

TEXT	LINE	LINE FROM BASE TEXT WITH VARIATIONS
01	0167	PUNISH A BODY WHICH HE COUD NOT PLEASE.,$
02	0167	
03	0167	
09	0167	
10	**0168	
17	0167	
04	0167V	COU'D NOT(
05	0167	
06	0167	
07	0167	
11	0167	
12	0167	
13	0167	
14	0167	
08	0167V	BABY WHICH HE COU'D NOT(
15	0167V	COULD NOT PLEASE, $
16	***	
11	0168A	**SAMPLE OF A LINE NOT IN TEXT 1.$

The line in text 1 is always given complete (the $ is an end-of-line marker, supplied by the computer if we happen to omit it; it is needed in case a line in another text differs from the base only in omitting a word or two at the end; without it such a line would print as a blank line). Texts 2, 3, 9, 10, and 17 agree with text 1 in this line, except that it is line 168 in text 10. Text 4 disagrees in spelling in a way that has made its line longer than the base, and texts 5–7 and 11–14 agree with text 4. Text 8 reads "baby" instead of "body," and also disagrees with the base in the same way as text 4; between the two disagreements are two words that do not vary from text 1 but have been printed for simplicity's sake (that is, simplicity in the program). Text 15 has disagreements in spelling and end-punctuation. The word "please" would be kept in any event to define the punctuation, but the word "not" has again been kept for simplicity's sake. The line in text 15 is the same length as the base, but even if it were not a (would not appear because the $ is a sufficient mark. Text 16 does not have this line. The asterisks at the head of the line supposedly added in text 11 show how indentation is indicated: one asterisk for each card-column indented. If several texts had this line or a variant of it, the same kind of entries as appear above it would appear below it. The program finds every difference between the texts; there is no way to signal that certain differences are of no interest.

The collation algorithm is as follows:

1. List the texts in register A (a register is a list).
2. Print a line from text 1.
3. Treat the line in the text just printed from as the base line.
4. If the corresponding line in the next text in register A is not the same as the base go to 7 (on return to this statement, "next" is redefined as "next after the former next").
5. Print the text and line numbers (only).
6. Go to 8.
7. List the next text as currently defined in register B.
8. If there are more entries in register A go to 4.
9. If there are no entries in register B, exit.
10. Clear register A.
11. Exchange registers A and B.
12. Print as much of the line in the first text in register A as is

required to show its differences from the corresponding line in text 1.

13. If there are more entries in register A go to 3.

The above does not account for misplaced, omitted, or added lines. At step 4, if the line in the base text is not the same as the line in the other text, the other text is searched ten lines backwards and forwards, or to the limit of the text if that comes sooner. If a line that is the same is found this way, two asterisks are printed before the line number, as in the example above, to call attention to the different line number. At step 12 the process is more complex if the lines are different enough to warrant a search for a better match. Here the base text is searched forward ten lines or to the end, if that comes sooner (the matches for the ten preceding lines are known from previous processing), and the results of the search are recorded before the search of the other text is undertaken. Then the algorithm is:

a. If the base and the other line have both been matched, lines have been interchanged in the other text; continue with step 12 using the match found for the base line.

b. If only the base line has been matched, the other text has omitted a line; enter its text number in register C and go to step 13.

c. If only the other line has been matched, the other text has an additional line; enter its text number in register D and go to step 13.

d. The lines are simply very bad matches; continue with step 12.

After exit from the collation routine, register C is checked and any texts there have their numbers printed with *** following, as shown above. Finally register D is checked; contents, if any, are transferred to register A, the line from the first text in the register is printed with an A after the line number, and the collation routine is reentered at step 3. This means that if a text has two lines added after line 97 of the base text, so that line 98 of the base matches line 100 of the other text, the added lines will be interfiled with the others as follows:

97, 98A, 98 and **100, 99A, 99 and **101, 100 and **102, etc.

When lines are interchanged and the displacement is more than ten lines, a line which is marked as omitted in one place will be found identified as added in another.

In Mr. Bland's version, backward search is simply backward, and the computer then sometimes stops short of the true match, having found a reasonable surrogate. There is, however, a clean-up routine in the program that periodically prints out lines that have not been matched with the bases before the limit of search passed beyond them. In Mr. Bandat's version, backward search starts ten lines backward and moves forward, but the clean-up routine is retained as precaution in case there should prove to be a machine error or an unrecognized logical error in the program.

There is no limitation on the length of the texts that can be compared, though we sometimes process long works in sections that are convenient for us, as in the example. Up to 99 texts can be compared unless there is a further limitation because of the size of the computer and the number of lines that must be read in to allow the computer to hunt for misplaced, added, or omitted lines. We have never had to process more than twenty texts, and have used large computers, so that our search-range of ten lines in each direction has always been much less than the number of lines in the computer at any one time.

It will be clear that corresponding parts of all texts must enter the computer together. We prepare our texts on 80-column punched cards. This is not necessarily better than preparing them on tape, but we think that it is easier to correct our files if they are on cards. In Mr. Bland's version of the program the cards must be sorted so that line 1 of text 2 follows line 1 of text 1, and so on. Each time the computer reads a card from text 1 it checks to be sure that there is room to store a corresponding card from each of the other texts. If there is not room enough, the computer compares what it has stored until it reaches the point at which processing one more line would reduce the search-range, and then it reads in the rest, or as much as there is room for given the number of lines from the last batch that must be retained to preserve the search-range.

There is, of course, a machine for sorting the cards; it occasionally appears on the television screen masquerading as a computer, but it is just a high-speed card-sorter.[2] But sorting the cards even with a machine takes an appreciable time, and there are special problems when text 1 is more than ten lines shorter than the rest and has to be fleshed out in the middle with dummy cards. Therefore Mr. Bandat's version accepts the cards in blocks, arranged so that block 1 of text 2 follows block 1 of text 1, and so on. We only need to be sure that the blocks are small enough so that one block from each text will fit in the computer; that the first card in the block from text 2, and so on, has a line corresponding to the line on the first card in the block from text 1; and that if there are any large omissions in any texts the gaps come at the ends of blocks.

In Mr. Bland's version of the program, the user specifies the number of texts to be compared. (There is, by the way, no limit to the number of works that can be processed in a single run as long as the number of texts in each does not exceed the specified number.) The storage area assigned to each text starts with a list of the locations in storage of the beginnings of its lines; the lines are stored in a single string, with extra blanks removed, following the list. In Mr. Bandat's version the storage area is a single three-dimensional block that can be thought of as a set of pigeonholes; the lines are stored one to the hole, the holes for the first text are in the first row and the rows for the other texts are below it. All holes are the same depth—enough for the longest possible line—all the rows are the same length—enough for the maximum lines per text to be processed—and there are enough rows for the maximum number of texts. I do not know which method is more efficient.

I have rewritten Mr. Bandat's version of the program to accept texts without standard lineation, i.e., in prose, using the following algorithm:

1. Store text 1.
2. Fill a buffer with lines from the next text. (On return to this statement from statement 16, "next" is redefined as "next after the former next.")
3. Count off a segment of the text in the buffer containing, if possible, the same number of words as the first line in text 1 not matched during a previous filling of the buffer from the same text or tested during the present filling.

4. If the last fifteen characters in the buffer segment are similar enough to the last fifteen characters in the line of text 1 go to 13.
5. If the foregoing test has failed more than once with the same filling of the buffer, go to 8.
6. Count off three more words in the buffer if possible.
7. Go to 4.
8. Count backwards one word in the buffer if possible.
9. If the head of the buffer has not been reached go to 4.
10. If there are more lines to test in text 1 go to 3.
11. Move the first line in the buffer to the text storage.
12. Go to 14.
13. Move the matched segment in the buffer to the text storage.
14. If there are more lines of the next text to move to the buffer go to 2.
15. If the buffer is not empty go to 3.
16. If there are more texts go to 2.

The next program we obtained was written for me by William P. Anderson in Fortran, so we have not had to rewrite it. We use it for proofreading, but it can also be used for collating.

Our texts are punched on the cards with the line number in columns 1–4, the text number in columns 5–6, the card number in column 7, and the line in columns 8-80. If the line is too long for a single card it may be continued on another card with a 2 instead of a 1 in column 7 and columns 1–6 the same as before. Our way of preparing the texts is to have two card-punch operators make duplicate copies, compare the duplicates with our proofreading program, correct the errors in both copies, and save copy 2 for a back-up in case we lose copy 1. That the only time I ever lost a deck of cards I had no back-up copy, merely proves the desirability of insurance.

When we use the program for collating, the columns with the text numbers are ignored. Only two texts can be collated at a time, of course. The general-purpose collating program provides a complete text by always printing out the whole line for text 1, and the whole of each added line as found in the first text to contain it. The resulting continuity is often helpful when deciding which variations are significant, for it is not necessary to turn directly to any of the texts to see what the surrounding context is. It also makes it possible to mix emendation with the analysis of the variants.

The proofreading program does not print unless it finds variations on the cards, and if the lines on the cards for the two texts do not stay in step the program will be unable to find the correspondences.

The out-put from this program looks as follows:

```
0001011FROM HARMONY, FROM HEAVENLY HARMONY
0001011FORM HARMONY, FROM HEAVENLY HARMONY,
    XX                                       X
```

It is useful to head the deck of cards for each copy with a card saying specifically THIS IS DECK 1 and THIS IS DECK 2. And in any case, since cards that match are not printed at all, it is well to provide a test that all cards have been processed, by ending each deck with a card saying END 1 and END 2.

The first deck is followed by a deck-separation card having zeros in columns 1–6 to identify it, another with any character in any column that the computer is to ignore in comparing the decks (this card may be blank but it must be there), and finally by the second deck. The computer sets up five 80-column storage spaces, one for the card recording the columns to be ignored, one for a list of the columns to be ignored, two for the cards to be compared, and one for the record of the results of the comparison. The algorithm is very simple:

1. Transfer the cards to a scratch tape (a tape for temporary storage) until the deck-separation card is read.
2. Rewind the scratch tape.
3. Store the card recording the columns to be ignored.
4. Print a list of the columns to be ignored.
5. Fill the storage area for the record of results with blanks and set a flag to signal no differences.
6. Read a card from each deck (halt if either has no more cards).
7. Reading left to right, if column is to be ignored go to 9.
8. If the column is not the same in both cards store an X in the corresponding column of the record of results and set the flag to signal difference.

[267]

9. If columns remain go to 7.
10. If the flag shows no differences go to 6.
11. Print a blank line, the two cards just compared, and the record of results.
12. Go to 5.

This is not the only way to read proof by machine by any means, but I prefer it to any other when the text has been prepared on cards, even though it takes extra effort to insure that the cards in the two decks have not somehow gotten out of step.[3] If one deck has one card too many or too few, a situation arises that is called in computer circles GIGO, "garbage in, garbage out." To prevent this divide the decks into blocks of 100 cards, according to the line numbers on the cards, and count each block with a card-sorter set to count without sorting. If there are more or less than 100 cards in the block, make a binary search to find the error: that is, divide the block in half, according to the line numbers on the cards, and count the first half; if this half has 50 cards, divide the other half in half again, according to the line numbers on the cards, and count the first half of this half; if this quarter does not have 25 cards, divide it approximately in half according to the line numbers on the cards and count its first half again. Having located the eighth where the error lies, fan the cards and read the line numbers on the cards until the error is located; this is quicker than using the card-sorter again. Occasionally there will be compensating errors within the hundred-word blocks, so that the decks get out of step for a time, but in these bad sections the corresponding lines are usually separated only by a line of garbage X's and a blank line, and so can be compared by eye without too much difficulty.

A conscientious card-puncher will normally make about one error in twenty lines. Since the errors are randomly distributed in the text about one line in eleven will have an error in at least one deck. Sometimes both decks will have the same error, but this will show up when the texts are collated. Experience in industry suggests that card-punchers will get more done if they rely on a proofreading program to find their errors, but that they will also make more errors and be less happy in their work than if they are encouraged to try to eliminate their own errors before the computer proofreading.

The third program in our suite I wrote myself, in the machine language of the 7090–7094. It makes an alphabetical list of the words in a text, with the location or locations in which each appears, e.g., the page and line. The alphabetizing process, which I learned from Martin Kay, is the most efficient I know when the words are not already partly alphabetized, as they are not in normal texts. The user can supply a list of words that are to be ignored, or are the only ones not to be ignored; he can have the words alphabetized as though they were spelled backwards, so that words ending in "a" come first; or he can supply a list of letter-pairs, such as "ie" and "ei," and words that do not contain any of the pairs will be ignored. This program was written to analyze Dryden's spelling as it appears in his autograph letters and is reflected in the printed and manuscript copies of his works. Sometime it ought to be used to test our hypothesis that the first edition will normally have more of Dryden's spellings than any other. The so-called concordance to Dryden's poetry is only a word list, and for textual editing a word list is all that is needed, since most of its use is to answer such questions as whether *Dramatique Poesie* is in italics every time it occurs in the copy-text of the *Essay*.

The main algorithm of the program is as follows:

1. Read a card and arrange its words in a tree.
2. If there is no more room for words in the computer go to 4.
3. If there are more cards go to 1.
4. Change the tree to a list.
5. If a list has been stored previously (on a scratch tape) merge the new list with it.
6. If there are no more cards to read, print the list and halt.
7. Store the list on a scratch tape.
8. Go to 1.

The alphabetizing process is thus in two parts. As each word is read it is arranged in a tree in which each node has at most two branches. The left branches contain words earlier in alphabetical sequence than those at the nodes, the right branches contain words later in alphabetical sequence. The first line of *The Hind and the Panther* would be arranged as follows:

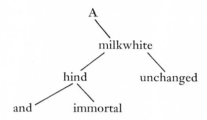

When all the words have been read, the last node before each left-running branch is connected with the other end of that branch, and the last node before each right-running branch has the other end of that branch connected to it. The result is an alphabetical series:

a and hind immortal milkwhite unchanged

The words are treated as types and tokens (in the first line of "A Song for St. Cecilia's Day,"

From harmony, from heavenly harmony,

harmony is a type and the two occurrences of it are tokens; the other words are both type and token). The words are stored in a type-list as they are read, with a space before each to record its length and the storage locations of the next words to the left and right in the tree. These location records I shall call left-pointers and right-pointers. The text-positions of the words, e.g., page and line, are stored in a token list as the words are read, together with the location of the type for each. These location records I shall call type-pointers. There is no way to tell the ideal proportion between the spaces to be alloted to the lists, so they are alloted the same space, the token list being stored backwards from the end of the space, and a record is kept of how close the ends of the lists are to each other.

The alphabetizing algorithms are as follows:

First Step

1. Store the first word in the type list, enter its position in the token list, and supply the necessary type-pointer.
2. Make the first word stored in the type list the base.
3. If the next word alphabetically precedes the base go to 8.
4. If the next word alphabetically follows the base go to 13.
5. Enter the text-position of the next word in the token list and supply a type-pointer to the location of the base.
6. If this is the last word on the card go to 18.
7. Redefine "next" as "next after the last next" and go to 2.
8. If the base has a left-pointer go to 11.
9. Enter the next word in the type list and supply the base a left-pointer to the location of the new type.
9a. Enter the text-position of the next word in the token list and supply a type-pointer to its location in the type list.
10. Go to 6.
11. Make the type pointed to by the left-pointer the base.
12. Go to 3.
13. If the base has a right-pointer go to 16.
14. Enter the next word in the type list and supply the base a right-pointer to the location of the new type.
15. Go to 9a.
16. Make the type pointed to' by the right-pointer the base.
17. Go to 3.
18. If there is not space in the lists for another card of words or if there are no more cards go to Second step.
19. Read another card.
20. Go to 7.

Second Step

1. Set a start-pointer to the first type and call it right-pointer of anchor type.
2. Find base type from right-pointer of anchor type.
3. If base type has left-pointer go to 7.
4. If base type has no right-pointer, exit.
5. Make the base type the anchor type.
6. Go to 2.
7. Find current type from left-pointer of base type.
8. Change right-pointer of anchor type to point to current type.

9. Remove left-pointer of base type.
10. If current type has no right-pointer go to 13.
11. Make type pointed to by right-pointer of current type the current type.
12. Go to 10.
13. Give current type a right-pointer pointing to base type.
14. Go to 2.

When alphabetizing is complete, there are no left-pointers, and their space is used to record instead the location of the first token for each type in the token list. These location records I shall call token-pointers. The type-pointers and token-pointers are adjusted by reading backwards through the token list, finding the type pointed to by each type-pointer, replacing the type-pointer by the token-pointer from the type (or by nothing if there is no token-pointer there), and giving the type a pointer to the new token. The right-pointers now give the alphabetical sequence of the types and the other pointers the textual sequence of the tokens for each type. In both lists, absence of a pointer signals the end of a sequence.

The algorithm for merging the alphabetized list in the computer with that on the scratch tape is:

1. If the test word in the computer and the test word on the scratch tape are the same go to 7.
2. If the word in the computer comes first alphabetically go to 5.
3. Print the entry for the word on the scratch tape (or write it on another scratch tape).
4. Go to 12.
5. Print the entry for the word in the computer (or write it on another scratch tape).
6. Go to 9.
7. Print (or write on another scratch tape) the entry on the scratch tape followed by the new information in the entry in the computer.
8. If there are no more words, exit.
9. If there are more words in the computer go to 11.
10. Print (or write on another scratch tape) the rest of the words on the scratch tape and exit.
11. Make the test word in the computer the next after the former test word.

12. If there are more words on the scratch tape go to 14.
13. Print (or write on another scratch tape) the rest of the words in the computer and exit.
14. Make the test word on the scratch tape the next after the former test word.
15. Go to 1.

I have written two programs for determining the family trees of texts, which we use when we have complex genealogical relationships among manuscripts. The simple one I intend to print in full elsewhere,[4] and the other is too complex to describe here. I have, however, described most of its operations in explaining how to do the same work with an abacus.[5] Where the second article mentions sorting, the program uses a routine exactly like the alphabetizing routine just described.

Programs of this kind rest directly on a theory and therefore cannot be any more useful than the theory. If the theory is incorrect, you get "garbage out" whatever you put in. On the other hand, a theory that has had a computer program built on it is likely to be at least internally consistent. First of all, the computer has been programmed by its manufacturer not to accept users' programs that have obvious inconsistencies. Secondly, well written computer programs perform the same tasks in exactly the same way always, by a maximum use of loops and of subprograms and subroutines that operate like loops. And in the third place, the wise programmer tests his work with problems of known solution and of every sort to be encountered, and if the program gives unexpected answers, he examines not only his program but also his other method of solution and the underlying theory of both processes.

Sometimes there is an even less direct value to a computer program. In my book, *A Manual of Textual Analysis* (1956), in which I suggested that computers could be used in textual criticism, the explanation of how to analyze variations with more than two alternate readings consists essentially of examples; no complete algorithm appears, and two of the examples are wrong precisely because I had no algorithm to insure their correctness. The much more precise explanations in my articles reflect the fact that a computer will not operate without detailed instructions. In my book, again, the explanation of how to deal with conflated texts is not only without an algorithm but would require a very complex one, essentially different in its underlying theory from the other methods espoused in the book. When I came to write my program, the difficulty of the algorithm struck me especially; just the thought of formulating it led me to look for other ways of doing the work. By this time I had worked out the algorithms for dealing with texts that were not conflated, and so I understood theory and practice well enough to recognize (gradually) that the theory comprehended conflation as well and that the practice needed only a little extension to deal with it. In my articles, therefore, the explanations of how to deal with conflation are not only much more precise but essentially different from the one in my book.

But the fact remains that the theory is more important than the program. For example, one of the manuscript copies of Dryden's *Indian Emperour* is a collateral of the first edition, an independent witness to Dryden's own manuscript, now lost. Which ought to be the copy-text, the extant manuscript or the first edition? The decision has to be made on the basis of their variations in spelling. Professor Bowers graded Dryden's spellings into more distinctive, less distinctive, and not distinctive, and concluded that the manuscript had the more distinctive of Dryden's spellings. I graded all the spellings equally, and using my word list program to help me identify and count them I concluded that the first edition had more of Dryden's spellings. So Professor Bowers chose the manuscript for his copy-text, and I chose the first edition.[6] The fact that I got accurate counts of all the spellings does not guarantee that my choice was correct.

Also, when there was evidence that Dryden's spelling habits had changed over a period of years before and after he wrote *The Indian Emperour*, I assumed that they changed gradually. On this basis I concluded that the probability that Dryden would use "hee," "bee," and so on when writing the play was about one in ten. In an autograph letter of 1653 we find 2 "bee," 1 "beeing," 1 "hee," 5 "mee," 2 "me"; in 1664, 6 "be," 2 "he," 1 "mee." These are the only letters we have that certainly precede *The Indian Emperour*. Dryden never used "-ee" again in the autograph letters and documents that we have; e.g., in 1666, the next letter to be preserved, we find 2 "be," 6 "we." When Lester Beaurline re-examined the matter, he assumed that Dryden's spelling habits changed in increments, so that his practice before writing the play could be assumed to continue through that time and his subsequent practice could be ignored. On this basis he concluded that the chances Dryden would spell "hee," "bee," and so on in *The Indian Emperour* were about one in three.[7]

My differences with Professor Beaurline, however, can perhaps be resolved by analogical reasoning, where my differences with Professor Bowers cannot. If I ever take up the subject of Dryden's spelling again it will be to test whether he changed his spelling habits gradually or by increments in later life, when we have more evidence. My program will make it easy enough to compile the necessary lists.

We have not reached the ultimate use of computers in our work, of course. The more complex of my text-critical programs builds textual trees, but reports its results as a series of line-segments, 1—2, 1—3, 2—4, and so on, which must be assembled into a tree by hand:

Machines are now available for drawing the trees by computer, and I intend to alter my program accordingly.

Also, machines for transcribing print directly onto computer tapes (optical scanners) are now in use, and when one is developed that will read seventeenth-century printing we shall want to avail ourselves of it. As soon as one mentions scanners, some serendipitist is sure to ask derisively whether it will not soon be possible for textual editors to avoid reading their texts entirely.[8] But the butterfly scholar can get at the dearest, sweetest, deep-down things without the textual scholar's constant risk of finding that all has become seared with his trade, bleared, and smeared with toil. After two weeks of working from nine to five, from Monday through Saturday, collating the seventeenth-century editions of *Absalom and Achitophel* in the Folger Library, I was still interrupting my work occasionally to savor the lines as verse. To collate seventeen editions of the same poem using a computer busied me for an afternoon at a card-sorter, and took the computer eleven minutes. I believe my appreciation of the poem, aside from my sense that the most minute and labored study of it will not entirely destroy its appeal, was no less, and certainly the accuracy of the results was greater.[9] I believe also, then, that the operators who punched up the poem seventeen times did not love it any better or produce more accurate copies than if they had spent a few hours feeding the texts to an optical scanner.

The output of an optical scanner will require a different kind of proofreading program, one that will call attention to unlikely sequences of characters as interpreted by the scanner, so that the Dryden program will eventually have six computer programs. Richard Bandat always speaks of his programs in masculine terms: "this man [i.e., subroutine] gets the lines, this man compares them." In the same idiom, then, with reference to our program yet to come, I say in the words of the Wife of Bath:

> Welcome the sixte, whan that evere he shal!

N O T E S

1. We make use of other mechanical aids, of course. The Library of the University of California, Los Angeles, purchased a Hinman collator in 1966, and before that we had developed a device of our own; see "The Poor Man's Mark IV, or Ersatz Hinman Collator," *PBSA*, LX (1966), 149–58, and George Robert Guffey, "Standardization of Photographic Reproductions for Mechanical Collation," *PBSA*, LXII (1968), 237–40.

2. With certain kinds of data a card-sorter can do the same work as a computer, cheaper, and, considering the relative waiting time to use the two, faster.

3. The brevity and general usefulness of this program warrant its being given in full:

```
        DIMENSION  COLUM(80), TABL1(80),  TABL2(80),
        XMARK(80), NKOLUM(80)
        INTEGER  COLUM,TABL1,TABL2,XMARK,BL,X
25      FORMAT (1H080A1/1H 80A1/1H 80A1)
44      FORMAT (14A6)
98      FORMAT (36H1COLUMNS DELETED FROM
        COMPARISON ARE / (40I3))
99      FORMAT (80A1)
        DATA BL,X/1H ,1HX/
 1      READ(5,44)(COLUM(I),I=1,14)
        IF(COLUM)5,10,5
 5      WRITE(8,44)(COLUM(I),I=1,14)
        GO TO 1
10      REWIND 8
        READ(5,99)(COLUM(I),I=1,80)
        K = 0
        NCOLUM(I) = 0
        DO 30 I=1,80
        IF (COLUM (I)–BL)31,30,31
31      K = K+1
        NKOLUM(K) = I
30      CONTINUE
        WRITE(6,98)(NKOLUM(I),I=1,K)
32      DO 33I=1,80
33      XMARK(I) = BL
        J = 1
20      READ(5,99)(TABL1(I),I=1,80)
        READ(8,99)(TABL2(I),I=1,80)
        DO 21 I=1,80
        IF(COLUM(I)–BL)21,22,21
22      IF(TABL1(I)–TABL2(I))23,21,23
23      XMARK(I) = X
        J = 2
21      CONTINUE
        GO TO (20,24), J
24      WRITE(6,25)(TABL2(I),I=1,80),(TABL1(I),I=1,80),
        (XMARK(I),I=1,80)
        GO TO 32
        END
```

For the IBM system/360, FORMAT statement 44 should read (20A4) and 20 should replace 14 in statements 1 and 5.

[277]

4. "A Thousand Klowns," forthcoming.

5. "Abaco-Textual Criticism," *PBSA*, LXII (1968), 547–78. See also "Some Routines for Textual Criticism," *The Library*, XXI (1966), 309–17, "Some Notes on Genealogical Methods in Textual Criticism," *Novum Testamentum*, IX (1967), 278–97, and "A New Calculus of Variants for Textual Genealogy," forthcoming.

6. Fredson Bowers, "The 1665 Manuscript of Dryden's *Indian Emperour*," *SP*, XLVIII (1951), 738–60; Vinton A. Dearing, "The Use of a Computer in Analyzing Dryden's Spellings," in *Literary Data Processing Conference Proceedings* (New York, 1964), pp. 200–210.

7. John Dryden, *Four Tragedies* (1967), pp. 32–33. Some of Professor Beaurline's remarks here arise from the fact that he did not have a computer-compiled list of Dryden's spellings, and when he wrote to ask me for more detailed information than I had published I replied only that I had lost my tables instead of offering to work them up again or to send him my computer-produced lists so that he could make his own tables.

8. In this connection I sense in the growing practice of printing a text with an apparatus but no explanatory notes a danger that the textual critic will not read carefully enough to avoid errors in his conclusions as to which variants are authorial or just plain correct.

9. In order to achieve a reasonable standard of accuracy, we normally do all collations made without the computer five times. Normally, too, once work is begun without using a computer it is finished in the same way; since the edition has been under way for a generation there is a backlog of work so begun, but the prospect of repeating or asking anyone else to repeat my work in the Folger was too much for me—the poem is over 1000 lines long.

WILLIAM M. GIBSON AND GEORGE R. PETTY, JR.

Project *OCCULT*: The Ordered Computer Collation of Unprepared Literary Text

WILLIAM M. GIBSON *and* GEORGE R. PETTY, JR. *report on a project designed to increase the accuracy and efficiency of collating. Project* OCCULT *promises to automate mechanical tasks and free textual scholars to spend more time on the art of editing.*

REVOLUTIONARY TECHNICAL innovations—and we believe OC-CULT is revolutionary—arise when the need for them is growing sharply, and someone succeeds in meeting the need. But the need comes first.

There is now an increasing interest in editing authoritatively the work of major American writers of the nineteenth century, and as those who have attempted such critical editions are aware, the part of the process which is at once most crucial and mechanical is collating—the exact comparison of all the details of the relevant forms of the text. When impressions have been made from standing type or from the same plates, an operator of the Hinman Collating Machine[1] will be able to find changes that have been made. But reading manuscript against print, or the first edition against a later reset edition demands reading aloud or comparison by eye; this chore is usually done by graduate students who work irregularly on an hourly basis. There is, inevitably, error, and the errors may easily be compounded because both kinds of collation are, for most collators, stupendously and nauseatingly dull.

Given the growing need for accurate collation and the "human use of human beings," we began in 1964 to experiment with a computer program that would uncover much more swiftly and accurately than graduate students could those variants on which the editor must exercise judgment.[2] We wrote out a group of nineteen rules on which the logic of collation by machine could be based—in mathematical terminology, an algorithm—and secured the services of Andrew Singer and Larry W. English, young programmers then associated with New York University, to write a collation program. Variant texts of Henry James's short novel, *Daisy Miller*, were chosen for comparison because James had essentially rewritten the story for the New York edition. That is, the first English edition (1879) and the New York edition (1909) differ more widely than any "collatable" text that editors are likely to want to establish. They constitute, in effect, not one but two distinct copy-texts, for the revised version is measurably a different story from the first edition: James altered ninety percent of his sentences in one way or another, and added about fifteen percent more material. In short we are *not* editing *Daisy Miller*, but have used the two texts to give our program an extreme test.

The upshot of this first effort was that Mr. Singer and Mr. English were finally unable to secure clear, meaningful print-out of the differences between the two variant texts. The print-out appeared in capital letters only, with many errors, with odd symbols for punctuation marks, and with words listed out of order. Furthermore, the program had stalled at sentence 390, and extensive debugging could not make it proceed further. But their work suggested to us that "ordered computer collation of unprepared literary texts" was possible.

Since one of the most trying difficulties of our first attempt had been the uncertainty of our communications with the programmers, Mr. Petty proposed that a second effort be made in which he would be the programmer.[3] We would thus be certain that decisions made by us as textual scholars would not be circumvented when they were translated into machine code. We realized that we would have to take a penalty in the reduced sophistication of our programming capability, but developments in computer language designed to handle strings of alphanumeric characters (a computer term which includes English language text) had made it much easier for students in the humanities to write programs.

At the suggestion of Mr. Petty we obtained the cooperation of Stockton Gaines, of the Institute for Defense Analyses at Princeton University, and Lee Varian, of the Princeton Computer Center. These men had been responsible for the implementation of the programming language called Snobol 4 at Princeton, and they were prepared to advise us if our problems befuddled us completely. They recommended Snobol 4 because it was designed to perform pattern matching and the concatenation of character strings by means of instructions whose syntax was close to written English.[4] We obtained a grant of $6,000 from the National Endowment for the Humanities and we started our work at the Princeton Computer Center in February 1968, continuing to use *Daisy Miller* as our experimental text.[5]

With the assistance of the Mohawk Data Sciences Corporation we produced a magnetic tape version of the two editions to be collated. This company has manufactured a machine which transforms the impulses from an electric typewriter keyboard into a machine-readable seven channel code on magnetic tape.[6] Because we did not want to use the long tapes repeatedly during the testing of the program, we also had the last few pages of the texts punched on machine-readable eighty character cards. The collation of these cards is printed at the end of this essay as a demonstration of the accuracy of the program.

Definition of the Problem

As a first practical step in the development of occult we had to define the concept of collation in data processing terms. We decided that the machine-readable form of the texts, whether cards, paper tape, or magnetic tape, should be as accurate and mechanical a reproduction of the visual appearance of the book or magazine as was humanly possible. No signs, signals, or numbers would be added to the text to assist the process of collation. This decision made the instructions to a keypuncher or typist perfectly simple and straightforward: copy the text as you see it on the page, line for line, as closely as your machine will permit. Where the machine did not provide a needed character, a suitable substitute would be inserted or a shift code established.[7] By refusing to become involved in pre-editing or structuring the input material we reduced the hazard of introducing new errors into the collation.

We further agreed that the machine ought to be able to proceed uninterrupted with the collation of two texts from beginning to end. This implied that the program would have to provide a method for keeping the scanning of one text synchronized with the other even if there were a substantial addition or deletion in either text. In other words, the machine would have to be able to "keep its place" in both texts. Many procedures for comparing two streams of characters, one character at a time, have been developed for the purpose of checking the accuracy of tape or card duplication or for similar editorial functions. However, these programs operate under the assumption that the location of corresponding characters in the input streams was sequential or otherwise predictable. Therefore, when a difference between two characters was discovered, the appropriate action could be taken and the comparison could proceed to the known location of the next corresponding characters. Some such programs assumed that the units of information in each input set, whether card images or tape records of fixed character length, corresponded in sequence, so that where an error was found in a card or record it could be corrected, and the comparison could continue secure in the knowledge that the next records would in fact correspond. Vinton Dearing, of the University of California at Los Angeles, has used a procedure like this to collate Dryden's poems, taking advantage of the fact that even if a line had so many variants that the machine lost its place during collation, the next line could be expected to correspond beginning with the first character.

The problem of collating unprepared literary prose is considerably more complicated than these comparison programs. Since line length varies with typography from one edition to another, and since there are no fixed syntactical units within which an author's revisions must fit, and no limit on the number of characters or words he might change, add, or delete, there is therefore no way to be certain where to begin the comparison after a sizeable difference had been found. The OCCULT program would have to include instructions for locating a place in both texts where the comparison could be resumed with the assurance that the material being compared was in fact logically comparable. Furthermore, since we had already decided that we would not pre-edit the texts by reading them through to number the corresponding sentences or by some similar procedure, the program would have to "find its place" by reference only to the characters supplied by the text.[8]

There was no question about the need for including in the collating procedure all marks of punctuation, including end-of-line hyphens, all upper and lower case characters, all diacritical marks, and all uses of italic or other non-standard type fonts. If at some point an editor might decide that a collation for substantives only was sufficient, the special marks could be eliminated during the reading in of the texts. Our present program is based on their inclusion, however, and would need to have a card or two altered to take account of the absence of the syntactical logic provided by these marks.

The number of significant editions to be collated would usually be more than two, but we saw no reason for the purpose of developing our process to undertake to compare more than two at any one run. If more needed to be included, they could be run individually against one of the texts previously collated, as long as all editions are collated against the same master text. There is no logical or technical objection to expanding the program to collate more than two texts at a time, but in the development stage the housekeeping required during coding to keep track of the extra material might be more than a harried amateur programmer could endure, particularly in the design of the output format.[9]

The collated material had to be arranged on a page in a format suitable for use by an editor. We selected a standard format for sight collation, in which space for the collated texts was provided side by side on the page. When a difference was found it had to be listed with page and line number directly opposite the corresponding page and line number of the other text, with the variant words printed out in order along with dots to indicate words in sequence that had been found to be identical, plus at least one word of context from the matched portion to show where the difference occurred.

The principal difficulties to be solved as a result of these decisions were keeping track of the text during processing, establishing reliable rules for locating corresponding parts of the text, comparing the corresponding parts, and finally arranging the results in a useful format.

Solution of the Problem

One of the first requirements for the solution of our problem was to limit the amount of text to be searched at any given time. Although the size of computer memories is becoming unbelievably large, the amount of memory space available for data to be used in efficient active processing is limited. We could not expect all of both texts to be available at once for scanning and cross-referencing. We therefore conceived the idea of establishing a limited block of words in one text, which we called the slave-text, in which an active search would be made for a selected group of words from the other text, called the master-text. It is unnecessary to search the slave-text from beginning to end for a given sentence in the master-text, for if identical sentences appear in widely separated locations in the two texts it seems sensible to treat them as entirely different sets of words because they figure in changed contexts. Therefore we can limit the range of forward search to a relatively small number of words, and the range of backward scan for transposed sentences to something less than half of the forward scan. When a block of words from the slave-text of the appropriate length is established in the memory of the machine, a group of words from the master-text is compared with that block. When the process of comparison is complete the block is extended by a unit of words, and the earliest unit of the block is dropped off. The scanning block is moved through the slave-text like the image projected from a microfilm reader. Thus the size of the memory required to scan the entire work is held to a practical minimum.

Logically only two kinds of change can be found by such a search: a deletion from the master-text or an addition to the slave-text. A rewritten passage is a simultaneous deletion and addition, and all unmatched material found between two matched groups of words may be considered as such. When the material is printed on the page it seems as if the computer has understood the subtle changes of meaning involved in the revision and identified the changed text as corresponding to the original. No such process has occurred, however. The program has simply taken advantage of the logical nodes that occur during the process of rewriting.

As a matter of efficiency the shorter text is selected as the master-text and the longer for the slave-text. This choice need not affect the selection of the copy-text into which an editor will emend, for the print-out will always show the copy-text in the left-hand column. The saving in search time comes about because only in the case of an extensive deletion in the slave-text of words from the master-text must the entire block of the slave-text be searched.

Because we are by nature literary scholars rather than computer experts, we began by thinking of the sentence as the unit of comparison in the collation. But when we tried to define a sentence ending in terms of punctuation conventions, character by character, we realized that there were many combinations of end punctuation —quotation marks, spaces, and carriage returns—to be accounted for, and that, in fact, it was impossible to find a definition of a sentence ending that was both comprehensive and discrete. If we relied on the typing convention of two spaces following a sentence end we avoided many ambiguities, but there was still no way to determine whether the sequence "letter-period-carriage return" is the end of a sentence or an abbreviation in the middle of one, like "Mr." or "Mrs."[10] These and other unimagined difficulties prompted us to give up the sentence as the unit of collation, and to substitute for it a set of twelve words. This number of words was small enough so that the probability of finding a false match was negligible, and large enough so that the comparison would proceed quickly through the text. Finally we determined that the slave-text block size should be fifteen sets of twelve words for forward scanning, and ten sets backward, giving a total context of three hundred words.

The basic procedure, then, is first to generate a block of three hundred words in the slave-text, keeping track of the line and page number for each set. Then, read in a set of text words from the master-text. Next, search the slave-block for a set of words like the test-set. If one is found, note the differences between the two sets, pass them on together with their line and page numbers to an output routine, and print them out in a format convenient for an editor. If no similar set is found, pass the test-set to the output routine as a set deleted from the slave-text, and read in the next set from the master-text as a test-set. When a number of master-text sets equal to the number of sets of forward scan in the slave-text has been tried without finding a match, the block of slave-text sets must be passed on as an addition and a new block generated. Of course, procedures must be established for adding a new set to the slave-block when a match is found, and for advancing all the unmatched sets to take up the place of the sets already matched.

The principal difficulty in this kind of continuous comparison is to make sure the machine does not lose its place after a series of failures to find a similarity.[11] In the method outlined above, we move from similarity to similarity so that we always have a pointer at the most recent matched location from which to proceed with collation.

In our first experiments we established several possible kinds of matches between the master-set and the slave-set:

1. The sets could be absolutely identical, including punctuation.
2. They could be identical except for punctuation.
3. They could be the same, including punctuation, but without regard to word order, as in the case of a transposed unpunctuated adverbial element.
4. They could be the same without regard to punctuation or word order.
5. They could be none of the above, but found similar because some percentage (we tried 75%) of their words were the same.

We found in practice that better than 90% of the matches were done on the statistical rule, which logically included the others. We therefore discarded all but the statistical procedure for matching. However, we felt that more weight ought to be given to the discovery of sequences of matched words within a set than to the simple unordered quantity of matched words. We therefore added an alternative statistical match which established the rule that if in the comparison of a set of twelve words from the master-text the sum of the number of words in the longest sequence plus the number of sequences was greater than or equal to 6, then the sets should be treated as matched. The following table shows the minimum possible matches. Our tests showed that this second rule did not produce false matches and that it was a more effective way to establish a match than the unordered rule, so it was finally adopted as the only rule for matching sets.

MINIMUMS FOR SUCCESSFUL MATCHING
OF TWO SETS OF 12 WORDS
Number of sequences found + number of words in largest
sequence = 6

1	5	6
2	4	6
3	3	6
4	2	6

Because we had been cautioned to be careful about keeping our place in the text, we had originally decided to divide the matching procedure into two parts: a first step to decide whether the pair of sets being considered were in fact the same, and then a second one to decide which words in the two sets would be retained for listing in the collation, and which omitted. In order to avoid being thrown off by punctuation changes, we conceived the first or locator step without punctuation. The second collator step had to be done with punctuation in order to provide all the information the editor might want. When it came to writing the program for the two steps, it became clear that they were so much alike as to be logically redundant. Since the editor had to see the variant words arranged in sentence order, with the words that were the same replaced by dots, and since there was not much point in omitting single words from the print-out, we found ourselves searching for sequences of two or more words in the collating routine exactly as we did in the locating routine. We therefore merged the two functions into one, which simultaneously determined whether the sets being considered were in fact the same logical sets, and if they were, which words had to be preserved for printing-out. If the statistical rule decided they were not logically the same, then of course the sets were preserved in their original form, without omitting coincidentally identical words, for the print-out. This merged step is done with the punctuation retained exactly as it is in the text.[12]

The program then resolved itself into the following steps:

1. Generate the slave-text block for comparison.
2. Locate and collate logically similar sets.
3. Adjust the block, and include routines for a discovered match and a discovered no-match.
4. Justify—that is, arrange all the computed information on the print-out page.

The actual coding of the program took about three months of trial and error, in which the machine repeatedly tried to explain how silly the instructions it had been given were.

Print-out Quality

The Princeton University Computer Center has a computer which allows the use of upper and lower case characters (see the sample collation at the end of this article); it does not, however, include italics or foreign language diacritical marks, which have to be provided for by means of shift codes. The decision to use a computer with this capability is not a trivial one, because to reproduce upper and lower case fonts on the keypunch which offers capitals only, a system of shift codes must be established and a translation program written to convert the keypunch information for the full character set. Furthermore, the program must be carefully coded to make the distinction between fonts during pattern matching and the program must be run only when a printer with a full character set chain is available. The use of a full character set chain slows the printing process, and in a busy computer center such a consideration argues against mounting the chain at all until a researcher who needs it makes his request in a very firm voice.

If the computed collation were listed on a magnetic tape it could be taken to a variety of graphic arts quality printing systems which could generate all the characters necessary for imitating the text as it was printed in the original. Typically these systems print the material on photographic negatives which are used in the preparation of photo-offset plates. We have observed such operations but are not now in a position to say that we have worked out the practical details of producing graphic arts quality print-out directly from our collation program. We need to find a machine that can read magnetic tape or punched cards produced from our program and translate them into the typical paper code system used by commercial printers. This is one of the many problems, labeled "trivial" by computer specialists, which take several months of time-consuming practical effort by someone interested in making them work. In the meantime, the sample provided in this text will illustrate the limitations and the usefulness of a standard computer character set with an upper and lower case print chain installed on the printer.

Preparation of Input Text

One of the most difficult aspects of project OCCULT has not been discussed here simply because it is too complex. In the course of our efforts we have prepared literary text in machine readable form by almost every variety of input device available today. All of them require an operator to read the text from the edition being collated, sometimes using special codes or characters for those not available on the keyboard. In order to reduce the number of errors in the input material a verification procedure may be used in which the taped or punched text is typed over again and typographical errors presumably located.[13] One promising by-product of our collation program is that it reveals all the typos, unless by an unlikely coincidence two different operators, working on different editions, happen to produce the same typo in exactly the same place. The input material can be updated (that is, corrected) following the first run, and a second run made with exceptionally accurate texts.[14]

TRIAL COLLATION OF LAST 8 PAGES OF DAISY MILLER USING VERSION 2 OF OCCULT, SEPTEMBER 16, 1968, PROGRAMMER G. PETTY

FIRST LONDON EDITION	COLLECTED NEW YORK EDITION
PAGE.LINE	PAGE.LINE
185.2 ..... Miss Miller, at midnight, ...	89.2 ..... Miss Miller at midnight .....
	89.3 gentleman; in spite of which deep discretion,
	however, the fact of the scandalous
185.4 gentleman; but nevertheless, ... later,	89.5 adventure was known ..... later,
185.5 the fact of her having been there under these	
circumstances was known	
185.7 ..... and	89.6 with a dozen vivid details, ... and
185.9 commented accordingly. Winterbourne reflected	89.7 was commented accordingly. Winterbourne
that they had of course known it at	judged thus that the people about the hotel
	had been thoroughly empowered to testify,
	and that after Daisy's return there would
	have
185.10 the hotel, and that, after Daisy's return,	89.11 .....
there had	
186.2 ..... man was conscious ..... moment	89.12 ..... man became aware ..... moment
186.5 that it had ceased to be a matter of serious	
regret to	
186.6	89.13 of how thoroughly it had ceased to ruffle
	.....

Economics

The collation of eight pages of *Daisy Miller* printed at the end of this article took eight minutes and thirty-eight seconds of computer time to perform. At this rate the collation of the whole work would take about an hour and ten minutes and would cost about $290, using the present rate of $250 per hour.[15] To this figure should be added the cost of preparing the texts for input, which costs at least as much as commercial typing, and frequently costs more. In the case of *Daisy Miller*, which is roughly thirty thousand words long, the cost of preparing two editions of tape (paper or magnetic) would be between $250 and $275. If the tapes are verified—that is, retyped, compared with the first typing, and corrected—the price will be nearly twice as much, about $500.

The cost of this collation is high because the texts used in our trial run are really two different novels, in which nine out of ten sentences were changed. By contrast, a complete collation of the *Cornhill Magazine* text of *Daisy Miller* against the first London edition, in which the only differences are likely to be punctuation, typos, and a few words, would take no more than twenty-five minutes, at a cost of approximately $105.

As we have suggested above, the sophistication of our programming leaves something to be desired, and we believe that the expense of the process can be reduced by as much as 40% by improved coding. Furthermore, the program may be applicable to the preparation of the input text in ways which could reduce the cost of that process as well. Collation by computer is a process which begins with the preparation of input text, and our program as presently used is only the central step in the complete system. We can say at this time that our program will provide an accurate collation of the input material, including whatever unduplicated errors have been introduced during its preparation. Occult is even in its present form a remarkable method for eliminating the drudgery and improving the accuracy of the task of collation.

The print-out of the last pages of *Daisy Miller* in the two variant texts appears below. It has been set in type to be clear and readable; however we intend to reproduce the complete print-out of three texts of *Daisy Miller* and the OCCULT program itself by photo-offset in a monograph within a year. The following shift codes are used (see note 7): #, begin italics; @, end italics. These would be converted to the appropriate type font when a printer with a suitable character set became available. The line numbers for the first page of collation are incorrect because the program was set up to begin collation at line 1 of each text, whereas this trial actually began at p. 185, line 8 of the London edition and p. 89, line 17 of the New York edition. After the first page the numbers are accurate.

TRIAL COLLATION OF LAST 8 PAGES OF DAISY MILLER USING VERSION 2 OF OCCULT, SEPTEMBER 16, 1968, PROGRAMMER G. PETTY

FIRST LONDON EDITION		COLLECTED NEW YORK EDITION	
185.2	. . . . Miss Miller, at mid-night, ...	89.2	. . . . Miss Miller at mid-night . . . .
		89.3	gentlemen; in spite of which deep discretion, however, the fact of the scandalous
185.4	gentleman; but nevertheless, ... later,	89.5	adventure was known . . . . later,
185.5	the fact of her having been there under these circumstances was known		
185.7	. . . . and	89.6	with a dozen vivid details, ... and
185.9	commented accordingly. Winterbourne reflected that they had of course known it at	89.7	was commented according-ly. Winterbourne judged thus that the people about the hotel had been thoroughly empowered to testify, and that after Daisy's return there would have
185.10	the hotel, and that, after Daisy's return, there had	89.11	. . . .
186.2	. . . . man was conscious . . . . moment	89.12	. . . . man became aware . . . . moment

186.5 that it had ceased to be a matter of serious regret to

186.6 . . . .

89.13 of how thoroughly it had ceased to ruffle . . . .

186.8 . . . . by lowminded . . . . These

89.15 . . . . by low-minded . . . . These

186.9 people, a day or two later, had serious information to give: the

89.16 sources of current criticism a day or two later abounded still further: the little American flirt was alarmingly ill and the doctors now in possession of the scene. Winterbourne,

186.10 little American flirt was alarmingly ill. Winterbourne, ...

90.3 . . . .

186.14 preceded him, ...

90.5 preceded him . . . .

186.15 by . . . . at

90.7 by the all-efficient . . . . at

187.1 night," said Randolph— "that's what . . . . her . . . .

90.8 night that way, you bet— that's what has . . . . her so . . . .

187.2 . . . . I shouldn't . . . . pla- guey

90.10 . . . . I should n't . . . . pla- guey

187.4 dark. You can't see anything here at night, except when there's a moon. In America there's always a moon!" Mrs. Miller was invisible; she

90.11 dark over here. You can't see anything over here with- out the moon's right up. In America they don't go round by the moon!" Mrs. Miller meanwhile wholly surrendered to her genius for unapparent uses; her sa- lon knew her less than ever, and she was presumably now at least giving her

187.7 was now, at least, giving her . . . . was

90.16 . . . . was

187.8 evident . . . . Winterbourne

90.18 clear . . . . Winterbourne

187.10 went often to ask for news of her, and once he saw Mrs.

90.20 constantly attended for news from the sick-room, which

[293]

Miller, who, though deeply alarmed, was—rather to his surprise—perfectly composed, and, as it appeared, a most efficient and judicious nurse. She talked a

reached him, however, but with worrying indirectness, though he once had speech, for a moment, of the poor girl's physician and once saw Mrs. Miller, who, sharply alarmed, struck him as thereby more happily inspired than he could have conceived and indeed as the most noiseless and light-handed of nurses. She invoked a good deal the remote shade of Dr. Davis,

187.15 good deal about Dr. Davis, ... of

90.27 . . . . of

187.17 saying to himself that she was not, after all, such a monstrous

90.28 taking her after all for less monstrous a goose. To this indulgence indeed something she further said

188.1 goose. . . . .

90.30 perhaps even more insidiously disposed him . . . .

188.3 day," she said to him. "Half the time she doesn't know what

90.31 day quite pleasantly. Half the time she does n't know what she's

188.5 message; . . . . She

91.2 message—. . . . She

188.7 told me to tell you that . . . . handsome

91.3 wanted you to know . . . . handsome

188.8 Italian. I am sure I am very glad; Mr. Giovanelli hasn't been

91.4 Italian who was always round. I'm sure I'm very glad; Mr. Giovanelli has n't been near us since

188.10 near us since . . . .

91.5 . . . .

188.11 gentleman; . . . .

91.6 gentleman, ...

188.13 that he was afraid I was angry with him for taking Daisy

91.8 he was afraid I had n't approved of his being round with her so much evenings. Of course it ain't as if their evenings were as pleasant as

ours—since #we@ don't
seem to feel that way about
the poison. I guess I #don't@
see the point now; but

188.14 round at night. Well, so I
      am; but . . . . a

91.12 . . . . a

188.15 lady. I would scorn to scold
      him. Any way, she says she's
      not engaged. I don't know
      why she wanted you to
      know;

91.13 lady and I'd scorn to raise a
      fuss. Anyway, she wants
      you to realise she ain't en-
      gaged. I don't know why she
      makes so much of it, but she
      said

189.1 but she said . . . . three
     times—'Mind . . . .

91.15 . . . . three times 'Mind
     . . . .

189.5 . . . . that castle, ... I

91.18 up . . . . that castle . . . .
     I

189.6 wouldn't . . . . as

91.19 would n't . . . . as

189.7 that. Only, if she is not en-
     gaged, I'm sure I'm glad to
     know it."
        But, as Winterbourne had
     said, it mattered very little.

91.20 #that@. Only if she ain't en-
     gaged I guess I'm glad to
     realise it too."
        But, as Winterbourne had
     originally judged, the truth
     on this question had small
     actual relevance. A

189.10 A . . . . been

91.23 . . . . been

189.11 . . . . the

91.25 indeed . . . . the

189.12 fever. Daisy's . . . . was
      cemetery,

91.26 #perniciosa@. A . . . . was
     found for her . . . .
     cemetery,

189.13 in . . . .

91.27 by . . . .

189.14 it, ...

91.29 it . . . .

189.17 . . . . career

91.30 . . . . career

190.2 would have led you to ex-
     pect. . . . . away.

91.31 might have made probable.
     . . . . away.

190.3 Giovanelli was very pale; on
     this occasion he had no
     flower in his button-hole; he
     seemed to wish to say some-
     thing. At last he

92.1 Giovanelli, in decorous
     mourning, showed but a
     whiter face; his button-hole
     lacked its nosegay and he
     had visibly something urgent

190.7   said, ...

190.8   . . . . amiable.”

190.9   And then . . . . a moment, "And she was . . . . Winterbourne

190.10 looked at him, and . . . . words, "And the . . . .

190.13 "The most innocent!" Winterbourne felt sore and angry. "Why

190.16 the devil," he . . . . take [take] . . . .

190.17 place?"

Mr. Giovanelli's urbanity was apparently imperturbable. He looked on the

191.2 ground a moment, and then he said, "For myself, ... and

191.4 she wanted to go."

"That was no reason!" Winterbourne declared.

The subtle Roman again dropped his eyes. "If she had lived, I

—and even to distress—to say, which he scarce knew how to "place." He decided at last to confide

92.5 it with a pale convulsion to Winterbourne. . . . .

92.7 . . . . amiable.”

92.8 To which . . . . a moment: "Also—naturally!—. . . . . Winterbourne

92.10 sounded him with hard dry eyes, but . . . . words, "The . . . .

92.12 "The most innocent!" It came somehow so much too late that our friend could only glare at its having come at all.

92.15 "Why the devil," he . . . . take . . . .

92.16 place?"

Giovanelli raised his neat shoulders and eyebrows to within a suspicion

92.19 of a shrug. "For myself . . . . and

92.20 #she@—she did what she liked."

Winterbourne's eyes attached themselves to the ground. "She did what she liked!"

It determined on the part of poor Giovanelli a further pious, a further candid, confidence. "If she had lived I should

191.9 should . . . . She would
never . . . . married

191.11 me, I am sure."
"She would never have
married you?"

191.13 . . . .

191.15 so. But no. I am sure."
Winterbourne listened to
him; he stood

191.15 . . . . turned

191.17 away again Mr. Giovanelli,
with his light slow step, had
retired.

192.3 Winterbourne almost immediately left Rome; . . . .
his

192.5 aunt, Mrs. Costello, at Vevey. Mrs. Costello was fond
of Vevey. In

192.6 . . . . of

192.8 Daisy Miller and her mysti-
fying manners. One day he
. . . . conscience

92.25 . . . . She never would
. . . . married

92.27 me."
It had been spoken as if to
attest, in all sincerity, his dis-
interestedness, but Winterbourne scarce knew what
welcome to give it. He said,
however, with a grace inferior to his friend's: "I dare
say not."
The

92.31 latter was even by this not
discouraged. . . . .

92.32 so. But no. I'm convinced."
Winterbourne took it in;
he stood staring

93.1 . . . . turned

93.3 round again his fellow
mourner had stepped back.
He almost immediately
left

93.5 Rome, ... his

93.6 aunt Mrs. Costello at Vevey.
Mrs. Costello extracted from
the charming old hotel there
a value that the Miller family had n't mastered the secret of. In

93.9 . . . . of

93.11 the most interesting member
of that trio—of her mystify-
ing manners and her queer
adventure. One day he

93.12 . . . . conscience

192.9	that . . . . injustice.	93.13	. . . . injustice.
192.11	"I am . . . . don't know," said Mrs. Costello	93.15	"I'm . . . . don't know"— that lady showed caution. . . . .
192.12	 I	93.17	 I
192.15	didn't . . . . at that . . . . But I have	93.18	did n't . . . . at the . . . . But I've . . . .
		93.21	"She took an odd way to gain it! But do you mean
192.16	"Is that a modest way," asked Mrs. Costello, "of say- ing	93.22	by what you say," Mrs. Cos- tello asked," . . . .
193.2	. . . . affection?" Winterbourne offered . . . . this	93.23	. . . . affection?" As he made . . . . this
		93.24	she after a little looked round at him—he hadn't been directly within sight; but the effect of that wasn't to make her repeat her ques- tion.
193.5	question; but he presently said, ...	93.27	He spoke, however, after a while. . . . .
193.7	I have . . . . foreign	93.29	I've . . . . foreign
193.9	parts." Nevertheless, he	93.30	parts." And this time she herself said nothing. Nevertheless he soon . . . .
193.11	. . . . that	94.2	. . . . that
193.13	he is "studying" hard . . . . that he is	94.3	he's "studying" hard . . . . that he's . . . .

COLLATION COMPLETE

N O T E S

---

1. The optical collator invented by Charlton Hinman. By an arrangement of mirrors this machine superimposes the image of one type
page on another so that points of difference between the pages appear
to the operator to waver and stand out. It appears unlikely that this kind

of mechanism will be superseded in detecting type-batter; but it cannot be used to compare one type-setting with another. See C. J. K. Hinman, "Mechanized Collation at the Houghton Library," *Harvard Library Bulletin*, IX (1955), 132–34, and Vinton A. Dearing, "The Poor Man's Mark IV, or Ersatz Hinman Collator," *PBSA*, LX (1966), 149–58.

2. Jess Stein of Random House, who had been using computers in making a new dictionary, encouraged us to believe such a program might be written. Lawrence Urdang, also of Random House, gave us technical advice. The Courant Mathematical Institute of New York University, through Eugene Isaacson, the associate director, gave us ten hours of free time on the IBM 7094; and Howard L. Walowitz and Jack Heller, also of New York University, told us that the developing program would work after several officials of a major computer company assured us it would not. Funds for our first effort were provided by an American Council of Learned Societies grant of $5,665.

3. During the first experiment I had learned Fortran II and had become familiar with FAP, the assembly language for the IBM 7094. G. Petty.

4. For a complete description of this language see R. E. Griswold, J. F. Poage, and I. P. Polonsky, *The Snobol 4 Programming Language*, Bell Telephone Laboratories, Inc. (1968). Interested scholars should write to the Publications Division, Bell Telephone Laboratories, Murray Hill, New Jersey, attention of J. L. Gregory. See also Allen Forte, *Snobol 3 Primer* (Cambridge, 1967), which describes a predecessor of Snobol 4.

5. Our debt to the American Council of Learned Societies for funds to support the initial experiment and to the National Endowment for the Humanities for a grant to make OCCULT operational is great, for the idea was extravagant. We owe the Modern Language Association of America and its officers thanks as well, for they administered the NEH grant without overhead.

6. The machine, the Mohawk 1181, produces a typescript as well as the magnetic tape. It creates a tape which must be translated by a special program before it can be used by a computer. We wish to thank William Starr of Mohawk Data Sciences Corporation, and his assistants Michael Henestofel and Arthur Johnson, for making two 1181 machines available to us; Karen Stein and Eileen Darby for learning to use the machines and making the magnetic tapes; and Hans Rütimann of the MLA headquarters staff for supervising the making of punch cards of the last few pages of the two texts.

7. A shift code is a symbol placed before a sequence of characters to indicate that all the following characters have been altered in some way not reproduceable by the input device; for example, the beginning

of a series of italicized characters, or the subsequent return to roman. These codes are deciphered in the program and can be used to reproduce the text exactly when an output printer with the needed characters is available.

8. It was this problem that led some of the computer experts we first consulted to be very discouraging about our prospects for success.

9. The only technical limitation on the number of texts to be collated simultaneously is the number of input devices available at the computer installation being used.

10. I was about to write a subroutine that would scan the line endings for all possible abbreviations ending with a period when we discovered a paragraph that ended with the string "letter-em dash-double quotes-carriage return." Who could tell what other combination might be lurking somewhere in James's pages to sabotage our program? And then we bethought ourselves of the problem of defining a sentence in Faulkner's *The Sound and the Fury*, and we gave up the whole procedure. G. Petty.

11. We were advised by computer specialists to pre-edit the text by numbering the similar sentences before reading them into the machine, so that the computer would have a place mark. This seemed to us self-defeating. If we had to read all the editions and number the similar sentences, we might just as well take the next step and collate by eye.

12. If for some reason an editor wanted a collation done without regard to punctuation at all, it would be a simple matter to eliminate those marks from consideration as the text was read in.

13. The preparation of natural language machine-readable text is a large and knotty problem which needs to be studied thoroughly very soon. Optical scanners which would read the text and translate it directly into machine-readable form have been constructed, but have not reached the necessary accuracy. The difficulty of preparing accurate text is now the major obstacle to the use of computer technology in the humanities.

14. The updating procedure for large quantities of text may be fairly complicated, however, and may require the development of an elaborate program to be operated from a typewriter or cathode ray input-output device.

15. In the future, editors at universities possessing computer centers ought to be able to secure free time on the computer for their research, as their colleagues in mathematics and the sciences already do.

Further Readings

THIS LIST IS SELECTIVE and intended to complement the essays in this volume. It is with this caution in mind that the comments on each entry should be read, for they are neither abstracts nor necessarily even fair indications of the main concerns of each article. Instead, the comments draw attention to those aspects of each essay, whether explicitly developed or not, which are important or useful to anyone concerned with textual editing as a discipline. These readings, together with the essays in the present volume, should be thought of as a compass, not as a chart, for exploring editorial problems.

BAENDER, Paul. "The Meaning of Copy-Text," *SB*, XXII (1969), 311–18.
Finds that "copy-text" is used to identify two often different items —the copy sent to a printer and the text which an editor regards as most authoritative—and argues that in its second application the term is prestige-loaded in a way that makes for confusion, especially where pre-publication forms of a work are involved.

BATESON, F. W. "Modern Bibliography and the Literary Artifact," *English Studies Today* (Bern, 1961), pp. 67–77.
Argues that the oral and temporal nature of the literary artifact imposes severe limitations on what a bibliographer can say about it. This attack on bibliography as a discipline which "battens on men's superstitious reverence for the written word" should be read in conjunction with Bowers' "Some Relations of Bibliography to Editorial Problems," with Archibald A. Hill's "The Locus of the Literary Work," *English Studies Today* (Edinburgh, 1964), pp. 41–50, and with Thorpe's "The Aesthetics of Textual Criticism."

BEARE, Robert L. "Notes on the Text of T. S. Eliot: Variants from Russell Square," *SB*, IX (1957), 21–49.
Demonstrates the prevalence and complexity of textual change in Eliot's works and raises questions about the meaning and application of the concepts "composition" and "final intention."

BIRCH, Brian. "Henry James: Some Bibliographical and Textual Matters," *The Library*, 5th ser. XX (1965), 108–123.

Explains variants in the text of *The Ambassadors* as the result of simultaneous American and British publication involving, for three different parts of the novel, three different paths of textual transmission. Cf. Hill, Jarvis, Kramer, and Welland.

BOWERS, Fredson. "Current Theories of Copy-Text, with an Illustration from Dryden," *Modern Philology*, XLVIII (1950), 12–20.
Defends Greg's rationale of copy-text against anticipated objections, the most important being the possibility that later authorial revision of accidentals will be missed by taking the first printed text as copy-text. The illustration from Dryden suggests that for accidentals the odds greatly favor the accuracy of the first edition over any later, even one authorially revised.

H. T. Swedenberg, Jr., in his "On Editing Dryden's Early Poems" in *Essays Critical and Historical Dedicated to Lilly B. Campbell* (Los Angeles, 1950), pp. 73–84, arrives at almost the same conclusions except that he adduces evidence that Dryden attended to accidentals and argues, accordingly, for more freedom to emend them.

BOWERS, Fredson. "Established Texts and Definitive Editions," *PQ*, XLI (1962), 1–17.
Differentiates techniques for establishing manuscript texts and for editing printed works, and argues that the bibliographical conditions which govern the latter may result in more than one definitive text, as in *Hamlet*, *Othello*, *Every Man in his Humour*, *The Prelude*, and *Leaves of Grass*, where usual eclectic practices are inapplicable.

BOWERS, Fredson. "Old Wine in New Bottles: Problems of Machine Printing," in *Editing Nineteenth Century Texts*, ed. John M. Robson (Toronto, 1967), pp. 9–36.
Displays a Pandora's box of bibliographical problems in modern printing where scholars accustomed only to hand printing had not expected them, and demonstrates how these problems effect editorial decisions.

BOWERS, Fredson. "A Preface to the Text" in the Hawthorne Centenary Edition of *The Scarlet Letter* (Columbus, 1962), pp. xxix–xlvii, and reprinted in later volumes.
Describes the editorial principles and procedures of the first truly critical edition of the works of an American novelist, and by implication challenges subsequent editions to do, not necessarily the same, but as well. For a record of the bibliographical work which lies behind this "Preface," see Bowers' "Hawthorne's Text" in *Hawthorne Centenary Essays*, ed. Roy Harvey Pearce (Columbus, 1964), pp. 401–425. Cf. Bruccoli.

BOWERS, Fredson. "Some Relations of Bibliography to Editorial Problems," *SB*, III (1950–51), 37–62.

Grants that textual criticism and analytical bibliography are independent arts, but argues that textual criticism cannot controvert applicable bibliographical findings and that definitive textual results are possible only by combining both disciplines. Cf. Bateson.

BOWERS, Fredson. "Textual Criticism," in *The Aims and Methods of Scholarship in Modern Languages and Literatures*, ed. James Thorpe (New York, 1963), pp. 23–42.
Offers the best concise account of the proper concerns and procedures of textual criticism.

BRUCCOLI, Matthew. "Concealed Printings in Hawthorne," *PBSA*, LVII (1963), 42–49.
Warns of the possibility for textual change within an edition of a modern book and notes thirty such variants, hitherto unrecorded, in *The Marble Faun*.

BRUCCOLI, Matthew. "Textual Variants in Sinclair Lewis's *Babbitt*," *SB*, XI (1958), 263–268.
Illustrates textual problems which arise from the unsuspected complexity of modern printing practices and argues that *Babbitt* contains an example of comparatively rare modern stop-press correction.

CENTER FOR EDITIONS OF AMERICAN AUTHORS. *Statement of Editorial Principles A Working Manual for Editing Nineteenth Century American Texts* (New York, 1967).
Establishes broad editorial procedures and standards for editions sponsored by the MLA's Center for Editions of American Authors. Manuals for individual editions supplement the CEAA *Statement*.

DEARING, Vinton A. "Dryden's *Mac Flecknoe*: The Case for Authorial Revision," *SB*, VII (1955), 85–102.
Argues of *Mac Flecknoe*, published in both manuscript and printed form, that it is possible to establish the history of revision by discovering the radiational relationship among its early texts.

DEARING, Vinton A. *Methods of Textual Editing* (Los Angeles, 1962).
Describes a new era in textual editing which combines principles developed by Greg and his successors with the economies of automation, and formulates the steps which an editor must take to prepare a critical text.

FRIEDMAN, Arthur. "The Problem of Indifferent Readings in the Eighteenth Century, with a Solution from *The Deserted Village*," *SB*, XIII (1960), 143–147.
Indicates what can be done with substantive variants whose authenticity can usually be determined by nothing more certain than personal taste or vague criteria of style.

HARKNESS, Bruce. "Bibliography and the Novelistic Fallacy," *SB*, XII (1959), 59–73.
Explains the anomalous conjunction in the study of modern fiction of close reading with carelessness in textual matters; demonstrates the dangers of this schizophrenic behavior by examining several often taught nineteenth- and twentieth-century novels, especially *The Great Gatsby*.

HILL, Hamlin. "Toward a Critical Text of *The Gilded Age*," *PBSA* LIX (1965), 142–149.
Shows how the facts of trans-Atlantic publication, further complicated by joint authorship and contradiction in authorial intentions, can be resolved only by reference to Twain and Warner's manuscripts and to the American Publishing Company agents' dummy of the novel. Cf. Birch, Jarvis, Kramer, and Welland.

JARVIS, F. P. "A Textual Comparison of the First British and American Editions of D. H. Lawrence's *Kangaroo*," *PBSA*, LIX (1965), 400–424.
Details variants between two nearly simultaneous editions printed from differently revised manuscripts. Cf. Birch, Hill, Kramer, and Welland.

KRAMER, Dale. "Two 'New' Texts of Thomas Hardy's *The Wood-landers*," *SB*, XX (1967), 135–150.
Shows how Hardy's effort to secure American copyright led to his sending two sets of successively revised proofs to Harpers, which were used as copy for two different editions of *The Woodlanders*. Cf. Birch, Hill, Jarvis, and Welland.

LAURENCE, Dan H. "A Bibliographical Novitiate: In Search of Henry James," *PBSA*, LII (1958), 23–33.
Narrates the less than likely places he looked and the luck he generated to get the facts straight about James's books.

MARSHALL, William H. "The Text of T. S. Eliot's 'Gerontion,'" *SB*, IV (1951–52), 213–217.
Describes how a living author reviewed the findings of his bibliographers, who then prepared a text which realized his intentions better than any previously printed edition.

MERIWETHER, James B. "Bibliographical and Textual Studies of Twentieth-Century Writers" in *Proceedings of the Conference on the Study of Twentieth-Century Literature* (East Lansing, 1961), pp. 35–51.
Calls upon libraries to acquire English editions essential to the study of contemporary writers and upon literary scholars to train themselves to deal with modern bibliographical and textual problems. Also points out that because publishers', printers', and agents' records will be destroyed, this work cannot be left to the future.

MERIWETHER, James B. "Some Notes on the Text of Faulkner's *Sanctuary*," *PBSA*, LV (1961), 192–206.
Studies the errors of the first edition of *Sanctuary* in the light of its composition and revision, and draws attention to the variants in the English edition which result from Bowdlerization. On the former, see also Linton Massey, "Notes on the Unrevised Galleys of Faulkner's *Sanctuary*," *SB*, VIII (1956), 195–208; on the latter, cf. Kramer.

MERIWETHER, James B. "The Text of Ernest Hemingway," *PBSA*, LVII (1963), 403–421.
Surveys the bibliographical and textual problems in Hemingway's published works and draws attention to some legal problems affecting these texts—copyright, testamentary restrictions, and the revenue laws applicable to unpublished literary property. For Hemingway, as for most other twentieth-century writers, the basic textual work remains to be done.

MERIWETHER, James B. "The Text of Faulkner's Books: An Introduction and Some Notes," *MFS*, IX (1963), 159–170.
Provides a model of advice on what text to quote until the definitive edition arrives.

ROBSON, John M. "Principles and Methods in the Collected Edition of John Stuart Mill" in his *Editing Nineteenth Century Texts* (Toronto, 1967), pp. 96–122.
Describes the logistics of editing a miscellaneous writer and argues, since interest in Mill is not primarily literary, that Greg's rationale of copy-text need not be applied and that no regular comparison of multiple copies within editions is necessary.

SANDERS, Charles Richard. "Editing the Carlyle Letters: Problems and Opportunities" in *Editing Nineteenth Century Texts*, ed. John M. Robson (Toronto, 1967), pp. 77–95.
Provides an account of what can be done with an embarrassment of riches—9,500 letters.

STILLINGER, Jack. "The Text of John Stuart Mill's *Autobiography*," *Bulletin of the John Ryland's Library*, XLIII (1960–61), 220–242.
Describes the three manuscript phases of the *Autobiography* and shows how the discovery of the last one, which Mill's daughter prepared for the press, provides crucial evidence towards establishing its text.

SWEDENBERG, H. T., Jr.—see Bowers, "Current Theories of Copy-Text."

TODD, William B. "Bibliography and the Editorial Problem in the Eighteenth Century," *SB*, IV (1951–52), 41–55.

Ingeniously suggests how press numbers and extracts quoted in reviews can be used to discriminate editions and impressions of eighteenth-century books.

WEINBERG, Bernard. "Editing Balzac: A Problem in Infinite Variation" in *Editing Nineteenth Century Texts*, ed. John M. Robson (Toronto, 1967), pp. 60–76.
Argues that the authority of Balzac's last revised edition and the extensive revision of virtually every edition preceding it render the principles of Greg and Bowers inapplicable; the alternative should be an edition based on a critical rather than a bibliographical assessment of what is significant evidence and one that is aimed more self-consciously in its apparatus at critical interests.

OTHER COLLECTED READINGS

Studies in Bibliography offers annually an enumerative bibliography of the year's work in textual editing and related areas.

BRACK, O. M., Jr., and Barnes, Warner, eds. *Bibliography and Textual Criticism: English and American Literature, 1700 to the Present* (Chicago, 1969).

ROBSON, John M., ed. *Editing Nineteenth Century Texts* (Toronto, 1967).
The relevant essays in this collection are described above; the volume also contains a useful annotated bibliography compiled by Warner Barnes, "Nineteenth-Century Editorial Problems: A Selective Bibliography," pp. 123–132.